SOCIAL DEMOCRATIC CRIMINOLOGY

This book argues that 'social democratic criminology' is an important critical perspective which is essential for the analysis of crime and criminal justice and crucial for humane and effective policy. The end of World War II resulted in 30 years of strategies to create a more peaceful international order. In domestic policy, all Western countries followed agendas informed by a social democratic sensibility. *Social Democratic Criminology* argues that the social democratic consensus has been pulled apart since the late 1960s, by the hegemony of neoliberalism: a resuscitation of nineteenth-century free market economics. There is now a gathering storm of apocalyptic dangers from climate change, pandemics, antibiotic resistance, and other existential threats. This book shows that the neoliberal revolution of the rich pushed aside social democratic values and policies regarding crime and security and replaced them with tougher 'law and order' approaches. The initial consequence was a tsunami of crime in all senses. Smarter security techniques did succeed in abating this for a while, but the decade of austerity in the wake of the 2008 financial crisis has seen growing violent and serious crime.

Social Democratic Criminology charts the history of social democracy, discusses the variety of conflicting ways in which it has been interpreted, and identifies its core uniting concepts and influence on criminology in the twentieth century. It analyses the decline of social democratic criminology and the sustained intellectual and political attacks it has endured. The concluding chapter looks at the prospects for reviving social democratic criminology, itself dependent on the prospects for a rebirth of the broader social democratic movement.

Written in a clear and direct style, this book will appeal to students and scholars of criminology, sociology, cultural studies, politics, history, social policy, and all those interested in social democracy and its importance for society.

Robert Reiner is Emeritus Professor of Criminology in the Law Department at the London School of Economics. He was President of the British Society of Criminology from 1993–6; Director of the LSE Mannheim Centre for Criminology and Criminal Justice from 1995–8; and convener of the Law Department from 2001–4. He is author of: *The Blue-Coated Worker, Chief Constables, Law and Order, Policing, Popular Culture and Political Economy, Crime: The Mystery of the Common-Sense Concept*, and *The Politics of the Police*, Fifth Edition (with Ben Bowling and James Sheptycki), and Editor (with Mike Maguire and Rod Morgan) of the first five editions of *The Oxford Handbook of Criminology*. He has also written numerous journal articles and book chapters. He received the British Society of Criminology Outstanding Achievement Award in 2011.

New Directions in Critical Criminology
Edited by Walter S. DeKeseredy
West Virginia University, USA

This series presents new cutting-edge critical criminological empirical, theoretical, and policy work on a broad range of social problems, including drug policy, rural crime and social control, policing and the media, ecocide, intersectionality, and the gendered nature of crime. It aims to highlight the most up-to-date authoritative essays written by new and established scholars in the field. Rather than offering a survey of the literature, each book takes a strong position on topics of major concern to those interested in seeking new ways of thinking critically about crime.

Queer Criminology
Carrie L. Buist and Emily Lenning

Crime, Justice and Social Media
Michael Salter

Southern Criminology
Kerry Carrington, Russell Hogg, John Scott, Máximo Sozzo and Reece Walters

Sex-Positive Criminology
Aimee Wodda and Vanessa R. Panfil

Social Democratic Criminology
Robert Reiner

For more information about this series, please visit: www.routledge.com/New-Directions-in-Critical-Criminology/book-series/NDCC

First published 2021
by Routledge
2 Park Square, Milton Park, Abingdon, Oxon OX14 4RN

and by Routledge
52 Vanderbilt Avenue, New York, NY 10017

Routledge is an imprint of the Taylor & Francis Group, an informa business

© 2021 Robert Reiner

The right of Robert Reiner to be identified as author of this work
has been asserted by him in accordance with sections 77 and 78 of the
Copyright, Designs and Patents Act 1988.

All rights reserved. No part of this book may be reprinted or reproduced or
utilised in any form or by any electronic, mechanical, or other means, now
known or hereafter invented, including photocopying and recording, or in
any information storage or retrieval system, without permission in writing
from the publishers.

Trademark notice: Product or corporate names may be trademarks or
registered trademarks, and are used only for identification and explanation
without intent to infringe.

British Library Cataloguing-in-Publication Data
A catalogue record for this book is available from the British Library

Library of Congress Cataloging-in-Publication Data
A catalog record for this book has been requested

ISBN: 978-1-138-23878-7 (hbk)
ISBN: 978-1-138-23879-4 (pbk)
ISBN: 978-1-315-29677-7 (ebk)

Typeset in Bembo
by Apex CoVantage, LLC

I dedicate this book particularly to the younger generations of my family: Toby and Meg, Charlotte and David, Ben, Jacob, and Ezra. May they experience a more hopeful future and contribute to its realisation.

CONTENTS

Preface	*viii*
Introduction: social democracy – the Utopia that worked	1
1 Social democracy: political history of a moral crusade	7
2 Social democratic criminology: the political *and* moral economy of crime and criminal justice	49
3 The strange death of social democratic criminology	84
4 Conclusion: born-again social democratic criminology	125
Index	*167*

PREFACE

The arc of justice has followed a sad trajectory in modern times. Two centuries of struggle and faltering progress towards the ideals of equality, liberty, and human solidarity culminated tragically after 1914, in three decades of economic depression and two bloody, brutal world wars. The widespread mood of 'never again' after 1945 shaped 'thirty glorious years' during which my generation enjoyed unprecedented (but incomplete) social democratic achievements in justice, security, welfare, and peace. As the book documents, this was stolen from subsequent generations by neoliberal globalisation, and we now face a series of existential threats to the very continuation of humanity. None of this is inevitable, but bending the arc of history back towards justice and harmony is a wicked bequest my generation is burdening our heirs with.

The conclusion of this book owes much to the inspiring scholarship and activism of a growing multitude of young writers and politicians, many proudly embracing the banner of democratic socialism. I have faith that they can fulfil the dreams that humanity has yearned for. As I write this the world is convulsed with anger over the brutal killing by police of George Floyd, an African American man, on 25 May 2020. It vividly illustrated the cruelty and suffering produced by injustice and oppression. But the massive demonstrations in his honour by people around the world, black/white, male/female, young/old, offer hope that the arc of history will bend towards justice. Black lives matter! No justice, no peace!

INTRODUCTION

Social democracy – the Utopia that worked

'We wuz robbed!' Most people alive today are the victims of a massive crime – the theft of their security and of their souls. After the cataclysm of World War II, including the most hideous crimes of all time, there was an almost universal sense of 'never again'. It resulted in 30 years of strategies to create a more peaceful international order, in the face of the Cold War and its nuclear threat. In domestic policy, all Western countries followed agendas informed by a social democratic sensibility, combining Keynesian economics and welfare state social policies. These were aimed at achieving significant reductions in inequality and insecurity, sheltering all people from the 'Five Giants' of 'Want, Disease, Ignorance, Squalor and Idleness' described in the seminal 1942 Beveridge Report (Timmins 2017). Although the report was met with some criticism from both Right and Left, it received massive popular enthusiasm. Its commitment to 'cradle to grave' protection for all was the cornerstone of the post-war consensus, echoed in all Western countries (Garland 2016). The result was three decades of growing prosperity, less inequality, and greater security, celebrated in France as *les trente glorieuses*. The evidence for this is detailed in Chapter 1.

This social democratic consensus has been pulled apart since the late 1960s, by the hegemony of neoliberalism: a resuscitation of nineteenth-century free market economics and laissez faire. The result (elaborated in Chapter 1, and magisterially in Piketty 2020) has been largely stagnant real earnings for all but the rich. This was disguised until the 2008 financial crash by a variety of devices, borrowing from the future to finance fragile living standards. Ever more evidently since the financial crisis this has produced a reinvigoration of the Five Giants that Beveridge had sought to defeat (Standing 2020). There is now a gathering storm of apocalyptic dangers from climate change, pandemics, antibiotic resistance, and other existential threats. To many people of my generation this snatching away of a once sunny future came as the shattering of a dream of unstoppable and inclusive progress, as

2 Introduction

set out by many powerful writers over the decade since 2010 (Judt 2010; Edgerton 2018; Ortolano 2019; Lawrence 2019; Maconie 2020).

The plight of the generations coming of age in the twenty-first century, experiencing a steady decline in living standards and life chances, has often been portrayed as a war between generations, with baby boomers (like myself) being portrayed as thieves of the futures of their children and grandchildren (Willetts 2010; Sternberg 2019). This book argues that the generational perspective, in which 'grandma' is 'mugged' for her crimes against her progeny (wrongly as Bristow 2019 argues) deflects attention from what really happened. The present and future welfare of the majority of all post-war generations has been stolen by a neoliberal political and moral economy that benefits only a tiny but dominant minority, setting the rest of us up to fight over the crumbs. This has succeeded thus far by divide-and-rule strategies, pitting generations, genders, ethnicities, sexualities, and religions against each other rather than realising common cause against the perpetrators.

The thesis of this book can be stated in a nutshell (but the complexities and evidence presented in later chapters are crucial too). During the 1970s there occurred a global transformation of political and moral economy, as neoliberalism swept away the social democratic consensus which had been dominant in the first three post-war decades. The stakes were at least as much moral as material, as one of the key figureheads of this revolution of the rich put it in a 1981 interview: 'Economics are the method: the object is to change the soul' (www.margaretthatcher. org/document/104475). Political economy shifted away from concern to provide decent and secure material provision to the many through Keynesian regulation of markets by fiscal and monetary policy coupled with welfare state protections. Instead, state intervention came to be castigated as inefficient and demoralising, and all were subject to a survival of the fittest struggle. This was thinly disguised and legitimated as spreading opportunities to participate in the fruit machine of casino capitalism. Neoliberalism constituted a revolution in moral economy, which supplanted reciprocal individualism based on the Golden Rule 'love your neighbour as yourself', with egoistic individualism, 'greed is good'. Egoism masqueraded as an ethic of responsibility and entrepreneurial risk-taking.

All this was echoed in the specific discipline of criminology and in criminal justice policy. There has never been an avowed school of social democratic criminology. But this book shows that a criminological perspective that can be called social democratic was widely held, especially during the post-war consensus decades, but also well before that. As with social democratic political and moral economy, it was a largely implicit, taken-for-granted social imaginary, held even by many who regretted or resisted it. Whether celebrated or castigated, many concurred with the view made famous by Martin Luther King that: 'The arc of the moral universe is long, but it bends toward justice' (www.si.edu/spotlight/ mlk?page=4&iframe=true).

In the criminology field, the essence of the social democratic perspective comprises five primary propositions: a) The problem of 'crime' (itself hard to define and usually enforced in unjust ways) must be kept in its place. It comprises some substantial, sometimes massively serious, harms. But usually these are dwarfed by many other problems, material, social, and psychological. Whether some of these should be criminalised is debatable because of the other propositions; b) the root causes of crime, both in the narrow legal sense and the broad sense of culpable harms, are the political and moral economy of capitalism, with its structural and cultural imperatives of ruthless egoism; c) penal interventions are justified if, but only if, they are restorative, restitutive, and reforming, removing or at least reducing further harms, not for revenge or punishment in itself; d) the criminal justice system is a blunt and largely ineffective tool for reducing crime overall, though its impact on the individuals caught up in it (usually the already disadvantaged) can be huge, for good or for evil; and e) whilst some harms may be perpetrated in any conceivable social system, by individuals who are mentally or physically sick, the vast majority of current offences, which are rooted in the unjust property relations of capitalism, will disappear if social democracy was achieved. Criminal justice would essentially become a branch of medicine.

In Chapters 2 and 3 we look at these propositions in more detail. But the basics of social democratic criminology were set out with characteristic pithiness by Oscar Wilde in his 1891 essay 'The Soul of Man Under Socialism':

> As one reads history, not in the expurgated editions written for school-boys and passmen, but in the original authorities of each time, one is absolutely sickened, not by the crimes that the wicked have committed, but by the punishments that the good have inflicted; and a community is infinitely more brutalised by the habitual employment of punishment, than it is by the occurrence of crime. . . . The less punishment, the less crime. When there is no punishment at all, crime will either cease to exist, or, if it occurs, will be treated by physicians as a very distressing form of dementia, to be cured by care and kindness. . . . When private property is abolished there will be no necessity for crime, no demand for it; it will cease to exist. . . . But though a crime may not be against property, it may spring from the misery and rage and depression produced by our wrong system of property-holding, and so, when that system is abolished, will disappear. When each member of the community has sufficient for his wants, and is not interfered with by his neighbour, it will not be an object of any interest to him to interfere with anyone else. Jealousy, which is an extraordinary source of crime in modern life, is an emotion closely bound up with our conceptions of property.
>
> *(www.wilde-online.info/the-soul-of-man-under-socialism-page9.html)*

Chapters 2 and 3 of this book amplify these claims, looking at the history and successes of social democratic criminology.

Chapter 1 first examines the ideas and history of social democracy itself. Nowadays the term has been hijacked by events in British political history during the 1980s, specifically the 1981 formation of a 'Social Democratic Party' that explicitly directed itself against a leftward move in the Labour Party. Thus, 'social democratic'

4 Introduction

came to be explicitly opposed to 'socialism'. This usage spread throughout the Western world in the 1990s, as a reaction against the red-in-tooth-and-claw neoliberalism of Reagan and Thatcher produced electoral success for self-labelled 'third way' parties, notably 'New' Labour and the Clinton Democrats.

It is this bastardised version of social democracy that leads the admirable resurgent carriers of the mantle today to call themselves 'democratic socialists' instead. As I show in Chapter 1, for most of its history social democracy did aim at socialism, albeit by evolutionary rather than revolutionary tactics. Contrary to the polemics of neoliberalism (Friedman 1962), socialism and democracy were seen as reinforcing, not contradicting, each other. Political democracy without a strong measure of social justice in effect becomes a mask for plutocracy (ever more clearly so today). Conversely, democracy, unclouded by the manipulations of propaganda, would result in support for socialism. This was believed both by opponents and advocates of the universal franchise. With the wisdom of hindsight this belief was wrong, and a substantial minority of working-class people have voted for conservative parties, (as Disraeli forecast when extending the franchise in 1867).

Chapter 1 sets out an ideal type of social democracy as a concept. It then details its achievements, before offering an analysis of why and how neoliberalism succeeded in casting it aside. This was not because of a failure of its basic values or model, as most commentators still believe. It was subverted from within by the rule-breaking, arguably unlawful, activities of financiers seeking to restore the rate of profits, which had been cut into by the small but real advances made by labour. In time these upset the foundations of the post-war financial and economic order achieved by Keynes and others. Thus the dreams of the neoliberal thought collective, formulated already in the 1930s but becoming an increasingly active and influential archipelago of think tanks and propagandists after the 1947 Mont Pelerin Conference, came in from the cold.

Chapters 2 and 3 of this book look in much more detail at the idea and history of 'social democratic' criminology. They document its success in achieving a more secure society, and more humane criminal justice rhetoric and to some degree practice. This was supplanted by a 'law and order' perspective, combining elements of neoconservatism and neoliberalism. Tough crime control was sold as the answer to problems like street crime, disorder, and drugs, that were largely of neoliberalism's own making, and certainly were exacerbated by its policies. The aim was primarily political and social control, however, not public safety. In Britain, the 1977 secret 'Ridley Plan' set out a right-wing agenda for destroying trade union power and paving the way for privatisation of nationalised industries (www.margaretthatcher.org/document/110795). In this strategy, provocative actions in co-operation with the police would generate militant strike action, that could then legitimate tough anti-union legislation and militaristic law enforcement. It was successfully implemented, especially during the 1984/5 Miners' Strike, which hugely weakened the trade union movement and consolidated the hegemony of neoliberalism.

US President Richard Nixon's conversion of the 'war against poverty' into a 'war against crime' and a 'war against drugs' was intentionally motivated by a wish

Introduction **5**

to erode the 1960s gains of the Civil Rights and anti-war movement. As his domestic policy chief advisor John Ehrlichman confessed in a 1994 interview:

> We knew we couldn't make it illegal to be either against the war or black, but by getting the public to associate the hippies with marijuana and blacks with heroin, and then criminalizing both heavily, we could disrupt those communities. We could arrest their leaders, raid their homes, break up their meetings, and vilify them night after night on the evening news. Did we know we were lying about the drugs? Of course, we did.
>
> *(www.history.com/topics/crime/the-war-on-drugs)*

Chapter 3 analyses in more detail the defeat of social democratic criminology by the law and order perspective.

Chapter 4 tackles the crying question prompted by the foregoing chapters. If social democratic political and moral economy were successful in terms of achieving greater social welfare, peace, security, and justice, what – if any – are the prospects of its restoration? That does not mean an obviously doomed attempt to put Humpty Dumpty together again. The specific institutional forms and policies that worked 70 years ago cannot be recreated. But the agenda of restoring social democratic values in terms of justice, democracy, security, and human interaction, informed by a bedrock belief in people's equal entitlement to respect and concern, must be revived. It is argued that there is no alternative (borrowing Margaret Thatcher's slogan) if any civilised existence is to be preserved. In Rosa Luxemburg's formulation a century ago, socialism or barbarism.

The obstacles to this are set out, but they all contain chinks of possible transformation. Above all, the accumulation of existential threats to human (indeed any) existence, all traceable to the excesses of neoliberalism – capitalism in its vulture phase – suggests not only that socialism is needed, but also that its elements are being formulated as the world struggles to tackle the current pandemic scourge and the looming apocalypse of climate change. The possibility that more benign forms of human co-operation can emerge from the effort to survive was vividly demonstrated by the moving 'clap for the carers' staged on 26 March throughout Britain, in tribute to the heroic and selfless staff of the NHS and other emergency services (www.theguardian.com/world/gallery/2020/mar/26/clap-for-carers-applauding-the-nhs-during-coronavirus-in-pictures). They provide the model of social democratic virtue in action for which this book argues in principle.

References

Bristow, J. (2019) *Stop Mugging Granny* New Haven: Yale University Press.
Edgerton, D. (2018) *The Rise and Fall of the British Nation* London: Allen Lane.
Friedman, M. (1962) *Capitalism and Freedom* Chicago: Chicago University Press.
Garland, D. (2016) *The Welfare State* Oxford: Oxford University Press.
Judt, T. (2010) *Ill Fares the Land* London: Allen Lane.

6 Introduction

Lawrence, J. (2019) *Me, Me, Me: The Search for Community in Post-war England* Oxford: Oxford University Press.

Maconie, S. (2020) *The Nanny State Made Me* London: Ebury Press.

Ortolano, G. (2019) *Thatcher's Progress* Cambridge: Cambridge University Press.

Piketty, T. (2020) *Capital and Ideology* Cambridge: Harvard University Press.

Standing, G. (2020) *Battling Eight Giants* London: Taurus.

Sternberg, J.C. (2019) *The Theft of a Decade* New York: PublicAffairs.

Timmins, N. (2017) *The Five Giants* London: Collins.

Willets, D. (2010) *The Pinch* London: Atlantic.

1

SOCIAL DEMOCRACY

Political history of a moral crusade

Social democracy has a strong claim to being the most successful form of socialism since the birth of both labels in the early nineteenth century. Despite being declared dead many times since the 1970s hegemony of neoliberalism, social democracy and its close cousin democratic socialism are vibrant contenders in the political and economic turbulence of the twenty-first century (Bhaskar 2019; Gilbert 2020). The meaning and influence of social democracy has gone through a variety of transformations in its 200 years of life, as this chapter analyses.

Many commentators and politicians saw 'a social democratic moment' in the wake of the 2007/8 financial crisis (notably Ed Miliband, leader of the British Labour Party from 2010–15 cf. Goes 2016; Cowley 2018). The attempt to save a silver lining from the clouds of economic recession was alas short lived, despite a widespread sense that it revealed fatal flaws in the neoliberal economic model that had been hegemonic since the 1970s (Gamble 2009, 2014; Crouch 2011; Schafer and Streeck 2013; Mirowski 2014; Streeck 2014, 2017; Davies 2016; Blakeley 2019). Within a few years a heroic rescue operation to avert total meltdown of the financial system was succeeded by a doubling down of neoliberalism, in the shape of austerity policies pursued by most Western governments (Blyth 2015; Mendoza 2015; Tooze 2018). These were purportedly justified by a dominant discourse, enthusiastically promoted in the largely right-wing mass news media. This blamed the rescuers – the governments that poured resources into the financial system – for profligate public spending, and shielded the perpetrators – the casino banking sector. Social democracy was villainised by the Right, and written off as dead even by many who are sympathetic to its aspirations (Lavelle 2008; Keane 2016; Marliere 2017; Barbieri 2017 (Foreign Affairs); Broning 2017 (FA); Lawson 2018).

Most current discussions of social democracy are beset by ambiguities and antinomies that have bedeviled the project since its origins in the early nineteenth century. These concern both the conception of social democratic aims and values,

8 Social democracy

and the strategies for achieving them. In essence, there is tension between espousing social democracy as a species of socialism distinguished by specific strategies to achieve it, or as mere sticking-plaster to ameliorate the evils of capitalism. Is social democracy a road to socialism or a perpetual Sisyphean struggle to reform capitalism? And in either case, what, if any, role is there for revolutionary tactics as distinct from legal and parliamentary campaigning? Are there circumstances when law-breaking or violence may be justified, as a necessary step towards realising democracy? Is social democracy primarily a foundational set of values or a historically variable cluster of political tactics and institutions?

Social democracy: a historical overview

This chapter aims to chart the history of social democracy and identify its core meanings. Social democracy has been an explicit label for a variety of different perspectives and movements since the middle of the nineteenth century. Four broad periods in its history can be distinguished.

Before World War I: social democracy is socialism

Social democracy's origins lie in the same maelstrom as all other versions of socialism: the tumultuous currents of conflict in political economy, ideology, and society generated by the advent of industrial capitalism and urbanisation. The intellectual and moral roots of socialism and social democracy go back much further still, to the Old and New Testaments (Dennis and Halsey 1988; Rogan 2018; Dorrien 2019), Greek and Roman philosophy (Gray 1946), and a host of social rebellions through the ages, from slave and peasant revolts in ancient and medieval times (Urbainczyk 2008; O'Brien 2016), to the ferment of crypto social democratic ideas during the English Civil War of the sixteenth century and the ensuing Commonwealth (Hill 1991; Gurney 2012; Rees 2017; Robertson 2018).

For much of the nineteenth century there was little to distinguish socialism, Marxism, and social democracy as labels. True, the Left was riddled by the narcissism of small differences, devastatingly lampooned in Monty Python's *Life of Brian*. But the terms 'socialist', 'social democrat', and 'Marxist' were used widely and almost interchangeably by most self-described champions of the working-class masses (Sassoon 1996 Chap. 1). Even Trotsky once declared that his nationality was 'Social Democratic' (Slezkine 2006 p. 169).

The roots of subsequent conflicts may be discerned in Marx and Engels' critique of the 'utopian' socialism of early pioneers such as St Simon (Taylor 2016) and Robert Owen (Owen 1991; Thompson and Williams 2011), although they were seen as important stepping stones to 'scientific' socialism (Marx and Engels 1848/1998; Engels 1880). Arguably the 'utopian' socialists were closer to the later meanings of social democracy, as it came to be distinguished from communism during the twentieth century, although social democracy's prime selling point paradoxically came to be non-utopian pragmatism and realism. But in the nineteenth century the term 'social democracy' was largely used as synonymous with socialism rather than a special brand of it.

Certainly the German Social Democratic Workers' Party, founded in 1869 and the first to carry the label, was primarily Marxist. Despite the twentieth-century connotations of the term, the Social Democratic Party was the most militantly socialist of the various organisations championing working-class unionisation and the political emancipatory struggles which emerged at that time. So too was the British Social Democratic Federation (SDF) founded in 1881 by Henry Hyndman. The SDF was one of the factions that came together to form the Labour Party at the turn of the twentieth century, although it was always at odds with the non-Marxist majority and disaffiliated in 1901.

In the late nineteenth century there began to emerge the seeds of conflict between revolutionary and reformist interpretations of socialism, laying the ground for the twentieth-century interpretation of social democracy as distinct from Marxism. For the past 100 years 'democracy' has mainly been seen as a limit on the legitimate tactics of socialism, and arguably on its aims as well. But hitherto the terms 'social' and 'democracy' were seen not only as fully compatible but indeed mutually necessary. Democracy, in the broadest sense of giving all people equal power to determine their lives and realise their aspirations (subject to the same for everyone else), requires rough equality in material resources and in social esteem. And the equalisation of formal political power signified by the universal franchise was regarded by most opinion, Left or Right, as bolstering the prospects of prosperity and security for the masses. Very few anticipated that, after gaining the franchise, significant proportions of the less well-off would support conservative parties. Disraeli, the driving force behind the 1867 Reform Act that began the enfranchisement of the working class, may have discerned angels in the marble (paraphrasing his obituary in *The Times*), but this optimism or pessimism – depending on political standpoint – was not shared by many contemporary commentators or politicians.

The foundation of Social Democratic parties, initially including many Marxists, was itself an indication that there was widespread belief that political participation in bourgeois democratic institutions could facilitate progress towards socialism. Soon after their foundation, however, Social Democratic parties began to experience conflict between 'revisionist' or evolutionary socialists on the one hand, and more orthodox Marxist and other revolutionary currents on the other.

The foremost figure in the emergence of an explicitly revisionist version of socialism within the German Social Democratic Party was Eduard Bernstein. A friend and protégé of Marx and Engels (who named him as one of his literary executors), Bernstein drafted the party's 1891 'Erfurt Programme' (together with Karl Kautsky and August Bebel). This postulated that the transcendence of capitalism by socialism, as well as reforms of immediate benefit to the working class, could be accomplished by legal participation in democratic processes (which attracted a forthright critique from Engels).

During the 1890s Bernstein became increasingly critical of Marx's analysis of capitalism, and in particular questioned the possibility or desirability of its

10 Social democracy

revolutionary overthrow. The actions of trade unions and social democratic parties, together with broader shifts in political economy and society, were considerably ameliorating the condition of the working class, argued Bernstein. This rendered revolution both less necessary and less feasible. The goals of socialism were being achieved by gradual evolution towards greater social justice and inclusion. These views were developed by Bernstein in a series of papers culminating in his seminal 1899 book, translated into English as *Evolutionary Socialism* (Bernstein 1899/1963). This attracted considerable criticism from erstwhile comrades such as Kautsky and Bebel, expressed most vigorously by Rosa Luxemburg in her *Social Reform or Revolution?* (Luxemburg 1899/2006. For fuller accounts of Bernstein and the revisionist debate cf. Gay 1962; Tudor and Tudor 1988; Steger 2008; Beilharz 2009 Chap. 3).

Similar conflicts occurred at the turn of the twentieth century in all social democratic parties. In France the French Socialist Party was founded in 1902 by Jean Jaures, merging a number of social democratic groups. However, it was opposed by Jules Guesde's revolutionary Socialist Party of France, although the parties united in 1905 and became the French section of the Second International. Under the leadership of Leon Blum, Jaures' protégé who succeeded him in 1914 when the anti-war Jaures was assassinated by a nationalist, the French Socialist Party continued on revisionist social democratic lines. In 1920, however, its more militant sections broke away and founded the French Communist Party (Colton 1987; Kurtz 2014; Birnbaum 2015).

In England the Labour Party has always been predominantly evolutionary. Indeed, one of its most influential constituents was the Fabian Society (Mackenzie and Mackenzie 1977; Beilharz 1992) which was predicated on gradual reformism (it had a considerable impact on Bernstein's development of revisionism during his exile in London). As seen from the foregoing, Hyndman's revolutionary Social Democratic Federation was also involved in the foundation of the Labour Party but rapidly split from it (Pelling 1966; Bevir 2011; Thorpe 2015).

The most fateful split occurred within the Russian Social Democratic Workers Party. In 1903, Lenin gained a temporary majority for his view that membership should be restricted to revolutionaries, as advocated by his pamphlet *What is to Be Done?* (Lenin 1901/1966). Henceforth he called his faction the 'Bolsheviks' (meaning 'majority'), dubbing his opponents 'Mensheviks' ('minority'). The Bolsheviks formally split off in 1912, and in October 2017 ousted the Menshevik government that had taken power in the February Revolution. In 1918, the Bolsheviks espoused the label 'Communist Party', and the distinction from social democratic became increasingly entrenched (Mieville 2017; Medhurst 2017; Ali 2017).

From World War I to II: social democracy vs. communism

Before the First World War, social democratic had been the predominant name used by Marxist and Socialist parties (the British Labour Party being a notable exception), all unequivocally espousing a goal of socialism. What this meant became increasingly controversial around the turn of the twentieth century, with serious splits about analysing the political economy of capitalism. Above all there were sharp divergences in political strategy, among advocates of revolution, evolution, or Fabian gradualism.

After World War I, social democracy came to be contrasted sharply with Communism, and to signify the revisionist and reformist project of taming the problems of capitalism through democratic methods. After 1917, with the establishment of the Bolshevik government in the Soviet Union, opposition between social democracy and communism grew fiercer. This split had fateful consequences, especially the failure to develop popular fronts in the face of the rise of fascism and Nazism in the 1920s and 1930s until it was too late (Jackson 1990; Preston 2016; Taylor 2019).

Social democracy signified at the very least a distinction of means from Bolshevism – the parliamentary road to socialism – and for many a change of ends too, reform of capitalism rather than its overthrow. The culmination of this latter evolution, seeking to extricate social democracy from socialism, was the founding of the British Social Democratic Party in 1981, as a breakaway from what its founding 'Gang of Four' perceived as an unacceptably radical and militant Labour Party (Bradley 1981; Crewe and King 1995). The transformation of Labour itself into New Labour, by Tony Blair after 1992, took this further in practice, under the rubric of the 'third way' (Giddens 1998, 2000; Callinicos 2001 offered a powerful contemporary critique). This trajectory has since been reversed under the leaderships of Ed Miliband and Jeremy Corbyn (Goes 2016; Beckett and Seddon 2019; Kogan 2019; Davis and Rentoul 2019).

For most of the twentieth century, however, 'social democratic' in Britain referred to a wide variety of socialist viewpoints distinguished from, on the left border, Soviet communism, and on the right, the 'new' liberalism inspired by T.H. Green in the late nineteenth and early twentieth centuries, and exemplified by L.T. Hobhouse (Clarke 1978; Freeden 1986; Collini 2009). Its intellectual centre of gravity was the English tradition of ethical socialism (Dennis and Halsey 1988), the quintessential exemplar of which was R.H. Tawney (Armstrong and Gray 2011; Goldman 2014; Rogan 2018) but which also included such thinkers as Graham Wallas (Wiener 1971), and T.H. Marshall (Bulmer and Rees 1996).

The heyday of social democracy: Les Trentes Glorieuses

With the arrival in power of social democratic parties in many countries after World War II, further ambiguity developed over whether their goal was democratically achieved socialism or a permanently mixed economy regulated by democratic governments concerned with social justice, security, and welfare. The hallmark achievements of social democratic governments were based on the maintenance of relatively full employment through the widespread adoption of Keynesian macroeconomic management (Keynes 1936; Skidelsky 2013; Crotty 2019; Mann 2019; Carter 2020). This supported the development of welfare states protecting people against economic and personal hazards from 'the cradle

12 Social democracy

to the grave' by delivering adequate public services and benefits (Timmins 2001; Renwick 2017; Garland 2016; Gamble 2016). The fundamental principle was 'bread for all . . . before cake for anybody' in the words of William Beveridge, architect of the British welfare state envisaged in his massively influential wartime report (Beveridge 1942).

The welfare state in Britain and elsewhere was only in part the product of post-war social democratic governments. Its origins came much earlier in many countries, in the late nineteenth and early twentieth centuries, sometimes promoted by conservative regimes for prudential reasons. In the USA, many elements found elsewhere, notably a publicly funded or supported health system, are still lacking. But even there the Depression and Second World War generated Franklin Delano Roosevelt's 'New Deal', continuing under both Republican and Democratic administrations, finally broadening in the early 1960s into Lyndon Johnson's 'Great Society' programme.

In the UK, although major elements were introduced by the post-war Labour government under Prime Minister Clement Attlee, notably the National Health Service, support ranged across the parties. William Beveridge was a Liberal (as was Keynes), and his report was commissioned by the wartime Coalition under Winston Churchill. Another key facet, free secondary education, was introduced by the Coalition's Education Minister, R.A. Butler, a Conservative, in his 1944 Education Act (Blatchford 2014).

A Keynesian and welfarist approach to economic and social policy became the norm in all Western countries for three decades after the Second World War, largely irrespective of which party was in power. The notion of a 'Butskellite' consensus in the post-war years remains the prevailing view amongst historians (Kavanagh 1992; Addison 1994; Kavanagh and Morris 1994; Fraser 2000; Hickson 2004; Toye 2013), although it has also attracted much criticism (Pimlott 1988; Kerr 1999; Jones and Kandiah 2014). The consensus interpretation was paralleled in the USA, with debates about 'the end of ideology' (Bell 1960; Lipset 1963). A 'social democratic compromise' (Wright 2006) was the reigning sensibility, always vigorously contested by the Right and Left flanks of the political spectrum, but nonetheless transcending overt or even conscious identification or affiliation as social democratic.

In view of the rapid and almost complete eclipse of the post-war Keynesian welfarist consensus (the causes of which are probed in the next section), it is important to review the considerable economic and social success it achieved. In France the period is widely called *les trente glorieuses* and British economists have referred to it as 'the Golden Age of capitalism' (Marglin and Schor 1990).

Between 1950 and 1973, growth in GDP was on average twice as high as from 1973–96 Maddison 1997 Tables 9, 10; Shaxson 2018 p. 283). The disparity between the two periods is even more marked in terms of GDP per capita. In Europe the growth rate per capita was 4.1% in 1950–73 (the social democratic heyday) but fell to 1.7% from 1973–96, as the neoliberal counterrevolution became embedded. GDP growth in the post-war decades was spectacularly high in the defeated Axis countries (9% in Japan, 6% in Germany, 5.6% in Italy), because of US aid and the building up almost from scratch of their shattered economies and societies. But by 1973–96 they had fallen back to close to average levels of growth. The war-ravaged countries that had been occupied by the Nazis (France, Belgium, the Netherlands, etc.) recovered nearly as fast. The two Allied victors that had not suffered invasion grew less well but still had historically fast rates and did significantly better than under neoliberalism. GDP growth was on average 2.9% in the UK and 3.9% in the USA 1950–73, but only 1.8% and 2.5%, respectively 1973–96.

Thus the neoliberals' favourite measure of economic success – GDP has many failings as a statistic – fared much better under supposedly sclerotic social democracy than business-friendly neoliberalism.

What makes the post-war growth in GDP especially remarkable historically is that it was spread throughout the population, as inequality fell during the social democratic period. The anaemic overall growth under neoliberalism went hand in hand with rapidly rising inequality. Growth since the 1970s has been hugely and increasingly concentrated in the upper economic levels, the 1%, and even more so, the 0.1%. Apart from inequality there has also been a resurgence of widespread poverty and deprivation, especially since the 2007/8 financial and economic crisis.

The share of the top 1% of income receivers in the UK fell from 35% before World War II to just over 20% by the early 1970s, whilst the shares of lower income groups rose, a clear indication that the growth of prosperity in the social democratic era was widely shared. As neoliberalism became entrenched, the share of the top 1% grew back to more than 30% by 2007, and the shares of the lowest groups fell continuously (www.equalitytrust.org.uk/).

The growth and extent of inequality in Europe was less than elsewhere (probably because some 'varieties of capitalism', such as Scandinavian social democracy and the corporate capitalism of Germany, France, and the Benelux countries, managed to resist the neoliberal onslaught to an extent cf. Esping-Anderson 1990; Hall and Soskice 2001). The sudden shift of Russia from the lowest to almost the highest inequality after 1990 and the collapse of the USSR is particularly striking.

The USA has long been the most unequal of Western societies. The share of top income receivers fell during the New Deal era, but since the advent of neoliberalism in the 1970s has returned to the heights of the early twentieth-century 'Gilded Age' (Saez and Zucman 2019 Chap. 1).

The success of *les trente glorieuses* of the social democratic era was remarkable, not only in reducing inequality somewhat, but also achieving rates of economic growth that put to shame the neoliberal claim to economic prowess (Piketty 2020 Chap. 11). Since the eclipse of the Keynesian welfarist consensus, inequality and poverty have increased everywhere (albeit varying with the extent of resistance to unleashing the full panoply of free market policies in some political economies, notably social democratic Scandinavia). In view of social democracy's achievements, the victory of the neoliberal onslaught against it thus poses something of a puzzle, which the next section addresses.

14 Social democracy

The strange decline of social democracy, 1970–2008

During the 30 years post World War II, there was widespread consensus in the Western world concerning Keynesian macroeconomic management policies. These were aimed at preventing the catastrophe of another Great Depression like the one that devastated the Western world after 1929. Not only had the worldwide slump brought widespread suffering in itself, but also it underlay the rise of Nazism and the massive loss of life and destruction wrought by World War II. The key purpose of Keynesian strategies was to minimise unemployment and economic instability.

In practice its main tools were counter-cyclical fiscal and monetary policy, which came to be pursued in all Western countries. These were crucially under-pinned by the system of international financial exchange negotiated at Bretton Woods in 1944 by Keynes, Harry Dexter White of the US Treasury, and repre-sentatives of 44 Allied countries (Conway 2015; Steil 2014). There were consider-able arguments between Keynes and White that were primarily won by the USA, clearly the dominant economy by then. The system that emerged was one under-pinned by the dollar, which became convertible into gold at a specified rate, and administered by the creation of crucial international financial institutions, notably the International Monetary Fund and the World Bank. The primary aim was to stabilise international monetary flows and in particular to prevent speculative cur-rency raids. Keynes' own plan had been more ambitious: an international unit of account, 'Bancor', for measuring trade and financial transactions, under the aegis of a substantive world bank, to be called the International Clearing Union. The alter-native US-promoted system adopted at Bretton Woods did nonetheless underpin the economic growth and the reductions in poverty and inequality, experienced in the three post-war decades. But since Bretton Woods collapsed in the early 1970s, and in particular after the 2008 financial crisis, several influential voices have sug-gested that Keynes' proposals would have been preferable. 'The collapse of the Bretton Woods system, which was based on the (Harry Dexter) White approach, indicates that the Keynesian approach may have been more farsighted' (Xiaochuan 2009 p. 2; see also IMF 2010 p. 27).

If *les trente glorieuses* deserved their name, how did the social democratic political and economic consensus collapse so rapidly and completely after the 1970s? How has neoliberalism become hegemonic in policy and culture, at any rate until the 2007/8 financial crisis and the ensuing recession? Conventional accounts in most media, political, and even academic discussion scarcely scratch the surface.

The standard narrative usually runs through a cursory catalogue of familiar land-marks but hardly tackles the roots of the problems. The global event that features most prominently in all versions is the oil crisis of 1973. This was triggered by the embargo imposed by OPEC (the association of Arab oil-producing countries), as leverage over the USA and other Western states that supported Israel in the 1967 and 1973 wars. There can be no doubt that the impact on the global economy was profound, triggering a recession that ended the substantial growth of the post-war decades.

Both unemployment and inflation rose rapidly, dubbed 'stagflation', something that was supposedly ruled out by Keynesian policies. The latter – or at any rate their rather simplistic version as captured by the prevailing image of the 'Phillips curve' – postulated that inflation was the product of excessive demand, and unemployment the result of inadequate demand (Forder 2014). Fiscal policy should be used in a countercyclical way to stabilise growth by injecting or withdrawing demand through adjusting taxation and public expenditure at appropriate points in the economic cycle. This simple account of Keynes' sophisticated analysis was not subscribed to by most economists in the emerging debate between 'Keynesians' and 'monetarists', but it was widely influential in political and public discourse and underlay the frustration when in the 1970s the policy levers seemed as inefficacious as pushing string.

In addition to the impact of the oil shock, accounts of the overturning of the social democratic consensus usually refer to political, social, and cultural changes that were widespread in the West by the 1970s, with local specifics in each country. The list would generally include the rise of individualism at the expense of communal attachments; a decline of deference and subordination to tradition and authority; the growth of culture wars about feminism, racism, sexual politics, and policies; and a return of militancy in collective protest, industrial relations, and trade unionism. The upshot was a growing panic, promoted by the media and conservative politicians, about an insidious ungovernability in society, culture, and the economy. In the UK, these threats to welfare and order were dramatically promoted by the mainly Conservative-supporting media, encapsulated during the 1979 general election campaign by images of garbage in the streets and unburied bodies during a prolonged strike of public sector workers in a 'winter of discontent'.

This narrative is descriptively true in its details. But it leaves open any explanation of why these changes occurred. What were the underlying causes undermining the successful social democratic consensus of the post-war decades? That the descriptive story is usually presented without any further questioning is due largely to the widespread acceptance of the crux of the neoliberal claim, not only by conservatives but also by many liberals and leftists. It is seldom questioned that the post-war welfarist and Keynesian strategies had failed in and of themselves, and thus there was a need for a fundamental backlash in political economy and social policy.

A full account of the great shift from post-war consensus to neoliberal hegemony has yet to be constructed. But the following sketch suggests that a more profound probing of the roots of change in political economy and culture is sorely needed.

Political economy

The fundamental problem with the application of Keynesian macroeconomic management techniques in the post-war period was not any technical deficiency. The root problem lay in the nature of the capitalist political economy that it was the avowed goal of Keynes to rescue – from the instability and inequality generated

16 Social democracy

by neoclassical free market economics, and from the authoritarian socialism he feared – in favour of a liberal democratic socialism (Crotty 2019; Mann 2019; Carter 2020). The sociological flaw in the Keynesian strategy was predicted by his contemporary, the Polish economist Michael Kalecki. Kalecki's relationship to Keynes is reminiscent of that between Alfred Russell Wallace and Charles Darwin. Kalecki developed an analysis of the sources of unemployment and economic cycles similar to Keynes, independently but with each aware of the other's work, albeit from different theoretical traditions (Robinson 1964; Toporowski 2011). A socialist steeped in Marxism, Kalecki incorporated a concept of classes into his analysis, and anticipated that the Keynesian revolution in macroeconomic management of capitalism would eventually be undermined by its own success (Kalecki 1943; Kaletsky 2010 pp. 52–53). The achievement of full employment would invigorate the economic and social power of the working class beyond a point acceptable to the upper class of capitalists and their political representatives. The latter would seek to reassert their dominance and restore a higher share of national income to profits, even if their absolute wealth had grown with general prosperity.

In the early stages of the eclipse of social democracy by neoliberalism, one key (albeit heavily debated) explanation offered by some Marxists was the falling rate and share of profits, with the consequences predicted by Kalecki (Glyn and Sutcliffe 1972a, 1972b; Yaffe 1973; Bowles et al. 1983; White 2008). In addition, the growing public expenditure on welfare, and on government-financed provision of services such as health and education, meant higher levels of taxation or state borrowing, generating a growing 'fiscal crisis of the state' (O'Connor 1973). Always hugely criticised by the upper class and neoliberals, the purchase of their arguments against welfarism became greater in the 1970s, as stagflation seemed to show that the Keynesian programme was no longer working. This was linked to the growing focus of the right-wing press and politicians on a supposedly excessive rise in trade union power and militancy, buttressed by the prioritisation of control of unemployment over inflation in fiscal and monetary policy up to the 1970s. As inflation and unemployment spiraled out of control, industrial conflict intensified, feeding the moral panic about ungovernability in the UK, USA, and elsewhere.

The abandonment of Bretton Woods, which had underpinned the post-war achievements of Keynesianism, owed far more to the activities of conservative business and governmental elites than to the right-wing bogies of excessive welfare, over-mighty trade unions, or even exogenous shocks like the oil crisis. The crucial date for the switch to neoliberal dominance was 15 August 1971, when President Richard Nixon issued the order that ended the direct convertibility of the dollar into gold at a rate pegged under the Bretton Woods agreement. This was followed by the abandonment of the system's pegs by other countries, making all currencies 'fiat' ones that floated freely in exchange value, with increasing instability in the face of cyclical trade currents and speculative flows. It was this that made it ever harder for governments to implement Keynesian demand management, when this required greater public expenditure with budget deficits that invited runs against their currencies. Trying to balance this by monetary policy and higher interest rates

Social democracy **17**

to attract foreign investment stoked inflation in turn. So stagflation had arrived, and ultimately the erosion of the post-war consensus by neoliberalism, which prioritised inflation and the interests of capital and finance over the employment and living standards of the mass of people.

But what had necessitated the 1971 'Nixon shock'? In essence it was the financial backlash of big business and bankers against the shift in favour of the mass of the population, symbolised by the falling share of profits. The immediate triggers were a growing American balance of payments deficit, and increasing speculative pressure on the dollar. The US Treasury's fiscal problems came partly from the benign Dr Jekyll side of the Kennedy and Johnson governments in the 1960s: the 'Great Society' programme and federal support for civil rights. But they came even more from the government's evil Mr Hyde aspect: the devastating Vietnam War.

The fiscal problems of the USA were exacerbated by financial developments in European money markets, spearheaded by some London banks' shenanigans as early as 1955 (Schenk 1998; Shaxson 2011; Green 2016; Bullough 2018; Blakeley 2019 pp. 40–42). During the 1960s a growing volume of dollars – 'Eurodollars' – were held in Europe by British and other banks, outside the jurisdiction and regulatory ambit of the US Federal Reserve. These generated higher earnings for business and financial players than the Fed-held dollars, although with greater risks. But the most significant attraction was their anonymity.

> 'These stateless dollars . . . could flow between countries unhindered . . . and the laws could not follow them' (Bullough op cit p. 35). By the early 1960s these 'deposits already amounted to $1 billion. . . $50 billion in today's money' (Shaxson 2018 p. 57). Twenty years later they were $1.6 trillion.
>
> *(ibid. p. 287)*

It is fascinating criminologically that the crucial weapon which dealt a fatal blow to the widespread growth and stability of the post-war consensus was rule breaking by plutocrats. They brought about a new normal as their deviance grew: a prime example of 'defining deviance down' to suit the powerful.

Soon the cunning of city bankers began to offer even more lucrative, and harder to unravel, varieties of financial instruments, notably Eurobonds and bearer bonds, developed by Warburg's in particular (Bullough op cit. Chap. 2). These innovations took advantage of jurisdictions like London, Switzerland, and a proliferation of tax and financial havens. They were prepared to furnish even warmer and ever less intrusive welcomes to footloose money. 'One of the main reasons the Euromarkets grew so fast was that their lack of controls made them a paradise for tax cheats, scammers and criminals' (Shaxson 2018 p. 56), as well as all wealthy people seeking tax shelters.

Thus was born the new world of 'offshore': 'the moment when clever London bankers conjured into existence a virtual country where, if you were rich enough, whoever you were, wherever your money came from, the laws did not apply to you'

18 Social democracy

(Bullough 2018 p. 42; Shaxson 2011, 2018 Chap. 2). Especially after the neoliberal governments of the 1980s poured rocket fuel on to the securitisation initiated by the limited deregulation of the 1970s, the complexity and ingenuity of increasingly ethereal financial instruments has exploded (Benjamin 2007 offers a definitive and lucid legal account of their sophistication on the verge of the 2008 crash).

This global financialisation was eventually to prove the trigger for the economic crisis of 2007/8, exposing the deeper failings of the neoliberal political economy and culture that spawned it (Tooze 2018 Parts I and II). The ramifications are still multiplying, most evidently the widespread alienation from the dominant form of political economy and public policy that produced the electoral shocks spearheaded by the 2016 UK Brexit vote and the US election of Donald Trump (Tooze ibid. Part IV; Lonergan and Blyth 2020).

The neoliberal assault on working-class post-war gains was spurred further by social democratic governments' attempts to advance democracy into the workplace itself during the 1960s and 1970s. The clearest case of this was the Swedish Rehn–Meidner plan (Blyth 2002 pp. 119–125; Harvey 2005 pp. 112–115; Berman 2006 pp. 184–186, 196–197). Under this:

> a 20 per cent tax on corporate profits would flow into wage earner funds controlled by the unions to be reinvested in the corporations. The effect would be to steadily reduce the significance of private ownership and to build towards collective ownership managed by the representatives of the workers. . . . However generous the terms of the buy-out may have been, the capitalist class was threatened with gradual annihilation as a distinctive class.
>
> *(Harvey ibid. pp. 112–113)*

No other country got as far down the road towards 'workers' control' in industry as Sweden, but the issue was on the agenda throughout Western Europe. In Britain, for example, in 1975 the Wilson government set up a Committee of Enquiry into Industrial Democracy, which reported two years later (Bullock 1977). Its terms of reference began:

> Accepting the need for a radical extension of industrial democracy in the control of companies by means of representation on boards of directors, and accepting the essential role of trade union organizations in this process, to consider how such an extension can best be achieved.

There were splits on the commission between the industrialists and the trade union and academic members. Its report was opposed on the one hand by business interests and company lawyers criticising the dilution of shareholder domination, and on the other hand by some socialists who felt it was too timid (Coates and Topham 1977; Coates 2003). In recent times there has been a revival of interest in industrial democracy, and in particular the Rehn-Meidner model, which continues to inspire current attempts to revive democratic socialism (Gowan and Viktorrson

2017; *New Socialist* 2017; Gowan 2018; Wray 2017; Pendleton 2018; McDonnell 2019 pp. xiv–xvi; Gowan and Lawrence 2019; Sunkara 2019 pp. 119–124).

If the birth of neoliberalism as governmental economic and social policy was attended by apparent economic crises, and by onslaughts on the conditions and power of workers, how was it successful in winning electoral majorities in the UK and USA by the turn of the 1980s? A superficial answer is tactical political superiority over the Left, facilitated considerably by the right-wing bias of most news media. As with the 2007/8 financial crisis, the Right were faster and smarter in putting over their narrative that the economic problems of capital should be blamed on profligate welfare spending (enough seems always to be found for war) and over-mighty trade unions greedily demanding higher wages, at the expense of the deserving rich who needed tax cuts (Klein 2007; Mirowski 2013). This was achieved in part by the successful promotion of free market perspectives by a growing proliferation of neoliberal intellectuals and think tanks, pushing simple analyses that had resonance with everyday problems of household budgeting, falsely presented as analogous with government budgets.

Ideology

The ideological undermining of the post-war consensus occurred in stages, accelerating after the late 1960s. There are a number of authoritative accounts of the origins of neoliberal perspectives, dating it back to the 1930s. The term 'neoliberalism' itself was coined at the 1938 Walter Lippman Colloqium. This was hosted in Paris by German philosopher Louis Rougier and co-organised by Friedrich von Hayek and German economist Wilhelm Ropke. Both were disciples of the Austrian economist Ludwig von Mises, a key figure in the neoliberal critique of Keynesian and socialist economics (Slobodian 2018 pp. 78–90). Von Mises was explicit in putting the 'democracy' of the free market above that of elections: 'the capitalistic market economy is a democracy, in which every penny constitutes a vote' (Zevin 2019 p. 27). It amounted to a 'consumer plebiscite' as the rich depended on the 'will of the people as consumers' (ibid.).

In England during World War II as a refugee, Hayek penned his best known book, *The Road to Serfdom*, a vigorous attack on the evils of totalitarianism. However, his primary target was neither Nazism (portrayed as a variant of socialism) nor Soviet Communism, but social democracy, presented as the slippery slope to totalitarianism.

After the war, Hayek was the leading figure in the establishment of the Mont Pelerin Society, named after the Swiss mountain resort where the first meeting was held in 1947 (Mirowski and Plehwe 2009; Jackson 2010; D. Stedman Jones 2012 Chaps. 2–4; Burgin 2012 Chap. 3; Peck 2013; Cahill and Konings 2017 Chap. 1; Slobodian 2018).

The Mont Pelerin Society (MPS) was the cradle of 'the neoliberal thought collective' (Mirowski and Plehwe op cit.). Its first meeting gathered a galaxy of economists and philosophers, including Hayek, von Mises, Milton Friedman, Karl

20 Social democracy

Popper, Lionel Robbins, Michael Polanyi, and Bernard de Jouvenel. All shared a generally liberal perspective, but not an undiluted faith in free markets. Popper, for example, left after the society rejected his suggestion that some socialists should be included (Stedman Jones op.cit. p. 40), and Michael Polanyi and de Jouvenel left within the first decade. So too did Raymond Aron who became a member only after the 1947 founding meeting, although he had attended the 1938 Walter Lippman Colloquium (Gane 2016). Over time the society became more dominated by economists with a free market position and was '*the* transnational think-tank that brought different strands of Austrian, German, British, French and American neoliberal thought into contact with one another' (Gane ibid. p. 263).

The MPS certainly contained a variety of perspectives, especially at the outset, and comprised a range of complex and sophisticated thinkers. However, it was rapidly supplemented by more polemical and populist free market think tanks and academic institutions, financed lavishly by corporate interests and wealthy right-wing individuals (Smith 1991; Cockett 1994; Jackson 2012). It was these that really carried neoliberalism from its intellectual roots at the MPS, through the wilderness years of the 1950s and '60s, when the post-war consensus remained dominant, to the increasing influence of free market ideas on political debates and governments from the 1970s onwards. Prominent US examples include the Hoover Institution, the American Enterprise Institute, the Heritage Foundation, and the Cato Institute (Fones-Wolf 1994; Carey 1996; Frank 2001; Burgin op.cit. p. 206). In Britain the brand leader was the Institute of Economic Affairs, founded in 1955 (Jackson 2012). Since then think tanks advocating free market and small-state perspectives have proliferated in Britain, such as the Centre for Policy Studies (founded 1974), the Adam Smith Institute (1977), Policy Exchange (2002), and the Tax Payers' Alliance (2004). Such think tanks were a crucial factor in the triumph of neoliberalism, symbolised above all by Margaret Thatcher's election victory in 1979 and the election as US President of Ronald Reagan in 1980. A particularly insidious aspect of these think tanks is that their innocuous names allow them to be presented in media debates as non-political. They also for the most part hide their primary sources of funding, flowing largely from corporate elites and intelligence agencies (Stonor Saunders 2000; Monbiot 2000, 2016; Mayer 2016; MacLean 2017).

'Buying time' for neoliberalism

Even more fundamentally, the potential resentment of the mass of people at the undermining of their prosperity and security by neoliberal policies primarily benefiting the rich, was defused by a variety of economic and financial tactics for 'buying time' (Streeck 2014). These repeatedly kicked down the road 'the delayed crisis of democratic capitalism' (ibid.). After the 1970s the real earnings of workers in the USA and UK remained static for the most part (and insecurity increased insidiously), although aspirations and consumption levels continued to grow generally. This conjuring trick was achieved by a succession of fiscal Ponzi schemes.

Four overlapping stages can be distinguished. The first was the unintended outcome of the forced destruction of Bretton Woods in the early 1970s: stagflation. Precarious social peace, at a time of real slump in overall growth and in the share of wages, was achieved *sotto voce* by the manipulation of what Keynes had called 'money illusion'. This was:

> a monetary policy that accommodated wage rises in excess of productivity growth, resulting in high global rates of inflation, especially in the second half of the 1970s. . . . The trick was to defuse the emergent distribution conflict between labour and capital by introducing additional resources, even if these existed only as money. . . . Inflation made the cake only seem larger.
>
> *(Streeck 2014 pp. 32–33)*

This was a way of borrowing from the future:

> Governments that sought social peace by means of inflation, introducing not yet existing resources into the capitalist distributional conflict, were able to draw on the magic of modern "fiat money", the amount of which may increase *ad libitum* depending upon political will and balances of power.
>
> *(Streeck ibid. pp. 33–34)*

By the late 1970s, high and rapid inflation came to be seen as problematic by all sides, but with the blame increasingly pinned by the media on excessively generous welfare spending by social democratic governments and their supposed weakness in the face of trade union militancy.

The neoliberal governments that swept to power in the 1980s, spearheaded by Margaret Thatcher in the UK and Ronald Reagan in the USA, were able to capitalise on that narrative. They adopted tough monetary policies which drove up unemployment, weakened trade unionism, and allowed cuts in welfare entitlements (although as the demand for support increased with growing unemployment and poverty, public expenditure on these services increased).

Backed up by strong state law and order tactics, particularly targeting trade union militancy and political protest, and a broadly sycophantic media, these policies signalled the destruction of the post-war consensus. The stronger state required by the 'freeing' of the economy (Gamble 1994) came with a hefty price tag for governments. Public debt as a share of national product in OECD countries went up by around a quarter in the 1980s (Streeck ibid. Figure 1.1 p. 8). 'Since tax increases would have been as politically risky as faster erosion of the social state, governments turned to debt as a way out' (Streeck ibid. p. 36), the second phase of 'buying time'. The rising extent of public debt became increasingly worrying for governments, producing pressure from money markets concerned about the prospects of repayment.

This led to the third stage of the Ponzi process of stealing from the future, already underway in the late 1980s in the wake of increasing deregulation of

22 Social democracy

financial institutions. The financial permissive society was symbolised above all by the 1986 'Big Bang', whereby the Thatcher government considerably relaxed the rules under which the stock exchange operated, and by the 1999 US repeal of the New Deal Era Glass-Steagall Act, which had erected strict barriers between retail and investment banking 'that prevented banks from gambling with their depositors' money' (Shaxson 2018 p. 159).

The 'third way' governments of the 1990s–2000s, notably Clinton's New Democrats and Blair's New Labour, presided over an era in which the proliferation of increasingly sophisticated financial products were widely touted as magic vehicles for taming risk. Bundling assets of variable riskiness into packages that were traded in ever more complex and opaque networks was believed to achieve the alchemy of eliminating the riskiness of the whole, as the good risks miraculously transubstantiated the bad (Tooze 2018). The belief in this miracle was sustained by a variety of theologies, from the 'efficient markets hypothesis' to the Black-Merton-Scholes formula for calculating the riskiness and value of derivatives and other financial instruments. The collapse in 2000 of Long-Term Asset Management, a hedge fund based on the supposed magic formula, demonstrated the hubris of trying to tame risk completely (Shaxson 2018 pp. 140–141).

The extent to which financialisation was a way of trying to protect the living standards of the most vulnerable sections of society, without the state having to increase public debt through welfare state or other public support measures, is indicated by the growth of subprime mortgages as a key aspect of the process. This was a way of relieving governments of the cost of providing public housing by extending to poorer people house purchase opportunities, as regulation of financial instruments like mortgages became ever weaker. This was notoriously the Achilles' heel of the securitisation process, which brought the whole house of cards tumbling down in 2007/8.

More generally, the third stage of the Ponzi scheme to defer a crisis of legitimacy for neoliberalism resulted in an explosion of private debt after the mid-1990s (Streeck 2014 Fig 1.9 p. 42). This has been aptly dubbed 'privatised Keynesianism' (Crouch 2009; Streeck ibid. pp. 38–39), boosting aggregate demand at a time of sluggish growth in real incomes by increasing private indebtedness.

The fourth stage of the 'buying time' saga has been the most unstable and least successful in its own terms, the often frantic and confused efforts to deal with the 2007/8 financial crisis and its ongoing ramifications (comprehensively analysed in the magisterial Tooze 2018). Streeck offers the gloomy prognostication that the governmental strategies to pull the world back from the brink of complete economic collapse after 2008 will struggle to maintain any vestige of liberal (let alone social) democracy. Tooze's detailed account shows that the financial fix of bailouts and quantitative easing in the decade since the crash was constructed and conducted largely behind the scenes of public discussion. It involved the deception, and sometimes setting aside, of democratic processes (e.g. at crucial stages in both Greece and Italy in 2011, replacing elected politicians by 'technocratic experts' with impeccable neoliberal pedigrees, cf. Tooze op.cit. pp. 410–412).

Social democracy **23**

The claim that liberal democracy is experiencing its greatest threat since the 1930s has become commonplace since 2010. After the victories in 2016 of the Leave campaign in the UK Referendum and the election of Donald Trump as US President, books and articles have poured out probing the rise of a new 'populism' at the expense of liberal democracy.

These frightening developments are the bitter fruit of the hegemony of neoliberalism, which although still in the saddle in terms of political control has run out of room in terms of legitimating itself by offering material benefits to the mass of people.

As Streeck warned:

> To continue along the road followed for the last forty years is to attempt to free the capitalist economy and its markets . . . from the kind of mass democracy that was part of the regime of postwar democratic capitalism. . . . In particular, the money magic of the past two decades, produced with the help of an unfettered finance industry, may have become too dangerous for governments to buy more time with it. . . . The utopian ideal of present-day crisis management is to complete, with political means, the already far-advanced depoliticization of the economy . . . with a population that would have learned, over years of hegemonic re-education, to regard the distributional outcomes of free markets as fair, or at least without alternative.
>
> *(Streeck ibid. p. 46; a pessimism reinforced in*
> *the preface to the 2017 second edition)*

The prospects for the future are considered in the conclusion of this book. But to complete this account of how *les trente glorieuses* were displaced by neoliberal hegemony, the foregoing political economy analysis must be augmented by consideration of the cultural shifts that eventually won over much of the population (and indeed the left-liberal politicians of the West in the era of Clintonian Democrats and New Labour).

Neoliberal culture

The cultural shifts developed in interaction with the political and economic changes outlined earlier. They can be summed up best by the title of a monumental work documenting the change: *The New Spirit of Capitalism* (Boltanski and Chiapello 2005). The old spirit was analysed by Weber's seminal classic *The Protestant Ethic and the Spirit of Capitalism* (Weber 1904/2001). In Weber's account the spirit of capitalism was embodied in a Puritan ethic of hard work, thrift, self-discipline, and deferred gratification. It was this attitude, of work now, reward later, that motivated sufficient labour and savings to make capital formation possible on a large-enough scale. Although indigence was frowned upon if it was seen as self-inflicted, charity to relieve the suffering of the deserving poor, who were victims of circumstances beyond their control, was a Christian virtue.

24 Social democracy

In Boltanski and Chiapello's analysis, following both Weber and Marx, capitalism's reproduction requires not only a successful political economy backed by force (of more or less legitimacy), but also it requires ideological acceptance, or better still enthusiasm, from the mass of people. However the exploitation, alienation, hierarchy, and managerial discipline inherent in capitalist industrial processes has also always generated incipient rejection. Critique of capitalism has been directed historically at four targets:

a   Disenchantment and inauthenticity;
b   Oppression and subordination, by the domination of the market and of management;
c   Poverty, inequality, and the suffering they bring;
d   Ruthless egoistic individualism (Boltanski and Chiapello op.cit. p. 37).

The first two generate an 'artistic critique' (ibid. Chap. 7) of capitalism (found e.g. in bohemian subcultures, and in Marx 1844/1975). The latter two generate the 'social critique' (Boltanski and Chiapello op.cit. Chap. 6), characterising the mainstream of socialism and social democracy. The two types of critique flourished simultaneously during the 1960s counterculture, reaching its apogee in May 1968 when uprisings, especially in France, brought together student protests and industrial strikes (ibid. Chap. 3). The 'new spirit of capitalism' developed since the 1970s, through the capture by capitalism of the 'artistic critique', and its severance from the 'social critique'. The latter was suppressed by the permeation of political discussion by neoliberal economic analysis suggesting TINA ('there is no alternative') and the variety of forms of 'buying time' outlined earlier which allowed mass consumption standards (but not real earnings or security) to be protected.

This was accentuated in the 1990s by the basic conversion of social democratic parties to the 'third way', accepting neoliberalism as inevitable. It is far from coincidental that this conversion of *soi-disant* social democratic parties to neoliberalism followed the collapse of the Soviet Union and its Eastern European empire in 1989. The existence of a rival form of political economy – however much it lagged behind Western competitors – worked to persuade capitalist elites that they needed to support the post-war social democratic consensus, or at least to postpone any collapse of mass living standards by the Ponzi schemes outlined earlier. The fall of the USSR, welcome in human rights terms, nonetheless allowed full-throttle free market capitalism to be unleashed.

The 'new spirit of capitalism' built upon 1960s countercultural values, based on the 'artistic critique' of inauthenticity and restrictions on individual liberty. To large swathes of people, especially the young, the counterculture offered a wondrously tempting mix of freedom, hedonism, erosion of unnecessary disciplines, and traditions: sex, drugs, and rock 'n' roll. These individualistic attractions were originally wrapped up with essentially Left ideals: equality (not only of class but race, gender, and sexuality), peace, justice, and concern for the environment (Vinen 2018). The uniting value was love, expressed explicitly by the 1967 hippy 'Summer of Love' in

Social democracy **25**

San Francisco, which spread across the world. 'All you need is love' sang the Beatles. 'Make love, not war' united an invitation to personal pleasure with an injunction not to act hatefully towards others.

The immensely seductive invitational edge of this new culture of love and freedom was rapidly prised away from its Left associations by the cunning of capitalism's genius for survival. The counterculture became commodified and commercialised as consumerism. It is commonplace that the second half of the twentieth century saw the rise of a consumerist society, generating a library of analyses celebrating or criticising it (Bauman 2004, 2007; Hall et al. 2008; Trentmann 2016). Consumerism signifies more than the growth of increasing levels of consumption, but rather that consumption becomes an aspect of a struggle for status, not just satisfaction of material wants – *conspicuous* consumption (Veblen 1899). In essence, it turns all goods into 'positional goods' (Hirsch 1977). But whilst Hirsch's original notion referred to things that are naturally scarce, such as a beautiful mountain-top view, a consumerist ethos turns everything into something valued because it enhances status rather than intrinsic pleasure. It is position in the league table that counts, not one's absolute position. Life becomes a zero-sum game of endless aspiration doomed to end in inevitable failure (Hall et al. 2020). But however many losers crowd the roulette wheel, the house of capitalism always wins.

Through an empirical analysis of management texts, Boltanski and Chiapello distil the essence of the new spirit of capitalism:

> Instead of the buttoned-down, self-disciplined and disciplinarian capitalists of old, the new model is buccaneering, adventurous, playful but bold. Charisma, vision, gifts of communication, intuition, mobility and generalism become the ideal traits of the new leaders – dressed-down, cool capitalists like Bill Gates or 'Ben and Jerry' . . . who refuse to surround themselves with the formal trappings of bureaucratic authority.
>
> *(Budgen 2000 p. 253)*

Discipline is exerted not by overt sanctions but by the embedding in most individuals of aspirations to follow these entrepreneurs to the top, which in the more laid-back environment of contemporary workplaces feels open to the talents – a new American Dream. Of course, this is not open at all to the many who service the primary workforce in a variety of ways, from cleaning to cooking to childcare to cab-driving, the precariat who are not even a reserve army of labour (Standing 2011).

The new spirit of capitalism flourished because of the export to 'emerging' economies of Fordist mass manufacturing, based on Taylorist models of rigid hierarchical management by networked firms operating in globalised webs of exchange (Boltanski and Chiapello op. cit. Chap. 4). There was an elective affinity between the less hierarchical forms of service organisations in Western countries and the new spirit of capitalism. The hidden price of this freedom for even the core workforce is their increasing precarity (Standing op. cit.). But would-be swashbuckling

26 Social democracy

masters of the universe can perhaps tolerate the thrill of risk and insecurity, at least for a while.

The core value of the new spirit is 'cool', which has been commercialised from an insider's minority culture of esoteric, artistic, or even spiritual superiority, into a badge of discernment and one-upmanship that is contradicted by its ubiquity (Pountain and Robins 2000). The game is kept going only because of constant commercial emphasis on the narcissism of small differences in style, preying on the insecurities of people desperate not to be caught out as uncool by sporting the wrong brands and logos (Klein 2000). Thus, commercial culture has bought up the counterculture in the service of capital (Frank 1997). The tropes and symbols of Left radicalism in the hippy era have been re-marketed as 'the rebel sell' (Heath and Potter 2005). Capitalism captured cool, appropriating dissidence into itself as a marketable commodity (McGuigan 2009).

However, just as the political economy of buying time ran out of road with the 2007/8 crash, the co-option of cool is an ever-harder sell in an age of austerity, insecurity, and ever-greater anxiety. The conquest of cool has had to go a stage further, with the increasing commercialisation of personal happiness and well-being by a new tribe of experts, purporting to teach us to be positive in the face of adversity (Ehrenreich 2010; Davies 2016, 2018).

Social democracy: core meaning and values

In the early 1980s, Britain's 'Social Democratic Party' (SDP) was founded by break-aways from the Labour Party, which they saw as moving too far towards socialism. The SDP later merged with the Liberal Party, and its splitting of political opposition to Thatcher was the proximate cause that gave the Conservatives four successive electoral victories. It also clouded the meaning of the term 'social democracy', which is now seen through the lens of the SDP as essentially a left wing of liberalism, without any hint of any deeper challenge to capitalism than minor reforms. During the 1990s this 'third way', pioneered by Tony Blair and his guru Tony Giddens, was espoused by many European leaders on the Centre Left. It had a tortuous relation to social democracy, which some still espoused as a label, but now was very much more in the mould of the 1980s SDP than the turn of the twentieth-century parties that had remained unabashedly socialist even in their revisionist wings.

Although the term 'social democracy' has thus been used in a variety of conflicting ways, and with varying relationships to cognate ideas such as liberalism or democratic socialism, it will be argued that there is a core concept and vision underlying these. Social democracy at root is the belief in an ethical ideal synthesizing the values of equality, liberty, and fraternity/community. These are regarded as interdependent rather than conflicting. Social democracy as a political movement stands for the possibility and indeed necessity of translating these values into government policy and everyday practice. On the basis of these aspirations, the chapter constructs an ideal type of 'social democracy' as a model for subsequent discussion. The intellectual roots of this lie in contrasting progenitors, originally primarily

Marxist and other Western European socialist movements. In the British Labour Party, arguably the most successful in the post-war period, the core inspiration was the English tradition of ethical socialism (Dennis and Halsey 1988), the quintessential exemplar of which was R.H. Tawney but which also included such thinkers as Graham Wallas, Hobhouse, and T.H. Marshall.

The 1990s' 'third way' of the two Tonys, Blair and Giddens, explicitly sought to triangulate this 'social democracy' with neoliberalism. Until then, however, 'social democracy' was always a species of socialism, although in the early twentieth century it had itself become a 'third way' between two poles, communism and liberalism. It was not, however, a *faut de mieux* or presentational splitting of the difference, but an anguished and internally contested terrain, an intellectual and moral Buridan's ass, torn between the powerful pulls of justice and liberty. There were, of course, many attempts to synthesise the two poles. The most fully developed of these remains John Rawls' magisterial theory of justice (Rawls 1971). This appeared just as the political and social influence of social democracy was about to dip below the horizon, a paradigm example of Hegel's owl of Minerva spreading its wings at dusk. Rawls is usually seen as a liberal theorist, but his arguments for principles that balance liberty and equality offer the most powerful case for the values underpinning social democracy. Recent scholarship (Edmundson 2017) has indeed shown that Rawls was a 'reluctant socialist', who moved towards more explicit identification with liberal and democratic socialism, as indicated by his last revisiting of his theory of justice (Rawls 2001).

'Social democracy' as an intellectual discourse, and *a fortiori* actually existing social democratic parties and governments, encompassed a wide variety of viewpoints and programmes. In its mid-twentieth century glorious decades, the heyday of European mixed-economy welfare states and the Rooseveltian New Deal in the United States, it stood for a broad consensus, albeit with vigorous opposition from unreconciled free marketers, old conservative nostalgists, and most Marxists.

This consensus also tacitly underpinned the analyses of crime and strategies for reform developed by most criminologists at that time (Garland and Sparks 2000 p. 195), as is explored in the next two chapters. There was a deep structure of shared assumptions amongst criminologists and practitioners that could be characterised as social democratic. This was shown by the quiet confidence of policymakers that, for all the problems of wartime and post-war crime, social progress would resolve these (Morris 1989 Chaps. 2, 3, 6; Bottoms and Stevenson 1992).

Social democracy: an ideal type

The terms 'social democracy' and 'democratic socialism' hitch together two words whose meaning has been debated over very long periods: democracy since antiquity, social and socialism since the early nineteenth century. They are all 'essentially contested concepts' in the terminology of the philosopher W.B. Gallie. These are 'concepts the proper use of which inevitably involves endless disputes about their proper uses on the part of their users' (Gallie 1956 p. 169). There are four

28 Social democracy

conditions constituting such concepts. They must be: 'appraisive' (i.e. necessarily involve some value judgements), 'internally complex', 'variously describable', and 'open' – they are liable to change considerably with changing circumstances.

Gallie specifically gives 'democracy' as a 'live example' (his others are 'religion', 'art', and 'social justice' pp. 183–187). Democracy is '*The* appraisive political concept *par excellence* in modern times'. Various complex meanings of democracy are postulated (e.g. majority choice of government, equal opportunity to acquire responsible leadership positions, citizen participation or self-government).

The fundamental meaning of democracy is vague:

> Certain political aspirations which have been embodied in countless slave, peasant, national and middle-class revolts and revolutions, as well as in scores of national constitutions and party records and programmes. These aspirations are evidently centred in a demand for increased equality: or, to put it negatively, they are advanced against governments and social orders whose aim is to prolong gross forms of inequality.
>
> *(Gallie op.cit.)*

Interpretations of democracy are contested between changing cultures and values, and conflicting interests and perspectives.

Today, the interpretation of democracy as dependent on formally free elections is paramount, although there is also widespread acknowledgement that voting may produce a 'tyranny of the majority' (as feared by de Toqueville and John Stuart Mill). Thus, some protection of minority rights is also seen as essential to democracy by most analysts. So too is the 'rule of law'. Neglected in much contemporary discussion is the idea of democracy as an expression of aspirations for equality more generally, or at any rate of suspicion of 'gross forms of inequality':

> Whereas the concepts of religion, of art and of democracy would seem to admit, under my condition (III), of an indefinite number of possible descriptions, the concept of social justice as popularly used to-day seems to admit of only two.
>
> *(Gallie p. 187)*

Of these the first rests on the ideas of merit and commutation: justice consists in the institution and application of those social arrangements whereby the meritorious individual receives his commutative due. The second rests upon, in the sense of presupposing, the ideas (or ideals) of co-operation, to provide the necessities of a worthwhile human life, and of distribution of products to assure such a life to all who co-operate. It is natural to take these two descriptions as characteristic of two facets of contemporary morality, which might be labelled liberal and socialist, respectively. But in fact these two facets would seem to appear in any morality or moral teaching worthy of the name: witness, for example, the opposed lessons of the parable of the

Social democracy **29**

talents and the parable of the vineyard . . . It is the sheer duality of these opposed uses that is of particular interest, since it suggests a bridge between those appraisive concepts which are variously describable and essentially contested and those whose everyday use appears to be uniquely describable and universally acknowledged.

(op.cit.)

Thus the ideas of social democracy (or democratic socialism) tie together two essentially contested concepts, and unsurprisingly have generated endless debate about their 'true' meaning. As seen earlier, their predominant usages have shifted over time.

Social democracy as an ideal type: nine thematic dimensions

Primacy of the ethical

In current political debate the language of morality has been captured by the religious Right in the United States, and by *Daily Mail* reading circles in the United Kingdom, and the politicians who fear them. This restricts the normative scope to an extremely narrow conception of 'traditional family values'. It blots out much broader conceptions of the moral universe, governing all spheres of human activity. Morality in wider spheres, including political economy and all social relations, has been the focus historically of many religious and secular philosophies, on the left as much as on the right of politics (Rogan 2018). As Michael Walzer has put it:

> For right-wing intellectuals and activists, values seem to be about sex and almost nothing else; vast areas of social life are left to the radically amoral play of market forces. And yet they "have" values, and we [the liberal left] don't.
>
> *(Walzer 2005 p. 37)*

The growing Republican domination of US politics since 1980, attributed by many analysts to the 'values' issue above all (Frank 2004), has prompted much discussion of the need for the left to recapture the language of ethics and passionate commitment to justice.

The left has often been uncomfortable with discussions of morality. Marx is said to have roared with laughter when he heard talk about morality (Lukes 1985 p. 27). He and Engels castigated ethically derived versions of socialism as 'utopian', rejecting them for a 'scientific' materialism (Marx and Engels 1848 [1998] pp. 72–75; Engels 1880). For the most part they espoused a political economy in which the course of human history was largely if not wholly shaped by the succession of modes of production. Such a deterministic perspective sat oddly with their lifelong commitment to vigorous political activism. It was also accompanied, even in the cornerstone of Marxist political economy, *Capital*, with analyses of specific

30 Social democracy

historical events. In these the functional prerequisites of capitalist development are mediated by relatively autonomous human actions and conflicts. A key example is the pivotal Chapter Ten, which explains the emergence of the Factory Acts. Nonetheless, an 'obstretic' view of history has been a deadly illusion for Marxists, whereby socialists act merely as midwives of communism, which will inevitably be born after the revolution generated by the contradictions of capitalism (G. Cohen 2000). This fatally underestimated the huge moral transformation that has to anticipate and accompany political and economic change if it is not to produce new forms of tyranny in the guise of liberation. It also skates over the depth of Marx and Engels' own moral sensitivity to the evils of industrial capitalism, redolent on almost every page of their writing. Arguably, it was a self *mis*-understanding. Their fervent desire to overcome the evils of capitalism paradoxically underlay their rejection of moralism, in favour of wishful thinking about an inevitable progression to communism.

The non-Marxist left has always been clearly driven by moral concerns. 'The Labour Party owes more to Methodism than to Marxism', the then General Secretary of the Labour Party Morgan Phillips said in 1953 (the words were actually written by his speechwriter, Dennis Healey cf Callaghan 1987). Harold Wilson, the Labour leader whose winning stance in 1964 was the utilitarian pragmatism of a vaunted 'white heat' of technological revolution, claimed, 'The Labour party is a moral crusade or it is nothing' (Hattersley 2014). Social democracy, indeed socialism in general, has been fundamentally idealist and ethical, combining a critical political economy with a moral economy of equality.

The ends that social democratic political action aimed at, and the means adopted for their pursuit, were derived from and subject to more or less explicitly stated moral values. Secular or religious, social democrats implicitly espoused the fundamental equality of value of all individuals, the ancient Golden Rule embodied in the biblical injunction to love your neighbour as yourself (Leviticus XIX p. 18; Wattles 1997; Gensler 2013). A Talmudic sage, Ben Azzai, specifically related the Golden Rule in Leviticus to the earlier biblical declaration that all people were created in the image of God (Genesis 1: 27), thus all individuals share in a common basis for equal concern and respect. This derivation makes it clear that the Golden Rule is intended to be universal, applying to all people and not just literal 'neighbours'. It also suggests that an element of objectivity underpins the concrete obligations of care flowing from the injunction 'to love'. These should be based on a notion of the common 'image' of humanity – what Marx referred to as 'species being'– not a projection of my own subjective preferences. If I am a masochist I do not follow the rule by flogging my neighbour. R.H. Tawney, perhaps the prime prophet of British social democracy, explicitly based his Christian socialism on 'the doctrine of the Incarnation and its implication that each person was of "infinite value" (Rogan 2018 p. 41). In Tawney's own words: 'The essence of all morality is this, to believe that every human being is of infinite importance, and therefore that no consideration of expediency can justify the oppression of one by another' (Winter and Joslin 1972 p. 67).

Shorn of its religious cloak, this principle continued to underlie most modern (and arguably post-modern) conceptions of morality and justice (Holland 2019). This is most evident in Kantian formulations of the ethical as the universalisable (Kant 1785). But it is also implied in utilitarianism (usually regarded as a fundamentally opposed perspective because it seemingly rides roughshod over the distinctness of persons). But utilitarianism, at least as a starting point, treats every individual's happiness as an equal input into the felicific calculus.

Nietzsche in the late nineteenth century, and some post-modernist and Foucauldian approaches in the late twentieth century, expressly reject both traditional religious and Enlightenment versions of such universalist ethics as restrictions on human autonomy and diversity. They advocate instead an aesthetic ethics and politics (Nietzsche 1885; Rose 1999 p. 282–284). However, rejecting the claims of transcendental moral codes, and of any absolute epistemological foundations for ethics, does not entail the rejection of the value of the Golden Rule. Several attempts at developing post-foundational ethics – for all their differences – nonetheless seem to echo the principle of what Dworkin calls 'equal respect and concern for others'(Dworkin 2000). Boutellier, for example, has made an impressive attempt to develop criminal justice ethics from Rorty's pragmatic conception of liberal irony (Rorty 1989, 1999; Boutellier 2000 Chap. 6). Rorty argued that the ironist, who recognises the contingency of her convictions, can still be a 'liberal', including among their 'ungroundable desires their own hope that suffering will be diminished, that the humiliation of human beings by other human beings may cease' (Rorty 1989, p. xv).

This is paralleled by Bauman's attempt to develop a post-modern 'morality without ethics', 'resurrecting the consideration of the Other temporarily . . . suspended by the obedience to the norm' (Bauman 1995 p. 7). It also recalls Levinas's notion of the ethical as the obverse of 'egology' – the assertion of the primacy of the self. 'We name the calling into question of my spontaneity by the presence of the other ethics' (Levinas 1969 p. 33).

Some liberals and social democrats may have thought their values were grounded in the self-evidence of intuition, scientific knowledge, the ineluctable march of history, or the will of God. But for many it was clear that there are no indubitable Archimedean points on which to ground ethical commitments in an objective, unanswerable way. This does not mean, however, that the values espoused by social democrats – liberty, equality, fraternity, in the now hallowed formula of the French and other democratic revolutions – were unreasonable or that there were no arguments that could be marshalled for them. But these arguments were always essentially contested and potentially endless.

Ethics were also primary for social democrats in considering legitimate means. Good ends did not justify 'dirty hands' (Sartre 1948). Violence in particular could not be adopted as a tactic of choice, however noble the cause pursued, but only defensively, and if a necessary and proportionate last resort. Just revolutionary violence was bound by criteria similar to just war theory (Walzer 1977; J.T. Reiner 2018, 2019). The use of morally dirty means was not only wrong in itself but also

32 Social democracy

counter-productive. It corrupted the users and frustrated the achievement of ethically desirable goals.

Social democratic criminology in particular has often been associated with explanations of crime in terms of economic factors (poverty, inequality, unemployment), as is seen in Chapters 2 and 3. But it was much more than just criminological Clintonism ('it's the economy, stupid'). Social democratic criminology was primarily concerned with ethical issues, not least in its attempts to define and explain crime. In the first place, crime, criminal justice, punishment, and anti-social behaviours (at all levels of the social hierarchy) were problems because they were sources of harm and suffering. Not only victims of crime but also perpetrators, and the social conditions that ultimately underlay crime, were all matters for ethical concern.

More specifically it is important to stress that economic factors such as poverty, inequality, or unemployment were seen as leading to crime primarily because they weakened support (in general and in potential offenders) for morality, in the sense of concern and respect for others. Willem Bonger's work, for example, is usually characterised as the most thorough-going example of Marxist economic determinism applied to crime (Taylor, Walton and Young 1973). But Bonger analyses the inequities of capitalism as criminogenic not in themselves but because they stimulate a culture of egoism.

Merton's anomie theory, the paradigm social democratic account of crime, is often reduced to a simplistic explanation in terms of structural inequalities in legitimate opportunities. But moral factors are basic to Merton's analysis. Merton stressed that a materialistic culture, in which success is primarily defined in money terms, encourages deviance at all levels of society. This is because monetary aspirations are inherently unlimited and prone to anomie. The materialist ethos also prioritises goal attainment over the legitimacy of means, and in itself erodes social and ethical controls.

Hermann Mannheim's analysis of how wartime and post-war conditions generated crime inextricably mixed together economic and moral issues (Taylor 1981 p. 45). The 1964 Labour Party study group document *Crime: A Challenge For Us All*, which informed the Wilson government's criminal justice agenda, adopted Tawney's analysis of the 'acquisitive society' to explain how Conservative economic policies had emphasised individual economic success, thus 'weakening the moral fibre of individuals' (Labour Party 1964 p. 5). Thus, to paraphrase Harold Wilson, social democracy (and social democratic criminology) are nothing if they are not moral crusades. And the morality can be nicely summed up by the Christian Socialist Charles Kingsley's homespun homily on the Golden Rule: 'do as you would be done by' (Kingsley 1863/2014).

Critique of capitalism

Social democrats saw capitalism as having systemic flaws that were intrinsic to it but might be mitigated. Capitalism's productive capacities were of course recognised, as

Social democracy **33**

well as its liberatory impact on the shackles of feudalism and slavery. Arguably there are few greater admirers of the material and social progress made by capitalism than Marx and Engels, and some passages of *The Communist Manifesto* read like a love poem to its wonders. To ethical socialists like Tawney, however, economic growth was a means to desirable ends such as the relief of poverty, not an end in itself. Indeed, material affluence posed moral dangers as it stimulated acquisitiveness and egoism (Tawney 1921).

Whatever its virtues, however, capitalism had several fundamental problems. Many social democrats differed from Marx's diagnosis of possible end states and how to achieve them. But they largely endorsed his critique of the perniciously unstable consequences of market anarchy, and the insecurity and injustice of a mode of production constructed on the basis of individual profit maximisation. The operation of unregulated markets inexorably generated inequality, as has been demonstrated time and again (most recently in Piketty 2014, 2020; Atkinson 2018). Whilst growth offers greater capacity to alleviate poverty, there is no automatic trickle-down effect. Increasing wealth and increasing poverty often march hand in hand at opposite ends of the economic pyramid, and notoriously what growth there has been since the 1970s has glued itself to the top social layers, especially the 1% (Dorling 2015), with massive ill effects (Wilkinson and Pickett 2010, 2019; Dorling 2018).

Indeed, the market price valuations that underpin measures of economic growth reflect differential economic power. Price is determined by *effective* demand (desire backed by the ability to pay), not social need. The conception of what to include in measures of national wealth such as gross national product is problematic and reflects specifically capitalist conceptions of value and well-being. Capitalists' pursuit of their own economic rationality can produce external diseconomies, wider social costs such as pollution, which do not figure in their own private calculations of efficient productive methods, nor in official calculations of wealth or illth. The neoclassical economists, such as Marshall and Pigou, who postulated that free market systems led to 'Pareto-optimal' allocation of resources in which (in the language of welfare economics) the 'gainers could over-compensate the losers', agreed with these criticisms. They endorsed political action to correct market dysfunctions. Capitalism also suffered from macroeconomic fluctuations, the cycle of depression and boom, which, following the arguments of Keynes and Kalecki in the 1930s, and Minsky in the 1970s/'80s (Minsky 1975/2008; Wray 2017), required government regulation to alleviate the ensuing misery.

Social democrats' criticisms of capitalism were not only aimed at its economic consequences but also the culture of amoral and possessive individualism that it accentuated.

It is this point that has stimulated the New Economics Foundation and others to explore alternative measures of economic welfare and growth, building in estimates for social costs of conventional economic activity, and forms of well-being that do not command an adequate market price (Jackson 2004; Coyle 2015; Jacobs and Mazzucato 2016; Mazzucato 2018; Raworth 2018; Bregman 2018).

34 Social democracy

The economic dysfunctions of capitalism that social democracy identified were seen by criminologists as leading to crime. The aetiology was not straightforward but mediated by intervening factors (such as their effects on morality, family life, and informal social controls). This has produced a plethora of research on the possible links between economic factors and crime (which are considered later in the book). The results of this research are complex, but there can be no doubt that the political economy plays a significant, if not straightforward, part in the explanation of crime and criminal justice. Certainly the turbo-capitalism of the Thatcher – Reagan years was a major causal factor in rocketing crime rates, and its slight attenuation under New Labour and other 'third way' approaches contributed something to subsequent falls in crime (Reiner 2007, 2016 pp. 164–185).

Gradualism

Despite the critique of capitalism offered by social democrats, most did not advocate its revolutionary overthrow. Specific reforms aimed at alleviating particular problems were to be argued for through the democratic process and implemented gradually, approaching socialism asymptotically. 'Gradualism' was explicitly espoused by the Fabian Society, which was founded in 1884 and named after the Roman general Quintus Fabius Maximus, legendary for his delaying tactics. Fabianism was a key component in the establishment and development of the British Labour Party (McBriar 2009; Pugh 2011; Hannah 2018), and a significant influence on Bernstein's evolutionary socialism. For many social democrats the accumulation of such reforms was intended to result ultimately in a qualitatively different social order, socialism. But for some social democrats capitalism was seen as beneficial, or at any rate inevitable, so that perpetual struggle was required to alleviate its egregious failings.

Gradualism was favoured in part to ensure by cautious experimentation that reforms worked without unintended negative consequences. But most fundamentally it was the necessary price of seeking to proceed democratically, by building consent, rather than through coercion. It was the price for avoiding the pains of violence and war, even if these were intended to bring about a better world.

The psychic cost of gradualism was living with the evils of injustice and oppression, whilst these were ameliorated in stages. This required patience, fortitude, and stoicism in the face of indefensible suffering. Piecemeal reform aimed at little dollops of jam today, rather than the promise of vats of it after the Revolution.

Social democracy sought gradual improvement in a forever messy and conflict-ridden world. This made social democracy a hard sell in competition with the glorious dreams of revolutionary rapture. As Leszek Kolakowski once put it:

> The trouble with the social democratic idea is that it does not . . . sell any of the exciting commodities which various totalitarian movements . . . offer dream-hungry youth. . . . It has no prescription for the total salvation of mankind. . . . It believes in no final easy victory over evil. It requires, in

addition to commitment to a number of basic values, hard knowledge and rational calculation. . . . It is an obstinate will to erode by inches the conditions which produce avoidable suffering, oppression, hunger, wars, racial and national hatred, insatiable greed and vindictive envy.

(Kolakowski 1979)

Social democratic criminology fundamentally sought to understand and reverse the macro causes of crime through economic and social policy. But it was also extensively involved in research and reform interventions aimed at effective and humane criminal justice and penal practice. The charge levelled both by Conservatives and by Left Realists in the 1980s that radical criminology was preoccupied with ultimate causes, not practical interventions to control crime, may have been true of the 'left idealism' of the 1970s. But it was certainly not true of earlier generations of social democratic criminologists, who were concerned as much with research ascertaining the humanity and fairness of penal intervention as with 'what works'.

Equality and *democracy*

Evolutionary social democracy sought to achieve greater equality through democratic and consensual means. More fundamentally, the bracketing together of 'social' and 'democracy' declares that they are mutually interdependent. 'Democratic' isn't just an Occam's Razor for ruling out certain tactics in the pursuit of equality. 'Social' as a qualifier to 'democracy' indicates a crucial point often overlooked by liberal discourse: the vital values of democratic institutions and processes, such as the rule of law, and free and fair elections based on the universal franchise, are undermined by inequality of economic condition or social status. Liberal democracy and socio-economic equality are not at odds with each other, *pace* the familiar conservative and liberal claim that equality can only be imposed by coercion. On the contrary, they are preconditions for each other. 'The free development of each is the condition of the free development of all' (Marx and Engels 1848/2015 p. 252).

Equality as a value espoused by social democrats does not mean calculating, let alone imposing, some ideal mathematical formula (although statistical demonstrations of the extent and trends in inequality of distribution of particular goods may be used as demonstrations of the absence of equality). As Marx argued in his 1875 *Critique of the Gotha Programme*, equality as an arithmetic algorithm is a bourgeois value reflecting the calculative competitiveness of capitalist society. The attainment of equality is only possible in conditions of abundance (made possible materially in the first instance by capitalist industrialisation, but also by the development of a more solidaristic ethos). Abundance makes possible the realisation of equality as 'from each according to their ability to each according to their needs' (ibid.). Marx's famous formulation has roots in earlier socialist thought, and indeed in both the Old and New Testaments (Ezra 2:69; Acts 11: 29; Avineri 2019).

36 Social democracy

There are, of course, extensive debates about how to interpret equality and democracy. But most social democrats have subscribed to a fundamental principle of treating everyone with 'equal concern and respect' (Dworkin 2000). Rawls' two principles of justice – equality of basic liberties and equality of material distribution (subject only to departures if they raise the position of the least well-off, the 'difference' principle) – expressed most explicitly the values of most social democrats. Rawls is usually regarded as a liberal, but his exposition of his two principles embodies the most succinct statement and defence of the idea of justice as conceived of by social democrats. Indeed, Rawls himself moved closer to social democracy in his later thought (Edmundson 2017).

Social democracy saw equality and liberal democracy as mutually reinforcing rather than in tension. In societies split by hierarchies of class (and gender, and ethnicity), equality was in the interest of the majority, so that ultimately the democratic process should produce a consensus for egalitarian measures. However, in a highly unequal society, it is only possible to have the 'best democracy money could buy' (Palast 2004). Substantive democracy is incompatible with gross inequalities, because of the influence of affluence (Gilens 2014; Paige and Gilens 2018), not to speak of the barely hidden outright purchase of the political process by the wealthy (Mayer 2016; MacLean 2017).

Social democrats certainly believed that a slow incorporation of all sections of society into civil, political, and social citizenship (Marshall 1950) had taken place since the late eighteenth century, and indeed this was the major basis for Bernstein's revisionism (Bernstein 1899). It was widely believed that this provided a foundation for social order and peace. The experience of the second half of the nineteenth century, during which recorded crime rates declined and then remained stable until after the First World War, seemed to confirm this, as Chapters 2 and 3 document. The 'dangerous classes' of the early Victorian period were progressively disciplined by the physically gentler, quotidian 'dull compulsion of economic relations' (Marx 1867 p. 737). Formal social control in the early twentieth century moved towards a more individualised, reform-oriented penal/welfare complex, informed by criminological research on the causation of offending and the requirements of rehabilitation (Garland 1985). Policing became more consensual both in everyday order maintenance and the handling of political and industrial disputes (Reiner 2010; Bowling et al. 2019 Chap. 4). The end of the social democratic era led to a crime and disorder explosion, although this was attenuated somewhat in the era of 'third way'–style social democracy (Reiner 2007 Chaps. 3–5; Reiner 2016 op.cit.).

Quiet optimism

Until the early 1970s, social democrats shared a tacit Whig theory of history. Whilst decrying any iron laws, there was a sense of continuing, albeit frequently broken and tentative, progress towards equality, liberty, and democracy, as is shown in detail in Chapters 2 and 3. This rested implicitly on a sense that there was a substantive historical agent, the working class, which constituted the majority of society and was receptive to the values of social democracy.

Even if the initial hook was self-interest in improving economic rewards and general social conditions, it could be hoped that there was an elective affinity between the social democratic ideals of liberty, equality, justice, and solidarity and the aspirations of the social majority.

Social democratic criminology shared this quiet optimism. However, this was challenged by the increase in recorded crime in the late 1950s. The rise in crime rates during a period of unprecedented mass affluence seemed to refute the expectation that crime would reduce with better social conditions. Jock Young famously called this an 'aetiological crisis' for social democratic criminology (Young 1986). But it is important to stress that social democratic criminology had not postulated a simple relationship between economic conditions and crime. This is not just reinterpretation with the benefit of hindsight. There are many examples of predictions by social democratic criminologists in the early 1960s of rising crime rates, resulting from the acquisitiveness, anomie, and relative deprivation sparked by the new consumerist culture (Labour Party 1964 p. 5; Downes 1966, 1988 pp. 103–109).

Dimensions of justice

Essentially creatures of their time, early social democrats for the most part did not speak about dimensions of inequality or oppression other than class, such as gender, ethnicity, or sexual preference. There were isolated examples who did, of course. John Stuart Mill (a liberal but with views that often were close to social democracy) was a famous early advocate of the rights of women, and Engels critically analysed the origins of the family (Engels 1884; cf. J.T. Reiner 2008). Criminologists can be proud of the example of Willem Bonger, the Dutch Marxist, Social Democratic Party activist, and academic criminologist, who championed the rights of gay people and of Jews in the face of Nazism, ultimately committing suicide in despair when the Germans invaded Holland (S. Cohen 1998; Moxon 2014 Chap. 3 later). Certainly the principles of social democracy demand justice for *all* forms of oppression, not just economic.

Social democratic criminologists primarily thought of issues of crime and justice in terms of class. The hope was that the gradual emancipation of the working class would alleviate progressively the other dimensions of criminal (in)justice. But differences of gender, race, and sexual preference were largely outside their attention until the 1960s. However, the general principle of equal concern and respect underpinning social democracy certainly lends itself to incorporating these dimensions of inequality and injustice into the analysis of crime, victimisation, and criminal justice. It is vital, moreover, not to neglect the continuing importance of class and economic inequality, not only in itself, but also as an underlying element in racial and other differences in crime and criminalisation. It is also important to remember that the crucial beginnings of legal and social justice for black and ethnic minority people, women, and gay people were laid in the social democratic era in Britain, the USA and elsewhere, during what right-wing writers castigate as the 'permissive society' and liberals and the Left celebrate as the civilised society (Newburn 1991; Reiner 2016 pp. 42–46, 182–183).

Since the advent of neoliberal hegemony, public debates about inequality have largely focussed on the dimensions hitherto neglected, notably gender, ethnicity, and sexuality, whilst overlooking economic class. Huge progress has been made in all of these, although much remains to be done (and the gains are fragile and patchy, largely restricted to liberal democratic Western societies). These achievements occlude the fact that progressive reforms were rooted in the heyday of social democratic hegemony, above all in the 1960s, and until recently were fiercely contested by conservative parties. The interdependence of different dimensions of power, inequality, and oppression has become increasingly analysed since the 1990s, in particular with the emergence of the concept of intersectionality (Potter 2015; Collins and Bilge 2016).

The state as instrument of justice

Social democrats have generally seen the democratic state as a necessary, and if not sufficient, at least a primary means of achieving greater equality and justice. This is not to say that they were not acutely aware of the dangers of state power. The two most widely celebrated dystopian novels about the dangers of totalitarianism, *Animal Farm* and *1984*, were written by a social democrat (albeit a highly idiosyncratic one), George Orwell.

There were always currents in social democracy that espoused non-state, bottom-up rather than top-down, routes to achieve social justice, such as the co-operative movement, the Friendly Societies, guild socialism (Cole 1920/2011), and versions of syndicalism and communitarianism. The 'local state' has also been, in theory and in practice, an important agent of social democracy (and has been hugely weakened under neoliberalism).

Social democratic criminology generally saw the liberal democratic state's criminal justice agencies as fundamentally benign, although there was an agenda of reform to make them more representative of, and responsive to, working-class concerns. But it was only from the mid-1960s that empirical socio-legal and criminological research began to focus on the way that policing and other parts of the criminal justice system discriminated in terms of class, age, gender, race, and sexuality (Heidensohn 2006; Heidensohn and Silvestri 2012; Burman and Gelsthorpe 2017; Phillips and Bowling 2017; Bowling et al. 2017 Chap. 6).

The state-centred character of social democratic criminology was called into question during the 1960s by the emergence of labelling theory, spearheading a broader proliferation of varieties of critical criminology (Becker 1963, 1967; DeKeseredy 2010; Ugwudike 2015; DeKeseredy and Dragiewicz 2017). Since the 1980s the centrality of the state in social democratic as well as other forms of criminology has been rendered problematic by the proliferation of non-state modes of criminal justice and social control (Jones and Newburn 1998; Bowling et al. 2019

Chap. 7). Post-modern theoretical perspectives, critically analysing state domination of security (Johnston and Shearing 2003; Holley and Shearing 2017), have developed and been vigorously debated (Loader and Walker 2007).

More recently, in the wake of the 2007/8 financial crisis and the neoliberal austerity policies ushered in by many governments, there has been some rehabilitation of the state as a necessary hub for social revival (Mitchell and Fazi 2017). As Michael Ignatieff put it powerfully:

> Most citizens . . . know they need a sovereign with the power to compel competing sources of power in society to serve the public good . . . to protect them from the systemic risks imposed on them by the powerful. They refuse to see why large corporations should privatise their gains, but socialise their losses.
>
> *(Ignatieff 2014)*

Science

Social democrats, in common with most other socialists and liberals, have viewed science as a positive force. Physical science and technology applied to productive processes offered the prospect of reducing the economic pressures underlying human drudgery and servitude. As seen earlier, for Marx the precondition of socialist distribution was abundance, enabled by the appliance of science to capitalist industrialisation. In addition, the piecemeal social engineering and regulation of markets aimed at by social democrats required social science to analyse problems systematically, and to predict and plan for the probable consequences of governmental policies.

This did not entail the simplistic positivism that has become a crude term of abuse by many contemporary sociologists. Social democrats recognised that observations are theory laden, that values affect the choice of study and the application of results, and indeed are hard to separate from the process of research.

For the most part they saw human behaviour as a dialectical outcome of structure and action, people making their own histories but not under conditions of their own choosing (paraphrasing Marx). But they would also have accepted that there are regularities that can be discerned in social interaction, even if these are probabilistic and not the product of iron determinism. Knowing and understanding as much as possible about these was necessary to guide practical reform. Whilst a vital element of the liberal democratic principles that social democrats believed in was tolerance, this did not entail relativism with regard to either 'facts' or values.

There can be no question that social democratic criminology was broadly 'positivist' in its approach to social science, and indeed to contemporary readers this is perhaps the most alienating aspect of the publications of 'actually existing' social democratic criminologists of the early twentieth century, such as Bonger, Hermann Mannheim, or Barbara Wootton (considered in more detail in Chapter 3). These social democratic criminologists felt it important to research as rigorously as

40 Social democracy

possible the causes of crime and the effectiveness, humanity, and justice of crime control policies. Occasionally, they even used numbers in their analyses (as, of course, did Marx himself)! But for the most part they would not have been guilty of the accusations routinely hurled at a straw person version of positivism by subsequent critics. They did not think that social science results could be regarded as absolute truth, completely objective representations of reality, or that they could resolve all issues. Most would have accepted Weber's analysis of the problems, limitations, ultimate impossibility, and yet importance and desirability as an ideal, of value-freedom in science (Weber 1918). Whilst they regarded it as useful to formulate and test empirical generalisations, few saw these as laws that determined individual behaviour.

Merton's analysis of deviant reactions to anomie, for example, has been criticised as a deterministic account that gives no space to individual interpretation of meaning and autonomy (Taylor et al. 1973 p. 108). However, it intended only to suggest probabilities, not certainties (Merton 1995), and raises rather than forecloses exploration of why people in similar structural situations develop different reactions (Reiner 1984 pp. 191–192).

There was unfortunately a dark side of social democrats' enthusiasm for science. Above all, the bastardised Darwinism that led to eugenics as a supposed 'scientific' solution to problems of inequality, poverty, and indeed crime certainly attracted enthusiastic support in some socialist circles, such as the Fabians. Since the adoption of these ideas wholesale by Nazism and their underpinning of arguably the greatest crime of all time, the attempted extermination of Jews, gypsies, gay people, the disabled, and other vulnerable, supposed 'inferiors', eugenics has largely disappeared, certainly on the Left. The experience of technology applied to mass destruction during and since World War II has also prompted a much greater suspicion of science. Nonetheless, social democracy still has something of an elective affinity with the broad ambition of science, the quest for rational and empirical research–based techniques to further understanding of the physical and social worlds.

Modernism

The values of justice and liberty, central to social democracy, have ancient origins. Many have perceived a long chain of inspiration going back to antiquity – the Hebrew prophets, Socrates, Jesus, Spartacus. Although no doubt the meanings of the terms change over time, writers and activists have drawn inspiration from the ancient sources throughout subsequent history. The chain continued through the Middle Ages and early modernity – John Ball ('When Adam delved and Eve span who was then the gentleman?'), Wat Tyler, Jack Straw, and other leaders of the Peasants' Revolt, Thomas More's Utopia, the Levellers and Diggers during the English Commonwealth.

The distinctly modern element in social democracy was the belief that these values were not a millenarian dream but capable of implementation as a practical

Social democracy **41**

political project, here and now, or in an imminent future. This was not necessarily part of a modernist 'grand narrative', though it was often tied to a view of history as (probably and unevenly) progressive.

Social democratic criminology, and its penological counterpart the rehabilitative ideal, were quintessential elements of 'penal modernism' (Garland 2001). However, the label 'modern' implies to some that they are discredited, dead, in an era of 'post' or 'late' modernity.

The rest of the book is concerned with examining this. The next chapter sets out the broad contours of social democratic criminology, assesses its strengths, and analyses its eclipse in the neoliberal era. The third chapter probes the 'strange death' of SDC in the neoliberal era. Finally, the concluding fourth chapter considers the possibility and desirability of resurrecting its core elements.

References

Addison, P. (1994) *The Road to 1945* London: Pimlico.

Ali, T. (2017) *The Dilemmas of Lenin* London: Verso.

Armstrong, G. and Gray, T. (2011) *The Authentic Tawney* Exeter: Imprint Academic.

Atkinson, A. (2018) *Inequality* Cambridge: Harvard University Press.

Avineri, S. (2019) *Karl Marx* New Haven: Yale University Press.

Barbieri, P. (2017) 'The Death and Life of Social Democracy' *Foreign Affairs* www.foreignaffairs.com/articles/europe/2017-04-25/death-and-life-social-democracy

Bauman, Z. (1995) *Life in Fragments* Oxford: Blackwell.

Bauman, Z. (2004) *Wasted Lives* Cambridge: Polity.

Bauman, Z. (2007) *Consuming Life* Cambridge: Polity.

Becker, H. (1963) *Outsiders* New York: Free Press.

Becker, H. (1967) 'Whose Side Are We On?' *Social Problems* 14/3: 239–247.

Beckett, F. and Seddon, M. (2019) *Jeremy Corbyn and the Strange Rebirth of Labour England* London: Biteback.

Beilharz, P. (1992) *Labour's Utopias* London: Routledge.

Beilharz, P. (2009) *Socialism and Modernity* Minneapolis: University of Minnesota Press.

Bell, D. (1960) *The End of Ideology* Glencoe: Free Press.

Benjamin, J. (2007) *Financial Law* Oxford: Oxford University Press.

Berman, S. (2006) *The Primacy of Politics* Cambridge: Cambridge University Press.

Bernstein, E. (1899/1963) *Evolutionary Socialism* New York: Schocken.

Beveridge, W. (1942) *Social Insurance and Allied Services* London: HMSO.

Bevir, M. (2011) *The Making of British Socialism* Princeton: Princeton University Press.

Bhaskar, S. (2019) *The Socialist Manifesto* London: Verso.

Birnbaum, P. (2015) *Leon Blum* New Haven: Yale University Press.

Blakeley, G. (2019) *Stolen* London: Repeater Books.

Blatchford, R. (2014) 'What is the Legacy of the Education Act, 70 Years on?' www.theguardian.com/education/2014/apr/22/1944-education-act-butler-policy-today

Blyth, M. (2002) *Great Transformations* Cambridge: Cambridge University Press.

Blyth, M. (2015) *Austerity* Oxford: Oxford University Press.

Boltanski, L. and Chiapello, E. (2005) *The New Spirit of Capitalism* London: Verso.

Bottoms, A.E. and Stevenson, S. (1992) 'What Went Wrong? Criminal Justice Policy in England and Wales 1945–70' in D. Downes (Ed.) *Unravelling Criminal Justice* London: Macmillan.

42 Social democracy

Boutellier, H. (2000) *Crime and Morality* Dordrecht: Kluwer.

Bowles, S., Gordon, D. and Weisskopf, T. (1983) *Beyond the Waste Land: A Democratic Alternative to Economic Decline* New York: Anchor.

Bowling, B., Iyer, S., Reiner, R. and Sheptycki, J. (2017) 'Policing: Past, Present and Future' in R. Matthews (Ed.) *What is to be Done About Crime and Punishment?* London: Macmillan.

Bowling, B., Reiner, R. and Sheptycki, J. (2019) *The Politics of the Police* 5th ed. Oxford: Oxford University Press.

Bradley, I. (1981) *Breaking the Mould?* Oxford: Blackwell.

Bregman, R. (2018) *Utopia for Realists* London: Bloomsbury.

Broning, M. (2017) 'The Future of Germany's Social Democrats' www.foreignaffairs.com/articles/germany/2017-09-25/future-germanys-social-democrats

Budgen, S. (2000) 'A New "Spirit of Capitalism"' 1 January/February, 149–156.

Bullock, A. (1977) *Report of the Commission on Industrial Democracy* London: HMSO.

Bullough, O. (2018) *Moneyland* London: Profile.

Bulmer, M. and Rees, A. (1996) *Citizenship Today* London: Routledge.

Burgin, A. (2012) *The Great Persuasion* Cambridge: Harvard University Press.

Burman, M. and Gelsthorpe, L. (2017) 'Feminist Criminology: Inequalities, Powerlessness, and Justice' in A. Liebling, S. Maruna and L. McAra (Eds.) *The Oxford Handbook of Criminology* 6th ed. Oxford: Oxford University Press.

Cahill, D. and Konings, M. (2017) *Neoliberalism* Cambridge: Polity.

Callaghan, J. (1987) *Time and Chance* London: Collins.

Callinicos, A. (2001) *Against the Third Way* Cambridge: Polity.

Carey, A. (1996) *Taking the Risk Out of Democracy: Corporate Propaganda versus Freedom and Liberty* Champaign: University of Illinois Press.

Carter, Z. (2020) *The Price of Peace: Money, Democracy, and the Life of John Maynard Keynes* New York: Random House.

Clarke, P. (1978) *Liberals and Social Democrats* Cambridge: Cambridge University Press.

Coates, K. (2003) *Workers' Control* Nottingham: Spokesman Books.

Coates, K. and Topham, T. (1977) *The Shop Steward's Guide to the Bullock Report* Nottingham: Spokesman Books.

Cockett, R. (1994) *Thinking the Unthinkable: Think-tanks and the Economic Counter-revolution 1931–83* London: Collins.

Cohen, G. (2000) *If You're An Egalitarian, How Come You're So Rich?* Cambridge: Harvard University Press.

Cohen, S. (1998) 'Intellectual Scepticism and Political Commitment' in P. Walton and J. Young (Eds.) *The New Criminology Revisited* London: Macmillan.

Cole, G.D.H. (1920/2011) *Guild Socialism Restated* Abingdon: Routledge.

Collini, S. (2009) *Liberalism and Sociology* Cambridge: Cambridge University Press.

Collins, P. and Bilge, S. (2016) *Intersectionality* Cambridge: Polity.

Colton, J. (1987) *Leon Blum* Durham, NC: Duke University Press.

Conway, E. (2015) *The Summit: Bretton Woods 1944* New York: Pegasus.

Cowley, J. (2018) 'The Left are now More Forgiving of Ed Miliband – But Many Labour MPs are Furious with him' www.newstatesman.com/politics/uk/2018/09/left-are-now-more-forgiving-ed-miliband-many-labour-mps-are-furious-him

Coyle, D. (2015) *GDP* Princeton: Princeton University Press.

Crewe, I. and King, A. (1995) *SDP* Oxford: Oxford University Press.

Crotty, J. (2019) *Keynes Against Capitalism* Abingdon: Routledge.

Crouch, C. (2009) 'Privatised Keynesianism' *British Journal of Politics and International Relations* 11/1: 382–399.

Crouch, C. (2011) *The Strange Non-Death of Neoliberalism* Cambridge: Polity.

Davies, W. (2016) *The Limits of Neoliberalism* London: Sage.

Davies, W. (2018) *Nervous States* London: Cape.

Davis, J. and Rentoul, J. (2019) *Heroes or Villains? The Blair Government Reconsidered* Oxford: Oxford University Press.

DeKeseredy, W. (2010) *Contemporary Critical Criminology* Abingdon: Routledge.

DeKeseredy, W. and Dragiewicz, M. (Eds.) (2017) *Routledge Handbook of Critical Criminology* 2nd ed. Abingdon: Routledge.

Dennis, N. and Halsey, A.H. (1988) *English Ethical Socialism* Oxford: Oxford University Press.

Dorling, D. (2015) *Injustice* Bristol: Policy Press.

Dorling, D. (2018) *Peak Inequality* Bristol: Policy Press.

Dorrien, G. (2019) *Social Democracy in the Making: Political and Religious Roots of European Socialism* New Haven: Yale University Press.

Downes, D. (1966) *The Delinquent Solution* London: Routledge.

Downes, D. (1988) *Contrasts in Tolerance* Oxford: Oxford University Press.

Dworkin, R. (2000) *Sovereign Virtue* Cambridge: Harvard University Press.

Edmundson, W. (2017) *John Rawls: Reticent Socialist* Cambridge: Cambridge University Press.

Ehrenreich, B. (2010) *Smile or Die* London: Granta.

Engels, F. (1880/1968) *Socialism: Utopian and Scientific in Marx and Engels – Selected Works* London: Lawrence and Wishart, 375–428.

Engels, F. (1884/2010) *The Origins of the Family, Private Property and the State* London: Penguin.

Esping-Anderson, G. (1990) *The Three Worlds of Welfare Capitalism* Cambridge: Polity.

Fones-Wolf, E. (1994) *Selling Free Enterprise: The Business Assault on Labour and Liberalism, 1945–1960* Urbana: University of Illinois Press.

Forder, J. (2014) *Macroeconomics and the Phillips Curve Myth* Oxford: Oxford University Press.

Frank, T. (1997) *The Conquest of Cool* Chicago: University of Chicago Press.

Frank, T. (2001) *One Market Under God* London: Secker and Warburg.

Frank, T. (2004) *What's the Matter With America?* London: Secker and Warburg.

Fraser, D. (2000) 'The Postwar Consensus: A Debate Not Long Enough?' *Parliamentary Affairs* 53/2: 347–362.

Freeden, M. (1986) *The New Liberalism* Oxford: Oxford University Press.

Gallie, W.B. (1956) 'Essentially Contested Concepts' *Proceedings of the Aristotelian Society* 56/1: 167–198.

Gamble, A. (1994) *The Free Economy and the Strong State* London: Macmillan.

Gamble, A. (2009) *The Spectre At The Feast* London: Macmillan.

Gamble, A. (2014) *Crisis Without End?* London: Macmillan.

Gamble, A. (2016) *Can the Welfare State Survive?* Cambridge: Polity.

Gane, N. (2016) 'In and Out of Neoliberalism: Reconsidering the Sociology of Raymond Aron' *Journal of Classical Sociology* 16/3: 261–279.

Garland, D. (1985) *Punishment and Welfare* Aldershot: Gower.

Garland, D. (2001) *The Culture of Control* Oxford: Oxford University Press.

Garland, D. (2016) *The Welfare State* Oxford: Oxford University Press.

Garland, D. and Sparks, R. (2000) 'Criminology, Social Theory and the Challenge of Our Times' *British Journal of Criminology* 40/2: 189–204.

Gay, P. (1962) *The Dilemma of Democratic Socialism* New York: Collier.

Gensler, H. (2013) *Ethics and the Golden Rule* Abingdon: Routledge.

Giddens, A. (1998) *The Third Way* Cambridge: Polity.

44 Social democracy

Giddens, A. (2000) *The Third Way and its Critics* Cambridge: Polity.

Gilbert, J. (2020) *Twenty-First Century Socialism* Cambridge: Polity.

Gilens, M. (2014) *Affluence and Influence* Princeton: Princeton University Press.

Glyn, A. and Sutcliffe, B. (1972a) *British Capitalism, Workers and the Profit Squeeze* London: Penguin.

Glyn, A. and Sutcliffe, B. (1972b) 'Labour and the Economy' *New Left Review* 1/76: 91–96.

Goes, E. (2016) 'The Labour Party Under Ed Miliband' *Renewal* 24/1: 29–40.

Goldman, L. (2014) *The Life of R.H. Tawney* London: Bloomsbury.

Gowan, P. (2018) 'Own the Future' https://jacobinmag.com/2018/07/labour-party-corbyn-manifesto-nationalization-democracy

Gowan, P. and Lawrence, M. (2019) 'A Cross-Atlantic Plan to Break Capital's Control' https://jacobinmag.com/2019/06/bernie-sanders-worker-ownership-funds-labour-party

Gowan, P. and Viktorrson, M. (2017) 'Revisiting the Meidner Plan' https://jacobinmag.com/2017/08/sweden-social-democracy-meidner-plan-capital

Gray, A. (1946) *The Socialist Tradition: Moses to Lenin* London: Longmans.

Green, J. (2016) 'Anglo-American Development, the Euromarkets, and the Deeper Origins of Neoliberal Deregulation' *Review of International Studies* 42/3: 425–449.

Gurney, J. (2012) *Gerrard Winstanley* London: Pluto.

Hall, P. and Soskice, D. (Eds.) (2001) *Varieties of Capitalism* Oxford: Oxford University Press.

Hall, S., Kuldova, T. and Horsley, M. (Eds.) (2020) *Crime, Harm and Consumerism* Abingdon: Routledge.

Hall, S., Winlow, S. and Ancrum, C. (2008) *Criminal Identities and Consumer Culture* Cullompton: Willan.

Hannah, S. (2018) *A Party With Socialists In It* London: Pluto.

Harvey, D. (2005) *A Brief History of Neoliberalism* Oxford: Oxford University Press.

Hattersley, R. (2014) 'Harold Wilson's Moral Crusade can Still be a Rallying Call for Labour' www.theguardian.com/commentisfree/2014/oct/14/harold-wilson-moral-crusade-rally-labour

Heath, J. and Potter, A. (2005) *The Rebel Sell* Chichester: Capstone.

Heidensohn, F. (Ed.) (2006) *Gender and Justice* Cullompton: Willan.

Heidensohn, F. and Silvestri, M. (2012) 'Gender and Crime' in M. Maguire, R. Morgan and R. Reiner (Eds.) *The Oxford Handbook of Criminology* 3rd ed. Oxford: Oxford University Press.

Hickson, K. (2004) 'The Old Left' in M. Beech, K. Hickson and R. Plant (Eds.) *The Struggle For Labour's Soul* Abingdon: Routledge.

Hill, C. (1991) *Change and Continuity in 17th. Century England* New Haven: Yale University Press.

Hirsch, F. (1977) *Social Limits to Growth* London: Routledge.

Holland, T. (2019) *Dominion: The Making of the Western Mind* London: Little Brown.

Holley, C. and Shearing, C. (Eds.) (2017) *Criminology and the Anthropocene* Abingdon: Routledge.

Ignatieff, M. (2014) 'Sovereignty and the Crisis of Democratic Politics' www.michaeligna tieff.ca/assets/pdfs/Sovereignty%20and%20the%20crisis%20of%20democratic%20poli tics_Demos%20Quarterly.pdf

IMF (2010) 'Reserve Accumulation and International Monetary Stability' *IMF Policy Papers* April 3 2010.

Jackson, B. (2010) 'At the Origins of Neo-Liberalism: The Free Economy and the Strong State 1930–1947' *Historical Journal* 53/1: 129–151.

Jackson, B. (2012) 'The Think-Tank Archipelago: Thatcherism and Neo-liberalism' in B. Jackson and R. Saunders (Eds.) *Making Thatcher's Britain* Cambridge: Cambridge University Press.

Jackson, J. (1990) *The Popular Front in France: Defending Democracy 1934–1938* Cambridge: Cambridge University Press.

Jackson, T. (2004) *Chasing Progress: Beyond Economic Growth* London: New Economics Foundation.

Jacobs, M. and Mazzucato, M. (Eds.) (2016) *Rethinking Capitalism* Oxford: Blackwell.

Johnston, L. and Shearing, C. (2003) *Governing Security* London: Routledge.

Jones, H. and Kandiah, M. (Eds.) (2014) *The Myth of Consensus* London: Macmillan.

Jones, T. and Newburn, T. (1998) *Private Security and Public Policing* Oxford: Oxford University Press.

Kalecki, M. (1943) 'Political Aspects of Full Employment' *Political Quarterly* 14/4: 322–331.

Kaletsky, A. (2010) *Capitalism 4.0* London: Bloomsbury.

Kant, I. (1785/1998) *Groundwork of the Metaphysics of Morals* Cambridge: Cambridge University Press.

Kavanagh, D. (1992) 'The Postwar Consensus' *Twentieth Century British History* 3/2: 175–190.

Kavanagh, D. and Morris, P. (1994) *Consensus Politics: From Attlee to Major* 2nd ed. Oxford: Blackwell.

Keane, J. (2016) 'Money, Capitalism and the Slow Death of Social Democracy' https://the-conversation.com/money-capitalism-and-the-slow-death-of-social-democracy-58703

Kerr, P. (1999) 'The Postwar Consensus: A Woozle that Wasn't' in D. Marsh, J. Buller, C. Hay, J. Johnston, P. Kerr, S. McAnulla and M. Watson (Eds.) *Postwar British Politics in Perspective* Cambridge: Polity.

Keynes, J.M. (1936/2007) *The General Theory of Employment, Interest and Money* London: Macmillan.

Kingsley, C. (1863/2016) *The Water Babies* London: Macmillan.

Klein, N. (2000) *No Logo* New York: Picador.

Klein, N. (2007) *The Shock Doctrine* London: Allen Lane.

Kogan, D. (2019) *Protest and Power* London: Bloomsbury.

Kolakowski, L. (1979) 'Social Democracy – Challenge' *Socialist Affairs* 3/1: 62–64.

Kurtz, G. (2014) *Jean Jaures: The Inner Life of Social Democracy* University Park, PA: Pennsylvania State University Press.

Labour Party (1964) *Crime: A Challenge to Us All* London: Labour Party.

Lavelle, A. (2008) *The Death of Social Democracy* Abingdon: Routledge.

Lawson, N. (2018) 'Averting the Death of Social Democracy' www.socialeurope.eu/averting-the-death-of-social-democracy

Lenin, V. (1901/1966) *What is to Be Done?* New York: Bantam.

Levinas, E. (1969) *Totality and Infinity* Pittsburgh: Duquesne University Press.

Lipset, S.M. (1963) *Political Man* New York: Doubleday.

Loader, I. and Walker, N. (2007) *Civilising Security* Cambridge: Cambridge University Press.

Lonergan, E. and Blyth, M. (2020) *Angrynomics* Newcastle: Agenda.

Lukes, S. (1985) *Marxism and Morality* Oxford: Oxford University Press.

Luxemburg, R. (1899/2006) *Reform or Revolution?* New York: Dover.

Mackenzie, N. and Mackenzie, J. (1977) *The First Fabians* London: Weidenfeld.

MacLean, N. (2017) *Democracy in Chains* London: Scribe.

Maddison, A. (1997) 'The Nature and Functioning of European Capitalism: A Historical and Comparative Perspective' *Valedictory Lecture, University of Groningen* www.ggdc.net/maddison/oriindex.htm

Mann, G. (2019) *In the Long Run We Are All Dead: Keynesianism, Political Economy and Revolution* London: Verso.

Marglin, S. and Schor, J. (Eds.) (1990) *The Golden Age of Capitalism* Oxford: Oxford University Press.

46 Social democracy

Marliere, P. (2017) 'The Strange Death of Social Democracy in Europe' Interview with A. Galanopoulos www.opendemocracy.net/en/can-europe-make-it/strange-death-of-social-democracy-in-europ/

Marshall, T.H. (1950) *Citizenship and Social Class* Cambridge: Cambridge University Press.

Marx, K. (1844/1975) *Economic and Philosophical Manuscripts (1844) in Early Writings* London: Penguin.

Marx, K. (1867/1976) *Capital* Vol. 1. London: Penguin.

Marx, K. and Engels, F. (1848/1998) *The Communist Manifesto* London: Verso.

Mayer, J. (2016) *Dark Money* London: Scribe.

Mazzucato, M. (2018) *The Value of Everything* London: Allen Lane.

McBriar, A. (2009) *Fabian Socialism and English Politics* Cambridge: Cambridge University Press.

McDonnell, J. (Ed.) (2019) *Economics for the Many* London: Verso.

McGuigan, J. (2009) *Cool Capitalism* London: Pluto.

Medhurst, J. (2017) *No Less Than Mystic: A History of Lenin and the Russian Revolution for a 21st-Century Left* London: Repeater.

Mendoza, K-A. (2015) *Austerity* London: New Internationalist.

Merton, R. (1995) 'Opportunity Structure: The Emergence, Diffusion and Differentiation of a Sociological Concept, 1930s-1950s' in F. Adler and W.S. Laufer (Eds.) *The Legacy of Anomie Theory* New Brunswick: Transaction.

Mieville, C. (2017) *October: The Story of the Russian Revolution* London: Verso.

Minsky, H. (1975/2008) *John Maynard Keynes* London: McGraw Hill.

Mirowski, P. (2013) *Never Let A Serious Crisis Go to Waste* London: Verso.

Mirowski, P. and Plehwe, D. (Eds.) (2009) *The Road From Mont Pelerin* Cambridge: Harvard University Press.

Mitchell, W. and Fazi, T. (2017) *Reclaiming the State* London: Pluto.

Monbiot, G. (2000) *The Captive State* London: Macmillan.

Monbiot, G. (2016) *How Did we Get Into This Mess?* London: Verso.

Morris, T. (1989) *Crime and Criminal Justice Since 1945* Oxford: Blackwell.

Moxon, D. (2014) 'Willem Bonger' in J.M. Miller (Ed.) *The Encyclopedia of Theoretical Criminology* Oxford: Blackwell.

Newburn, T. (1991) *Permission and Regulation: Law and Morals in Post-War Britain* Abingdon: Routledge.

Newburn, T. (2003) *Crime and Criminal Justice Policy* 2nd ed. London: Longman.

New Socialist (2017) 'Labour's Alternative Models of Ownership Report' https://newsocialist.org.uk/labours-alternative-models-of-ownership-report/

Nietzche, F. (1885/2000) *Beyond Good and Evil* New York: Random House.

O'Brien, M. (2016) *When Adam Delved and Eve Span* London: Bookmarks.

O'Connor, J. (1973) *The Fiscal Crisis of the State* New York: St. Martin's.

Owen, R. (1813/1991) *A New View of Society* London: Penguin.

Paige, B. and Gilens, M. (2018) *Democracy in America?* Chicago: University of Chicago Press.

Palast, G. (2004) *The Best Democracy Money Can Buy* New York: Plume.

Peck, J. (2013) *Constructions of Neoliberal Reason* Oxford: Oxford University Press.

Pelling, H. (1966) *The Origins of the Labour Party* Oxford: Oxford University Press.

Pendleton, A. (2018) 'Inclusive Ownership Funds Will Build Better Businesses' https://neweconomics.org/2018/09/inclusive-ownership-funds-will-build-better-businesses

Phillips, C. and Bowling, B. (2017) 'Ethnicities, Racism, Crime, and Criminal Justice' in A. Liebling, S. Maruna and L. McAra (Eds.) *The Oxford Handbook of Criminology* 6th ed. Oxford: Oxford University Press.

Piketty, T. (2014) *Capital in the Twenty-First Century* Cambridge: Harvard University Press.

Piketty, T. (2020) *Capital and Ideology* Cambridge: Harvard University Press.

Pimlott, B. (1988) 'The Myth of Consensus' in L. Smith (Ed.) *The Making of Britain* London: Macmillan.

Potter, H. (2015) *Intersectionality and Criminology* Abingdon: Routledge.

Pountain, D. and Robins, D. (2000) *Cool Rules* London: Reaktion Books.

Preston, P. (2016) *The Spanish Civil War* London: Collins.

Pugh, P. (2011) *Educate, Agitate, Organise* Abingdon: Routledge.

Rawls, J. (1971) *A Theory of Justice* Cambridge: Harvard University Press.

Rawls, J. (2001) *Justice As Fairness* Cambridge: Harvard University Press.

Raworth, K. (2018) *Doughnut Economics* London: Random House.

Rees, J. (2017) *The Leveller Revolution* London: Verso.

Reiner, J.T. (2008) 'The Philosophical Foundations of Gender Equality in Liberalism and Marxism: A Study of Mill and Marx' *Twenty-First Century Society* 3/1: 13–30.

Reiner, J.T. (2018) *New Directions in Just War Theory* Carlisle, PA: Strategic Studies Institute.

Reiner, J.T. (2019) *Michael Walzer* Cambridge: Polity.

Reiner, R. (1984) 'Crime, Law and Deviance: The Durkheim Legacy' in S. Fenton (Ed.) *Durkheim and Modern Sociology* Cambridge: Cambridge University Press.

Reiner, R. (2007) *Law and Order: An Honest Citizen's Guide to Crime and Control* Cambridge: Polity.

Reiner, R. (2010) 'Citizenship, Crime, Criminalization: Marshalling a Social Democratic Perspective' *New Criminal Law Review* 13/2: 241–261.

Reiner, R. (2016) *Crime: The Mystery of the Common-Sense Concept* Cambridge: Polity.

Renwick, C. (2017) *Bread for All* London: Allen Lane.

Robertson, G. (2018) *The Levellers* London: Verso.

Robinson, J. (1964) *Economic Philosophy* London: Pelican.

Rogan, T. (2018) *The Moral Economists* Princeton: Princeton University Press.

Rorty, R. (1989) *Contingency, Irony and Solidarity* Cambridge: Cambridge University Press.

Rorty, R. (1999) *Philosophy and Social Hope* London: Penguin.

Rose, N. (1999) *Powers of Freedom* Cambridge: Cambridge University Press.

Saez, E. and Zucman, G. (2019) *The Triumph of Injustice* New York: Norton.

Sartre, J.-P. (1948/1985) *Les Mains Sales* London: Routledge.

Sassoon, D. (1996) *One Hundred Years of Socialism* New York: New Press.

Schafer, A. and Streeck, W. (Eds.) (2013) *Politics in the Age of Austerity* Cambridge: Polity.

Schenk, C. (1998) 'The Origins of the Eurodollar Market in London: 1955–1963' *Explorations in Economic History* 35/1: 221–238.

Shaxson, N. (2011) *Treasure Islands* London: Macmillan.

Shaxson, N. (2018) *The Finance Curse* London: Bodley Head.

Skidelsky, R. (2013) *John Maynard Keynes* London: Penguin.

Slezkine, Y. (2006) *The Jewish Century* Princeton: Princeton University Press.

Slobodian, Q. (2018) *Globalists* Cambridge: Harvard University Press.

Smith, J. (1991) *The Idea Brokers* New York: Free Press.

Standing, G. (2011) *The Precariat* London: Bloomsbury.

Stedman Jones, D. (2012) *Masters of the Universe* Princeton: Princeton University Press.

Steger, M. (2008) *The Quest For Evolutionary Socialism* Cambridge: Cambridge University Press.

Steil, B. (2014) *The Battle of Bretton Woods* Princeton: Princeton University Press.

Stonor Saunders, F. (2000) *Who Paid the Piper?* London: Granta.

Streeck, W. (2014) *Buying Time* London: Verso.

48 Social democracy

Streeck, W. (2017) *How Will Capitalism End?* London: Verso.

Sunkara, B. (2019) *The Socialist Manifesto* London: Verso.

Tawney, R.H. (1921) *The Acquisitive Society* London: Bell.

Taylor, E. (2019) *The Popular Front Novel in Britain 1934–1940* Chicago: Haymarket.

Taylor, I. (1981) *Law and Order: Arguments for Socialism* London: Macmillan.

Taylor, I., Walton, P. and Young, J. (1973) *The New Criminology* London: Routledge.

Taylor, K. (2016) *The Political Ideas of the Utopian Socialists* Abingdon: Routledge.

Thompson, N. and Williams, C. (Eds.) (2011) *Robert Owen and His Legacy* Cardiff: University of Wales Press.

Thorpe, A. (2015) *A History of the British Labour Party* London: Red Globe Press.

Timmins, N. (2001) *The Five Giants* London: Collins.

Tooze, A. (2018) *Crashed* London: Allen Lane.

Toporowski, J. (2011) 'Shared Ideas and Mutual Incomprehension: Kalecki and Cambridge' in P. Arestis (Ed.) *Microeconomics, Macroeconomics and Economic Policy* London: Palgrave.

Toye, R. (2013) 'From "Consensus" to "Common Ground"' *Journal of Contemporary History* 48/1: 3–23.

Trentmann, F. (2016) *Empire of Things* London: Allen Lane.

Tudor, H. and Tudor, J.M. (Eds.) (1988) *Marxism and Social Democracy* Cambridge: Cambridge University Press.

Ugwudike, P. (2015) *An Introduction to Critical Criminology* Bristol: Policy Press.

Urbainczyk, T. (2008) *Slave Revolts in Antiquity* Abingdon: Routledge.

Veblen, T. (1899/2009) *The Theory of the Leisure Class* Oxford: Oxford University Press.

Vinen, R. (2018) *The Long '68* London: Penguin.

Walzer, M. (1977) *Just and Unjust Wars* New York: Basic Books.

Walzer, M. (2005) 'All God's Children Got Values' *Dissent* Spring: 35–40.

Wattles, J. (1997) *The Golden Rule* Oxford: Oxford University Press.

Weber, M. (1904/2001) *The Protestant Ethic and the Spirit of Capitalism* London: Penguin.

Weber, M. (1918/2004) *"Science As A Vocation" and "Politics As A Vocation", The Vocation Lectures* Indianapolis: Hackett.

White, S. (2008) 'The Economics of Andrew Glyn' http://renewal.org.uk/articles/the-economics-of-andrew-glyn

Wiener, M. (1971) *Between Two Worlds: Political Thought of Graham Wallas* Oxford: Oxford University Press.

Wilkinson, R. and Pickett, K. (2010) *The Spirit Level* London: Penguin.

Wilkinson, R. and Pickett, K. (2019) *The Inner Level* London: Penguin.

Winter, J.M. and Joslin, D. (1972) *R.H. Tawney's Commonplace Book* Cambridge: Cambridge University Press.

Wray, L.R. (2017) *Why Minsky Matters* Princeton: Princeton University Press.

Wright, E.O. (2006) 'Compass Points: Towards a Socialist Alternative' *New Left Review* 41/September–October: 93–124.

Xiaochuan, Z. (2009) 'Reform the International Monetary System' *BIS Review* www.bis.org/review/r090402c.pdf

Yaffe, D. (1973) 'The Crisis of Profitability: A Critique of the Glyn-Sutcliffe Thesis' *New Left Review* 80/July–August: 45–62.

Young, J. (1986) 'The Failure of Criminology: The Need for a Radical Realism' in R. Matthews and J. Young (Eds.) *Confronting Crime* London: Sage.

Zevin, A. (2019) 'Every Penny a Vote' *London Review of Books* 41/16. www.lrb.co.uk/the-paper/v41/n16/alexander-zevin/every-penny-a-vote

2

SOCIAL DEMOCRATIC CRIMINOLOGY

The political *and* moral economy of crime and criminal justice

Criminology texts are usually organised around a fairly standard list of perspectives said to have characterised criminology's history, with a proliferating array of labels to describe contemporary approaches. The most respected US and UK theoretical criminology texts (e.g. McLaughlin and Newburn 2013; Bernard et al. 2015; Lilly et al. 2018; Hopkins Burke 2018) are typically organised around some 20-plus main chapters reviewing distinct traditions – from classical to critical criminology, many of which are subdivided into a dozen or more variants.

Social democratic criminology (SDC) is not one of these traditional categories. Nonetheless it was an implicit set of ideas, imaginaries, and sensibilities detectable in mainstream sociological criminology for most of the twentieth century. The term 'SDC' has been used by various histories (notably Taylor 1981a, 1981b; Rock 2019 Chap. 1; Downes and Newburn 2020 forthcoming), primarily to characterise the predominant discourse about crime during the era of the broadly social democratic consensus in the Western world. What is referred to is an approach to characterising crime, its causation, and control, that was not limited to academic criminologists (there were few at that time) but included politicians, criminal justice policy-makers, and practitioners. Nor was it restricted to avowed Social Democrats, although – as shown in the previous chapter – there was a broad policy consensus that at least tacitly reflected social democratic principles. It is thus better conceived as an implicit sensibility, lifeworld (Habermas 1996), habitus (Bourdieu 1990), or social imaginary (Taylor 2004) than an explicit theory, ideology, or academic 'ology'. As Bourdieu says of his notion of habitus, it is that which 'goes without saying' in a particular culture and time (Bourdieu op.cit. pp. 66–67). It reflects and reproduces particular social structures, and can be inferred from discourse and practical activities, but it is seldom, if ever, explicitly expressed.

The label 'social democratic criminology' is thus not one that has been espoused or advocated by believers (except for me), but by more or less friendly critics. They

50 Social democratic criminology

respect the achievements of the 30 post-war years but celebrate the transcendence of social democratic criminology by a spectrum of other Left and liberal egalitarian approaches, ranging from more full-blooded socialism to pragmatic revisionism and realism.

This chapter discusses what SDC stands for in relation to the broad history of criminological perspectives: a political economy of crime and criminal justice, tacitly inspired by a social democratic moral economy of justice. Since the 1970s the rise of neoliberal hegemony has pushed aside analysis of crime from the perspective of social democratic political economy. The emphasis became either pragmatic policy-oriented research or culturalist interpretation and appreciation. This chapter traces the roots in political economy of criminology – in the broad sense of organised thinking about crime and criminal justice, and as an explicit subject of academic research and teaching. It argues for the continuing relevance of political and moral economy in understanding patterns of crime and control. The concept of moral economy has long informed political economy and history (Rogan 2018), indicating that economic and social activities are embedded in various concepts of morality. It was introduced to criminology by Karstedt and Farrall (2006) in their analysis of 'crimes of everyday life', dishonest practices engaged in by people who deemed themselves, and were seen as, respectable citizens.

It also offers evidence that neoliberal political economies are associated with more serious violent crime, and less humane modes of control, than social democracies. The era in which SDC tacitly constituted a widespread consensus was successful in maintaining relative social peace, utilising comparatively humane criminal justice policies. However, this achievement declined rapidly with the advance of neoliberal hegemony in governmental thought and practice after the late 1960s. How and why this occurred is probed in Chapter 3. The prospects for revival are considered in the concluding chapter.

Social democratic criminology: the essentials

SDC is an intertwining of political and moral economy, with detailed analysis of a variety of community, family, and individual processes. These generate and shape the behaviours which are authoritatively labelled as crimes by state-organised criminal justice agencies. Although often operating with a sincere veneer of scientific objectivity, it is usually not difficult to detect the ethical values of social democracy in the assumptions and prescriptions of SDC. Perhaps most fundamental is a tacit assumption of the common humanity of those people labelled as offenders. This implies their redeemability if the sources of their condemned actions are unravelled. In SDC, penal responses are aimed ultimately at reintegration, not exclusion.

SDC is a 'root cause' perspective on crime, of the kind that conservatives revile (Wilson 1975), but this does not mean a single-factor reductive determinism. Rather, SDC aims at a complex understanding of root causes, involving many interacting and interdependent pathways between macro-level political economy and culture and their culmination in micro-level criminal or criminal justice actions.

Social democratic criminology **51**

Although most specific theories and research projects focus on the micro and meso levels, in SDC these are seen as stemming fundamentally from two macro 'root causes': conflicts and contradictions in political economy, and a moral economy blighted by social injustice in myriad forms. As we will see, there have been political economies of crime and justice that are not at all social democratic, and many critical analyses focus on specific dimensions of injustice which are not directly reducible to political economy. Actually existing social democratic criminologists (in the sense of criminologists who explicitly espoused social democracy politically, e.g. Bonger 1916/1969 Chaps. 1C, III, 1943; Mannheim 1946 Chap. 4, 1965 Chaps. 23, 26; Wootton 1959 pp. 30, 318; Wootton 1981/1992 Chap. 1) were well aware of the relationship between crime and gender, ethnicity, and sexuality, often campaigning for the reforms that began to gather pace in the late 1950s. Nonetheless, their empirical and policy focus was on the young working-class males who were (and are) the mainstay of criminal law in action. But the distinctive claim of SDC is that the practical and the ethical problems of crime and criminal justice are shaped at root by the core injustices of capitalist political economies, which it believes can be reformed, and perhaps even eliminated ultimately.

This analysis leads to a critique of punitive 'law and order' criminal justice policies. The problems driving crime cannot be suppressed in the long run by the harshness of the executioner's axe or noose, nor by the police officer's truncheon. This is partly for ethical reasons – the offender is ultimately made from the same crooked timber as all humanity (in Kant's phrase), and thus should be seen as fundamentally deserving equal concern and respect, even if their misdeeds merit a reintegrative albeit painful penal response in the first place. It is also because of the practical limits of criminal justice in terms of preventive, detective, and rehabilitative techniques, above all because these cannot tackle the 'root causes' of crime. Criminal justice reform must proceed in tandem with broader political-economic projects to achieve social democratic ideals. As put by Black Lives Matter T-shirts: 'No justice, no peace'.

Social democratic criminology: what needs to be explained

On the face of it, the name 'social democratic criminology' – like any criminology – implies a concern with 'crime' and its understanding. Frequently begged by all criminologies, however, are some fundamental questions: What is crime? What are the elements of criminological understanding of 'crime'? How can they illuminate overall trends and patterns of criminalisation?

What is crime?

The word 'crime' is usually used as if its meaning is clear, uncontested, and unproblematic. Yet most arguments about it involve people talking past each other (for more detailed discussion of the concept of crime, see Henry and Lanier 2001;

52 Social democratic criminology

Reiner 2007 Chap. 2; Reiner 2016; Lacey and Zedner 2017). At least five different conceptions of crime can be distinguished, as follows.

Legal conceptions of crime

If asked to define 'crime', most people would probably invoke the criminal law. And they would have the authority of the Oxford English Dictionary on their side (crime is 'an action or omission which constitutes an offence and is punishable by law'). But there is significant divergence and contradiction among legal, moral, and social constructions of crime.

Defining criminal law itself in substantive terms is problematic, because of the vast, rapidly growing and shifting corpus of criminal law. The UK list of 'Notifiable Offences' (which the police have a statutory obligation to record) includes more than 1,500 types of criminal offence (each type containing many separate offences), continuously being added to.

Given this vast, shifting corpus of substantive law, most criminal law texts define crime formalistically, in an essentially tautologous way. For example, 'crime is an act capable of being followed by criminal proceedings having a criminal outcome' (Williams 1955 p. 107). Some critical legal theorists have sought to transcend the divide between legal and sociological interpretations of crime by the concept of 'criminalization', recognizing that the boundaries between legal and social constructions of crime are contingent, socially created and culturally variable (Lacey and Zedner 2017).

Normative conceptions of crime

Critical criminologists have frequently argued that law fails to define as criminal very serious and wilful harm committed by powerful people, states, and corporations (Hillyard et al. 2004; Nelken 2012; Green and Ward 2017; Levi and Lord 2017; Brisman and South 2017; Bittle et al. 2018). A key contemporary example is tax 'avoidance', ways of minimising payment that are technically legal. In 2016 leaks of files from the Panamanian bank Mossack Fonseca revealed the massive extent to which global political and financial elites used tax havens for avoidance and evasion. President Obama remarked caustically: 'The problem is that a lot of this stuff is legal, not illegal' (www.theguardian.com/news/2016/apr/05/justice-department-panama-papers-mossack-fonseca-us-investigation). The huge growth of offshore finance with devastatingly damaging consequences has been well documented (Shaxson 2012, 2018, 2019; Brooks 2014; Zucman 2016; Harrington 2016; Bullough 2018). Comparative research on the 'finance curse' has calculated that 'the total cost of lost growth potential for the UK caused by "too much finance" between 1995 and 2015 is in the region of £4,500 billion. This total figure amounts to roughly 2.5 years of the average GDP across the period' (Baker et al. 2019).

Don't 'banksters', whose reckless practices have wrecked the lives of so many since the 2007 credit crunch (Clark and Heath 2015; Tooze 2018), deserve

Social democratic criminology **53**

criminalisation alongside the most heinous gangsters? But despite their depredations the rich and powerful largely flourish behind a de facto shield of impunity
(Reiner 2016 Chap. 4), 'too big to jail' (Garrett 2014). Far from seriously curbing
the egregious financial dealings of giant corporations and those who run them,
neoliberal governments award most of their contracts to multinational corporations
operating in tax havens, thus starving exchequers of funds for public expenditure
(Lasko-Skinner et al. 2019).

This isn't just a matter of massive economic harms attributable to the wealthy.
The 'austerity' policies adopted by neoliberal governments, supposedly because of
the impact on public funds of the 2007/8 financial crash, have resulted in thousands
of avoidable deaths in Britain alone, not to speak of much wider physical and men-
tal disease (Stuckler and Basu 2013; O'Hara 2015; Cooper and Whyte 2017; Ryan
2019; Case and Deaton 2020). This has rightly been described as 'social murder' by
many commentators, reviving the term coined by Engels a century ago. It vividly
describes the unnecessary and usually very cruel deaths of many of the most vulnerable sections of society resulting from neoliberal governmental economic policy
(Engels 1844; Chernomas and Hudson 2008; Chakrabortty 2017; Grover 2018).
Vastly more numerous than these social murders is the scarcely countable grievous
and actual bodily harm attributable to austerity, deregulation and the whole ghoul-
ish package of neoliberal economics.

These arguments have developed into the influential claim that criminology
should be replaced by 'zemiology', the study of serious culpable harms, whether
or not they are proscribed by criminal law (Hillyard et al. 2004; Pemberton 2016;
Hillyard and Tombs 2017; Boukli and Kotze 2018). The definition of 'harms' is, of
course, as socially contentious as notions of 'crime', but it explicitly invites normative evaluation, not authoritative declaration.

Conversely, the law criminalises conduct that arguably should not be sanctioned
at all, or that would best be regulated without criminal penalties. Liberal political
philosophers have long claimed that, for both principled and pragmatic reasons,
'private (im)moral behaviour' should not be subject to criminal law. This was the
subject of two famous debates, the first between John Stuart Mill and Judge Fitz-
james Stephen in the nineteenth century, and the second between H.L.A. Hart and
Lord Justice Devlin in the 1960s, following the Wolfenden Report's recommenda-
tion that the criminal law regulation of homosexuality and prostitution should be
liberalised (Mill 1859/1998; Hart 1963; Devlin 1965). Currently, fierce debates
flourish about whether certain activities should be decriminalised – for example,
drug taking or assisted suicide of terminally ill people. Criminal law and competing
moral notions of what should or should not be criminalised thus frequently are in
conflict.

Social/cultural conceptions of crime

Emile Durkheim made an influential attempt to construct a sociological definition
of crime: 'Crime shocks sentiments which, for a given social system are found in all

54 Social democratic criminology

healthy consciences . . . an act is criminal when it offends strong and defined states of the collective conscience' (Durkheim 1893/1973 pp. 73, 80).

As Durkheim himself recognised (anticipating contemporary critical criminology's 'labelling theory'), conceptions of the criminal vary considerably among and within societies, and over time. What is socially sanctioned as deviant will vary from the formal definitions of law and is hotly contested. Jeremy Clarkson fans may complain that the police and courts harass motorists, not 'real' criminals. Are speeding or driving using a mobile phone socially deviant? They are certainly against criminal law and sometimes prosecuted, but many people engage in them. Drink-driving is socially deviant in most circles nowadays but was not in England until some three decades ago, although it was even then in Scandinavia. Who is 'really' criminal – the 'honest, victimized' householder or the young burglar she or he shoots in the back? Who is perceived and stigmatised as 'criminal' only partially overlaps with formal criminalisation.

Criminal justice conceptions of crime

Analysis of who gets processed formally by the criminal justice system suggests another contrasting social construction of crime and criminality. Recorded crimes and criminals form a tiny, unrepresentative sample of all law-breaking – let alone culpable harm and wrongdoing not sanctioned by law. The overwhelming majority of those in prison are young males from economically underprivileged groups, and there is a huge disproportion of black and other ethnic minority people. They are in prison mainly for street crimes, not suite crimes – car theft, burglary, drug offences – not insider trading, pensions mis-selling, tax evasion, or snorting coke in luxury. As the title of a celebrated critique of criminal 'justice' puts it, 'The Rich Get Richer and the Poor Get Prison' (Reiman and Leighton 2012). This pattern not only mocks the fairness of our self-described system of justice, but also calls into question a vast swathe of traditional criminological research, which is based on analysis of those unlucky enough to lose in the criminal justice lottery.

Mass media and policy conceptions of crime

The constructions of crime offered by the mass media indicate yet another pattern. Mass media representations follow a 'law of opposites' (Surette 2014) compared with official crime statistics. Mass media stories ('factual' or 'fictional') focus overwhelmingly on the most serious violent and sexual offences, above all murder, even though these are thankfully rare (Greer and Reiner 2012). The media identify criminal justice primarily with the police, who are portrayed as effective, law-abiding, and morally virtuous. Negative depictions have increased since the 1950s but remain a minority. In news and fiction stories the police almost invariably catch the perpetrator, although in reality only a tiny proportion of crimes are cleared up.

It is this mass media picture that informs most public and policy debate. The media focus on the suffering of a (thankfully) small minority who are the massively

Social democratic criminology **55**

injured, vulnerable, angelically innocent victims of sensational but rare crimes. Politicians are highly sensitive to such reporting, thus distorting policy-making. By contrast, the widespread and devastating suffering inflicted on the mass of the population by wealthy corporations, governments, and the global elite of super high-worth individuals is almost never framed in a crime perspective.

In view of these complexly conflicting, yet sometimes overlapping, conceptions of crime, how is the object of study in any criminology (including SDC) to be defined? Many, if not most, criminological studies avoid any formal definition but implicitly assume a legal conception, studying a criminal justice-defined object: actions which are recorded as crimes, following victim reports or discovery by the police themselves.

As noted earlier, however, the criminal law definition ignores what many, perhaps most, people would regard as very serious and blameworthy harms and wrongs. Moreover, many criminal law offences are commonly regarded as either not wrong or harmful at all, or at any rate as not very serious matters. Even worse, the criminal justice definition is vitiated by the easily demonstrated serious biases in the system. Those criminal acts which are recorded at all represent only a tiny proportion of all offences in the law books. And those people who are processed as suspects or offenders are overwhelmingly drawn from the least powerful and poorest sections of society. More misleadingly still, political and popular crime discourse is focussed mainly on the even more atypical offences portrayed in the mass media.

It is arguable, therefore, that the idea of crime is not a cognitive concept, referring to an ontological reality outside itself, but an expressive one 'embodying an attitude of revulsion, fear, pain or disapproval' (Reiner 2016 p. 5). Some of these behaviours become subject to formal criminalisation, but whether they do or not depends on the very unequally distributed power to influence law creation and enforcement, rather than the degree of harm or pain caused.

This does not mean that the feelings of disgust, fear, suffering, and condemnation levelled at conventionally defined crimes are not merited. In many instances, what is officially treated as crime *does* inflict severe and utterly unjustifiable pain, anxiety, hardship, and loss. Arguably, there is a core of these offences that would be condemned and sanctioned in any social or moral order (Cowling 2008). Rules and institutions seeking to control such core offences may even be functional prerequisites of any form of order, any viable society, a 'minimum content of natural law' (Hart 1961).

However, the process by which harms and wrongs are criminalised is far from a neutral, consensual, or objective process. As critical lawyers and criminologists (including social democratic ones) have shown, making the law in the books and enforcing the law in action reflects the unequal structures of political power and material resources that have besmirched all known societies. Law and its enforcement has the dual function of dealing out 'parking tickets and class repression' (Marenin 1982), reproducing simultaneously the necessary conditions of both *general* order (patterns of co-operative civilised living in the interests of all) and *particular* order (hierarchies of privilege and power). And when push comes to shove

56 Social democratic criminology

(often literally), it is usually the interests of the powerful – the few, not the many – that are embodied in law and its enforcement.

This suggests it is necessary to distinguish 'crime' – actions that cause what someone perceives as culpably wrong and harmful – from 'Crime' – actions labelled as such by criminal law and/or in practice by criminal justice agencies. Most criminology (including SDC) concentrates on the latter, but critical criminologists (including SDC) recognise that it is the former that primarily needs explanation and control, as do the biased criminalisation processes turning crime into Crime. The next section outlines a framework for approaching these issues, in terms of what are the necessary conditions of 'Crime' and 'crime'. It also suggests that the two fundamental aspects of SDC – political economy and moral concern for social justice – play a part in all of them.

Crime's complex preconditions

Several logically necessary preconditions must be met before a crime in any of the aforementioned senses can occur: labelling, motive, means, opportunity, and the absence of control. These conditions can shed light both on the micro factors generating criminal acts, and also on broader macro changes in overall levels and patterns of crime.

Labelling

Actions cannot be meaningfully called 'crimes' unless someone perceives or experiences them as such. At the very least, they must be aware of pain or deprivation being suffered, even if the source is not clear to the victims. Certainly for 'Crimes' (i.e. officially labelled offences) to occur the actions involved must first become part of criminal law, and then become subject to criminal justice processes recording them.

Apparent shifts in crime rates and patterns are frequently the result of changes in criminal law, or in patterns of reporting and recording incidents. In the 1970s, for example, the spread of household contents insurance induced more victims to report burglaries, sparking an apparent surge in crime (Reiner 2016 pp. 123–125). Changes in the official rules for counting offences in 1998 and 2002 (Reiner 2007 pp. 50–51, 70–71) drove up the police-recorded crime rate.

Labelling may also act as a cause of criminal behaviour itself. Changes in how people treat identified offenders (whether stigmatisation, ostracism, denial of jobs, or glorification as a cool guy or a 'made man') may contribute to further offending, as may alterations in a convicted person's self-identity. Whether the crime-producing consequences of official reactions to deviance outweigh their crime-control effects is an open empirical question with varying answers.

Motivation

Detective fiction, as well as newspaper and 'true crime' stories, usually portray the motives driving crime as complex, puzzling, often bizarre, requiring the sensitivity of Dostoevsky or Freud – or at least Agatha Christie or Sherlock Holmes – to unravel them. This is because the media focus on extremely unusual, very serious, pathologically violent or sexual cases. Most offences are committed for conventional, readily comprehensible reasons, motivated by desires that are widely shared – money, fashionable goods, sex, excitement, thrills, intoxication by alcohol, adrenalin, or other substances. Offenders are driven not by deviant cultures but by immersion in contemporary consumerism (Hall et al. 2008). Their moral values are usually conventional, and they frequently invoke narratives gleaned from common mitigatory tropes to neutralise potential guilt feelings about violating dominant norms which they share (Sykes and Matza 1957).

The fact that most crime is motivated by mundane aspirations and desires does not mean that understanding motives is simple or unimportant. It also facilitates unravelling the links mediating micro interactions and macro structural pressures and processes. Social, cultural, and economic changes affect the attractions of behaviour labelled as criminal, increasing or decreasing the numbers of people motivated to commit them.

Means

As lovers of detective mysteries know, in addition to motive, committing crimes requires means and opportunity. The necessary means of specific crimes encompass a variety of personal, emotional, and technical resources.

Changes in political economy, culture, technology, and social patterns can expand or contract the means of committing crimes (Ekblom and Tilley 2000; Gill 2005). New types of crime become possible, old ones may be blocked off, and novel techniques for carrying out old offences are created. Innovative means of exchange and finance, from cheques to credit cards and, more recently, the internet and bitcoin, have supplied new techniques for the old art of relieving people of their money and possessions (Harrington 2016; Zucman 2016; Bullough 2018). Cyberspace has enabled many new types of offence and novel ways of committing old offences, such as terrorism, piracy, fraud, identity theft, stalking, sexual offences against children, hacking security codes, and sexist or racist harassment (Wall 2007; Jewkes and Yar 2009; McGuire and Dowling 2013; Yar and Steinmetz 2019). The increased speed and extent of travel and communications signified by globalisation facilitates a variety of crimes – for example, trafficking in people, drugs, arms, money laundering, and terrorism (Sheptycki and Wardak 2005; Dragiewicz 2014; Findlay et al. 2013; Franko 2017, 2019; Glenny 2017).

Opportunity

Motivated and sufficiently equipped offenders require suitable opportunities, attractive and vulnerable targets ranging from people to property, before crimes can be accomplished (Mayhew et al. 1976; Felson and Clarke 1998; Clarke 2012). The availability and extent of such criminal opportunities vary over time and space, shaped and reshaped by socio-economic, cultural, and lifestyle differences

58 Social democratic criminology

(Natarajan 2011; Ekblom 2018). They may be expanded by a proliferation of tempting targets (e.g. the spread of car ownership, televisions, videos, DVD players, home PCs, laptops, and, more recently, mobile phones and iPads – each in turn becoming the hottest items for theft).

Many studies have charted surges in particular kinds of theft following the development of new 'must-have' consumer goods. For instance, there was a sharp rise in robberies of mobile phones from early 2000 to early 2002 (whilst thefts of other goods remained roughly static), tracking the rapid rise in ownership (Curran et al. 2005).

Absence of controls

One additional ingredient is necessary before a crime can be committed against suitable targets – the absence of controls, informal and formal. A potential burglar, say, may be eager to find a property to burgle, perhaps to feed her children or a habit. Equipped with house-breaking tools and know-how, she comes across a relatively secluded house, undelivered mail stuck in the letterbox, indicating absent owners, and she spies the flashing LEDs of tempting electronic equipment through the ground-floor window.

But her progress up the garden path may be arrested by the plod of a patrolling police officer's feet or the sound of a siren. Even in the likely event that the not so long, overstretched arm of the law is deployed elsewhere, one final intervention may hold her back. On the shelf she spots a Bible, and recalls the still, small voice of her Sunday School teacher, 'Thou shalt not steal' – and goes home for tea and reflection.

Changes in the efficacy of formal criminal justice controls may alter the attractions or possibility of crime. The 1990s recorded drop in crime in the USA has been popularly attributed to harder, smarter, or simply more policing. 'Crime is down, blame the police', boasted former NYPD Chief William Bratton (Bratton 1998). 'Law and order' politicians often gave the credit to tougher punishment, claiming vindication for Michael Howard's 'prison works' slogan. Both claims are vigorously disputed, and the evidence supporting them is dubious (Tonry 2014; Farrell et al. 2014; Roeder et al. 2015; Reiner 2016 pp. 164–185). The very fact that in the two decades after 1995 a decline in recorded crime was universal throughout the Western world, despite substantial variations in policing and penal policies in different jurisdictions, calls the parochial assertions of Bratton, Howard, and their ilk into question. There is a plethora of research evidence and historical experience to cast doubt on the simplistic promises again being made by right-wing governments in the USA, UK, and elsewhere that they can crack crime by 'law and order' toughness to make potential offenders 'literally feel terror at the thought of committing offences' (www.theguardian.com/politics/2019/aug/03/priti-patel-home-secretary-wants-criminals-to-literally-feel-terror). Nonetheless, external formal controls do play some part in shaping crime trends.

Informal social controls are also important in interpreting crime trends and patterns. The thesis that informal controls – family, school, socialisation, community, or 'social capital' – are the fundamental basis of order has a long pedigree, in both SDC and most mainstream criminology. Indeed, it has in recent decades been proposed as the basis of a general theory of crime (Hirschi 1969; Gottfredson and Hirschi 1990), that has generated both expansion and critique (e.g. Tittle 1995; Braithwaite 1997). Since the 1970s, conservatives have commonly claimed that increasing 'permissiveness' in the wake of liberalising legislation and the anti-authoritarian counter-culture of 'the 60s' was a major cause of rising crime. However, this argument has a problem explaining why recorded crime fell after the 1990s, despite continuing cultural liberalisation (Reiner 2016 pp. 171–173).

Multiple causes and crime trends

Crime has complex more or less loosely coupled causes, so no single-factor accounts (such as the conservative 'permissiveness' thesis) can withstand close examination. The foregoing analysis in terms of five necessary conditions of crime provides a variety of tools for explaining particular trends and turning points. For example, the explosion of crime in the 1980s and early '90s (confirmed by both police statistics and victim surveys) was attributable above all to the pernicious effects of neoliberal economic policies: rapidly rising inequality and social exclusion in a consumerist culture of heightened acquisitiveness (Reiner 2007, 2016; Hall et al. 2008). The subsequent fall in recorded crime in the 1990s remains somewhat mysterious, as it is difficult to see any attenuation of 'criminality' (the tendency of society to produce criminals). The right's bête noir, 'permissiveness', has continued unabated, indeed arguably accentuated. So too has the economic and social polarisation attributable to neoliberal globalisation (Reiner 2016 pp. 164–185).

The most plausible account of the falling crime rates since the mid-1990s is the 'security hypothesis': the huge expansion in the use and efficacy of technical crime-prevention techniques, especially car and home security devices (Farrell et al. 2011, 2014). These have held the lid down on a continuing underlying pressure towards 'criminality'. The 2011 British riots showed dramatically what happens when the lid is temporarily lifted (Newburn et al. 2015; Winlow et al. 2015). Smart and fair criminal justice may suppress offending, but only as first aid in the absence of political-economic policies to tackle root causes.

The digital age has offered new means and opportunities for criminality in the form of cybercrime and cyberterrorism. A big business has grown around security technologies which aim to protect against cyberattacks, which in some cases have hit high-profile targets, creating cybercrime/security arms races. Ultimately, however, new forms of offending are likely to regularly outstrip new controls, as long as pressures in political and moral economy generate more criminality.

It is necessary to be tough not only on crime but also on its underlying causes, which lie way beyond the ambit of cops, courts, and corrections. As expressed by fictional private eye Philip Marlowe, 'Crime isn't a disease, it's a symptom. Cops

60 Social democratic criminology

are like a doctor that gives you an aspirin for a brain tumour' (Chandler 1953/1977 p. 599). This is a core tenet of SDC. Before putting SDC to work in analysing crime trends in more detail, we first examine the fluctuating fortunes of political economy as a criminological perspective.

Political economy and the history of criminology

The term 'political economy' is used in contradictory ways nowadays. Although it most frequently indicates a perspective that is distinct from 'economics', it is also sometimes treated as synonymous with it. *The Journal of Political Economy*, for instance, is the title of the house journal of the Chicago School, most famously associated with Milton Friedman and other exponents of neoclassical economics. Stemming from this position is the interpretation of political economy as the application of neoclassical economics to the analysis of politics and policies (Weingast and Whitman 2008), including crime and criminal justice (Becker 1968; Albertson and Fox 2012).

However, what is now taught as 'economics' is very different from the 'political economy' that was its origin. The most famous work of eighteenth-century political economy, Adam Smith's *The Wealth of Nations*, was part of a much wider exploration of social structure and relations, inextricably bound up with moral philosophy. Marx saw himself as heir to this tradition, synthesising it with the dialectical philosophy of Hegel and with French St Simonian socialism. Indeed, 'political economy' is often used nowadays as virtually a synonym for Marxism.

'Economics' grew out of political economy in the late nineteenth century as a distinct discipline, focussing on the economic in abstraction from these wider dimensions. It now refers to a supposedly apolitical, value-free, 'scientific' enterprise, analysing the 'economic' using primarily mathematical models based on highly abstract and simplified axioms about human motivation, decision-making processes, and forms of social organisation. Since the 2007/8 financial crisis this approach has increasingly been questioned by students, academics, and some policy-makers and politicians (cf. the movements www.neweconomics.org, 'real-world economics' www.paecon.net, www.evonomics.com, and Fullbrook 2007; Aldred 2010, 2019; Keen 2011; Chang 2011; Haring and Douglas 2012; Earle et al. 2017; Fleming 2017, 2019; Raworth 2018; McDonnell 2018). Nonetheless, it remains the dominant mode of teaching, research, and policy advice.

During the late nineteenth century, liberal capitalist economies became relatively firmly established and hegemonic, after protracted and turbulent birth pangs and teething pains. Specialist social science disciplines developed from the broad discourses of political economy and philosophy: economics, political science, sociology, psychology – and indeed, criminology. This was interrelated with the growing separation between what came to be seen as different social and institutional fields.

Liberal capitalism was characterised by ideal and institutionalised distinctions between the spheres of the 'private' and 'public'; 'civil society' and 'state'; 'the

Social democratic criminology **61**

economy' and 'the polity'; 'criminal' and 'civil' law, each constituted and studied by an autonomous discipline (Neocleous 2000 pp. 13–14; Lea 2002 Chaps. 1–3). 'Political economy', by contrast, generally stresses the *embeddedness* of the 'economic' in wider networks of political, social, and cultural processes.

Political economy has been an important influence in modern attempts to understand crime and its control (Reiner 2012a, 2012b, 2018), although its influence has been eclipsed at times – in particular during the last three decades of neoliberal hegemony. It was also occluded in the late nineteenth century, when the term 'criminology' was first coined to refer to the emerging 'science of the criminal' pioneered by Lombroso and his associates. David Garland's magisterial analysis of the discipline's origins argued that

> criminology is structured around two basic projects – the governmental and the Lombrosian . . . oriented towards a scientific goal, but also towards an institutional field; towards a theoretical project, but also towards an administrative task. Whatever fragile unity the discipline achieves emerges from the belief that these two projects are mutually supportive rather than incompatible, that etiological research can be made useful for administrative purposes, and that the findings of operational research further the ends of theoretical enquiry.
>
> *(Garland 2001 p. 16)*

The term 'criminology' as such came into being as the label for the Lombrosian version of the quest for theoretical understanding of the aetiology of crime (Mannheim 1960 p. 1). But the project of developing criminological analysis using the intellectual tools of political economy and social science, partly to further the policy ends of achieving order and justice, predated the label. The eighteenth-century criminologies *avant la lettre*, the 'classical' school of criminal law and the 'science of police', were closely linked to political economy. They were sidelined in the later nineteenth century by the rise of the positivist 'science of the criminal', with its aura of scientific rigour, objectivity, and dispassionate expertise. The late twentieth-century downplaying of political economy in criminology was the result of the opposite one-sided accentuation: an attempt to marginalise theoretical questions for the sake of 'realism' – a pragmatic pursuit of policies that 'worked', denying the relevance of any consideration of deeper causes.

The eclectic, broad-ranging account of crime, criminals, and control that political economy offers is necessary both for understanding the sources of crime (and control efforts), and for effective and just policy. The continuing relevance of political economy will be illustrated by a brief demonstration of its utility in illuminating crime and control trends. It will be argued that both historical analysis and macro-comparisons of contemporary crime and control patterns show that variations in crime and criminal justice phenomena are associated with different types of political economy. Most specifically, whilst the growing neoliberal hegemony in the last quarter of the twentieth century generated growing crime threats and

62 Social democratic criminology

tougher criminal justice policies, social democracy has been associated with greater safety and more humane social control.

Criminology's roots in political economy and the 'science of police'

The standard account of the history of criminology sees its origins in the 'classical' perspective associated with Beccaria's 1764 book *Dei Delitti e Delle Pene*, and its profound influence, via Blackstone, Bentham, and others, on the Enlightenment movements for reform of criminal law and punishment. It has often been argued that the 'classical' perspective is not fully criminological (apart from lacking the label) because it was not concerned with aetiological questions, assuming a voluntaristic, rational economic actor model of offenders. Beirne has shown that this was not true of Beccaria, who was strongly influenced by the emerging 'science of man' in the discussions of the philosophers and political economists of the Scottish Enlightenment, notably Hume, Adam Ferguson, and Adam Smith (Beirne 1993). This was a deterministic discourse concerned with explaining the causes of human conduct and society. Histories of criminology often neglect the relationship between political economy and Enlightenment discussions of crime and criminal justice, reflected only partly in the work of Beccaria (who was appointed to a chair of 'Political Economy and Science of Police' at Milan in 1768, where he delivered lectures on the 'Elements of Political Economy' (Pasquino 1978 p. 45).

Political economy was intertwined particularly with the 'science of police' that flourished in the eighteenth and early nineteenth centuries but has been overlooked by criminologists until recently. It is well known that the term 'police' originally had a much broader meaning, essentially coterminous with the internal policies of governments. What is less acknowledged is the intimate intertwining of 'police' and political economy. In his 1763 *Lectures on Justice, Police, Revenue and Arms*, Adam Smith defined 'police' as

> the second general division of jurisprudence. The name is French and is originally derived from the Greek *polis*, which properly signified the policy of civil government, but now it only means the regulation of the inferior parts of government, viz: cleanliness, security and cheapness or plenty. The two former, to wit, the proper method of carrying dirt from the streets, and the execution of justice, so far as it regards regulations for preventing crimes or the method of keeping a city guard, though useful, are too mean to be considered in a general discourse of this kind. . . . We observe then, that in cities where there is most police and the greatest number of regulations concerning it, there is not always the greatest security. . . . Upon this principle, therefore, it is not so much the police that prevents the commission of crimes as having as few persons as possible to live upon others. Nothing tends so much to corrupt mankind as dependency, whilst independency increases the honesty of the people. The establishment of commerce and

Social democratic criminology **63**

manufactures, which brings about this independency, is the best police for preventing crimes. The common people have better wages in this way than in any other, and in consequence of this a general probity of manners takes place through the whole country.

(Smith 1763/1898)

In short, it is broader political economic policies that offer the best prospects of controlling crime and disorder, not explicit policing tactics aimed at this.

The eighteenth-century 'science of police' was a vast body of work that flourished across Europe but has been almost totally ignored by criminologists until fairly recently (Radzinowicz 1956; Pasquino 1978; Reiner 1988; Neocleous 2000, 2006; Dubber 2005; Dubber and Valverde 2006). In England the leading exponent of the 'science of police' was the magistrate Patrick Colquhoun. Colquhoun is most commonly remembered as a pioneer of the modern British police in the narrow sense (Stead 1977). However, he wrote extensively on political economy, crime, and criminal justice, and his work can be seen as a precursor of criminology (Colquhoun 1797, 1800, 1806). To Colquhoun crime and criminal justice were not independent phenomena that could be considered in isolation from broader issues of social and economic structure (paralleling Adam Smith's analysis, cited earlier). His proposals for the prevention and control of crime were rooted in empirical investigation of crime patterns.

Colquhoun's analysis located the ultimate causes of crime in the overall structure of economy and society, but he was concerned to unravel the social and cultural mediations generating criminality and conformity. Crime was 'the constant and never-failing attendant on the accumulation of wealth', providing the opportunities and temptations for misappropriation (Colquhoun 1800 pp. 155–156). Crime (mainly theft) was attributable to the poor, but poverty did not determine crime. Crime had both structural and cultural sources. Structural factors included variations in the opportunities for training available to different ethnic groups due to downturns in the economic cycle. But cultural and informal moral controls (such as religion and the promotion of uplifting rather than 'bawdy' forms of popular pastimes) were also important to encourage 'manners' that were 'virtuous' rather than 'depraved'.

The reform of formal policing arrangements for which Colquhoun is best known was only a relatively minor aspect of the policies he saw as required to prevent crime. Effective deterrence by regular police patrol was important and more effective than harsh punishment after the event. But the operation of formal policing was primarily significant in symbolic and cultural rather than instrumental, utilitarian terms. The beneficial effects of police patrol were more attributable to their encouraging moral discipline than deterring or catching perpetrators. The terrain of police was to be 'upon the broad scale of General Prevention – mild in its operations – effective in its results; having justice and humanity for its basis, and the general security of the State and Individuals for its ultimate object' (Colquhoun 1800 p. 38).

64 Social democratic criminology

Overall, the broad analysis of security, order, crime, and policing, advanced by the staunch conservative Colquhoun as the 'science of police', was more sensitive to the interplay of politics, law, morality, and justice with criminality than the later nineteenth-century 'science of the criminal' was. Like the contemporaneous displacement of political economy by economics, the apparent gain in 'scientific' rigour was bought at a high price in terms of obscuring the political, economic, and ethical dimensions of crime and welfare. The present-day focus of conservatives on 'toughness', deterrent policing, and punitive penality in a war on crime, grotesquely oversimplifies the much more complex analysis and prescriptions of their forebears.

During the late nineteenth-century heyday of individualist positivism, there continued to be attempts to analyse crime from macro-sociological perspectives informed by political economy. Durkheim's 1897 classic *Suicide*, for example, offered a template for later theoretical analyses of fluctuating rates and patterns of deviance, as well as two seminal concepts, egoism and anomie (Durkheim 1897/1951).

In the early twentieth century there were scattered attempts to develop political economies of crime and punishment. The most significant were the attempt to develop a systematic Marxist analysis of crime by Willem Bonger, a Dutch professor (Bonger 1916), and Rusche and Kirchheimer's influential political economy of punishment (Rusche and Kirchheimer 1939).

To Bonger the main way in which capitalism was related to crime was through the stimulation of a moral climate of egoism, at all levels of society. In terms that anticipated Merton's seminal analysis of anomie (Merton 1938), Bonger talked of the stimulation of material desires by modern marketing, explaining not only proletarian crime but also crimes of the powerful.

Merton's anomie theory remains the most influential formulation of a political economy of crime (Merton 1938). Most accounts portray it as 'strain' theory and focus on its analysis of crime patterns *among* social groups. A society that *culturally* encourages common material aspirations by a mythology of meritocracy, against a *structural* reality of unequal opportunities, generates anomic pressures and deviant reactions. More fundamentally, however, Merton suggested that anomie was related to the very nature of aspirations in particular cultures. A highly materialistic culture – especially one that defines success almost exclusively in monetary terms – is prone to problems of moral regulation and crime, at *all* levels. This is not an economically determinist account; the *cultural meaning* of material factors such as poverty or inequality is crucial.

Merton's perspective, particularly as developed by Cloward and Ohlin (1960), was a major influence on the criminological application of New Deal political economy during Lyndon Johnson's 'Great Society' programme and war on poverty declared in 1964. Despite its strengths, however, Merton's analysis fell out of fashion after the mid-1960s. Its social democratic critique of unbridled capitalism was too cautious for 1970s radical criminology, too radical for post-1980s neoliberalism, and too structuralist for Foucauldians and postmodernists. Soon the war on

Social democratic criminology **65**

poverty transmogrified into the war on crime under the banner of law and order (Hinton 2016). Mertonian anomie theory has, however, recently re-emerged in attempts to analyse variations in crime rates and patterns over time and among different types of political economy (Messner and Rosenfeld 2012; Reiner 2007 pp. 14–15, 84, 92–93, 109; *Theoretical Criminology* Special Issue February 2007; Rosenfeld and Messner 2013).

The criminological perspective most explicitly rooted in political economy was the 'fully social theory of deviance' sketched in *The New Criminology* (Taylor et al. 1973 pp. 268–280), stressing the interdependence of macro, meso, and micro processes. This was explicitly intended as 'a political economy of criminal action, and of the reaction it excites', together with 'a politically informed social psychology of these ongoing social dynamics' (ibid. p. 279). It was an attempt 'to move criminology out of its imprisonment in artificially segregated specifics . . . to bring the parts together again in order to form the whole' (ibid.).

Most research studies inevitably focus on a narrower range of phenomena, but the checklist of elements for a 'fully social theory' is a reminder of the wider contexts in which deviance and control are embedded. This was illustrated by *Policing the Crisis*, the closest attempt to incorporate all these elements into the study of one specific phenomenon, a magisterial study of mugging and the reaction to it (Hall et al. 1978). Hall et al. moved out from an account of a particular robbery in Birmingham to a wide-ranging analysis of British economic, political, social, and cultural history since World War II, charting the deeper concerns that 'mugging' condensed, and the impact of transformations in the political economy on young black men in particular.

The eclipse of political economy in criminology

Political economy has been sidelined in the neoliberal era since the late 1970s by a number of 'turns' in intellectual, cultural, and political life. It was caught in a pincer movement from both right and left, denying the reality of 'society', or at any rate structural causes and grand narratives. Criminology reflected this shift, beginning with the right-wing 'realist' critique initiated by James Q. Wilson's polemic against 'root cause' perspectives (Wilson 1975, p. xv). Left realism as it developed in the 1980s also claimed that rising crime in a more 'affluent society' constituted an 'aetiological crisis' for social democratic criminology (Lea and Young 1984; Young 1986).

Mainstream criminology, for its part, became dominated by pragmatic concerns about immediately practicable policies. This was partially linked to theoretical analysis that saw crime as driven not by any deep causes, but asserted that 'opportunity makes the thief' (Felson and Clarke 1998). Research became grounded in concerns about improving security to prevent such opportunities. Causal explanation concentrated on individual and situational levels (Mayhew et al. 1976), which are more amenable to policy interventions and do not raise questions of wider social justice. Whilst realism ousted political economy, it was

66 Social democratic criminology

also associated with a broader revival of perspectives based on economic models, such as rational choice theory (Cornish and Clarke 1986; Tilley and Farrell 2011), as well as a rejuvenated neoclassical economics of crime (Becker 1968; Albertson and Fox 2012).

More recently, 'cultural criminologists' have claimed that political economy cannot comprehend the subjective seductions of crime and the romance of deviance (Katz 1988; Presdee 2000; Ferrell et al. 2004, 2015; Muzzatti and Smith 2018). There is no necessary contradiction between political economy and cultural analysis, however, and some have argued for a synthesis with structural perspectives (Young 2003; Hayward 2004; Hall and Winlow 2003, 2004, 2007; Ferrell 2007; Hall et al. 2008). Nonetheless, the 'cultural turn' in general, especially in its postmodern incarnations, rejects the determinism and 'grand narratives' they attribute to mainstream Marxism and other approaches based on political economy (Jameson 1991, 1998; Bonnell and Hunt 1999; Milovanovich 2018). Interpretation of experience and culture came to be seen as the function of intellectual analysis, rather than explanation, or policy advocacy, or designing legislation (Bauman 1989).

In the 1980s these critiques were buttressed by a belief (strongly promoted by the Thatcher and Reagan governments) that econometric evidence called into question any postulated relationships between crime and economic factors. More recent studies, however, generally show that economic factors are now closely related to crime trends and patterns. This change is largely due to the quite distinct social meaning, extent, and impact of unemployment, poverty, and inequality during the post-war Keynesian, welfare-state compromise, contrasted with their devastating impact following the social tsunami of neoliberalism (for a summary see Reiner 2007 pp. 79–80, 97–110, 2016 pp. 173–176, 2018 pp. 25–26).

Historical and comparative studies also demonstrate that political economy shapes patterns of crime and of crime control policy, with a major contrast between social democracies and neoliberalism (Reiner 2007, 2016, 2018; Hall 2007, 2012; Lacey 2008; Hall et al. 2008; Hall and McLean 2009). Political economy constitutes a holistic approach, encompassing the dialectical complexity of interactions between macro structures and individual actions. As Weber put it long ago, explanation has to be both 'causally adequate' *and* 'adequate at the level of meaning'. *Verstehen* and structural analysis are complementary, not contradictory. This is illustrated by a consideration of how crime trends and patterns in Britain can be understood.

Crime, criminalisation, and the growth of citizenship

Criminal justice systems are based on the delivery of doses of pain where this is deemed necessary, although this is projected as procedurally and even substantively fair and appropriate. Between the mid-nineteenth and mid-twentieth century in Britain, however, there developed a system of modern criminal justice that broadly sought to emphasise welfare, rehabilitation and re-incorporation, consensus, and legitimacy (especially as compared to what came before and after). There was an attempt, always imperfectly realised and often hypocritical, at minimising force, pain, and violence, and thus seeking to gain a substantial measure of popular consent. Welfarist social policy together with inclusive economic and political citizenship, not exclusion and harsh sanctions, were seen as the basis of social and political order, and of crime control. Policing and punishment, the first and last stages of the formal criminal process, both based ultimately on physical force, were seen as regrettably necessary stopgaps until root causes could be tackled. This was the heyday of the governing tactics that have been analysed as policing by consent and penal welfarism (Garland 1985, 2001; Reiner 2010; Bowling et al. 2019; Downes and Newburn forthcoming). These strategies were formulated, applied, and regulated by policy-makers and practitioners that Ian Loader has characterised as 'Platonic Guardians' (Loader 2006). The political affiliations of these officials varied. However, their heyday was the post-World War II era of Butskellite consensus infused with a broadly social democratic sensibility (Rock 2019; Downes and Newburn op cit). Crime was committed by human beings who were not qualitatively set apart from normal humanity, even if various causes led them to commit unacceptable and sometimes grossly harmful acts. The task of criminological research was to ascertain these causes. The purpose of policing and penal policy and practice was to prevent and repair the damage done. Ultimately crime control meant tackling the root causes of the problems (which often lay outside the sphere of criminal justice).

The relatively liberal approach to crime and justice practiced by the 'Platonic Guardians' was a form of liberal elitism (Loader 2006). The majority of public opinion tended to be much harsher in its view of how to deal with offenders, at any rate after the mid-nineteenth century as policing and criminal justice gradually ceased to be experienced by the masses as a form of oppression. The backdrop and necessary condition of relatively inclusive and 'civilised' penal approaches was that crime and disorder seemed to be contained and indeed diminishing problems. It began to disintegrate as the rise of neoliberalism eroded the consensus political economy based on a social democratic sensibility (analysed in Chapter 1):

> Liberal elitism made sense in, or was at least fitted to, a world where crime was less prevalent as an act and more settled as a cultural category; a world where people evinced trust and deference towards social authority and had more patient expectations of government; a world marked by greater equality and solidarity and less ambient precariousness and insecurity. Such an outlook speaks less well to a society where crime has become a recurrent feature of everyday life; where the anxieties and demands it generates are widely and excitedly disseminated by the mass media; where reduced levels of trust in the institutions of government coincide with heightened public demands of them; where consumerism threatens to eclipse citizenship as the organizing political principle – and symbol of belonging – of the age.
>
> *(Loader 2006 p. 581)*

68 Social democratic criminology

Whether this bleak assessment still holds true, in the face of the challenges to belief in neoliberalism since the 2007/8 financial and economic crash, is discussed in the conclusion. But first it is necessary to probe the extent of success of the long-term progress towards more inclusive and forward-looking socio-economic and criminal justice policies from the mid-nineteenth century until the rise of neoliberalism in the 1970s.

In part this can be marked by official criminal justice statistics, although these are of notoriously debatable validity and value (Coleman and Moynihan 1996; Reiner 2007 Chap. 3, 2016 Chap. 5; Maguire and McVie 2017). National crime statistics began to be collected and published by the Home Office after the 1856 County and Borough Police Act, which established modern police forces throughout the country. From the 1850s until the 1920s the crime levels recorded by the police remained on a plateau. Although there are no figures for crimes that were not prosecuted before 1856, on the basis of the judicial statistics historians generally believe that the mid-Victorian levels represent a decline from much higher levels in the early nineteenth century (Gatrell 1980).

There is some debate about whether the flat trend from the 1850s to the 1920s is attributable to a low level of actual offending. It has been cogently argued that supply-side rationing of the figures resulted in data that were a statistical illusion. This was driven by fiscal parsimony and by successive governments' concern to present an appearance of success for the new police, and other nineteenth-century criminal justice reforms (H. Taylor 1998a, 1999; for a cogent critique cf. Morris 2001).

But what is clear is that there was a steady state of criminalisation, and at any rate the *appearance* of success in crime control. Criminologists and policy-makers at the turn of the twentieth century (like their counterparts in the early twenty-first century) were vexed about how to explain the great crime drop (Radzinowicz and Hood 1986; H. Taylor 1998b). Political and industrial disorder also seemed both less frequent and less violent – a match rather than a battle – compared with the earlier nineteenth century, or indeed the later twentieth century (Geary 1985). As the mass of the population came to be included to some extent in a commonly shared status of political and socio-economic citizenship, so class conflict became somewhat attenuated and institutionalised. This has been charted and analysed as a 'civilising process', the taming of the more violent aspects of human behaviour by cultural and governmental progress freeing the 'better angels of our nature' (Elias 1939/1994; Pinker 2011). However, given the preconditions of this process in the political economy of more inclusive capitalism, and the reversal of the trend towards less violence as neoliberalism has become dominant, it is apt to analyse this as a 'pseudo pacification process' (Hall and Winlow 2003, 2004; Hall 2007, 2012; Horsley et al. 2015).

Thus, during the century between the 1850s and 1950s there came to be embedded the system of policing celebrated as 'policing by consent' (Bowling et al Chap. 4). Over the same period, 'penal welfarism' (Garland 1985, 2019) became the prevailing response to apprehended offenders. Although these strategies had

Social democratic criminology **69**

complex conditions of existence, the underlying context was the gradual incorporation of the mass of the population into social as well as civil and political citizenship –
what David Garland has called the 'solidarity project' (Garland 2001 p. 199. The
classic account is Marshall 1950; cf. Reiner 2010). And it has been the reversal of
the trend towards greater inclusion resulting from the advent of neoliberalism since
the 1970s that generated the crime and disorder explosions of the 1980s, and a
harsher politics of law and order (Reiner 2007, 2016 Chap. 5, pp. 158–185). An
inverse association between violent crime levels and US presidents whose policies
are more inclined towards social democracy has also been demonstrated (Gilligan
2011). In short, the closer the political and moral economy approaches the social
democratic sensibility which prevailed during the three post-war decades, the
greater the extent of social peace. The next section probes the official statistics that
lend some support to that interpretation (however tenuous they are in themselves).

The calculus of crime: charting recent trends

Criminal statistics are notoriously riddled with pitfalls. Above all, there is a huge
extent of unrecorded crime, due to non-reporting by victims, non-recording by
the police, and an incalculable volume of offending that victims and police never
even become aware of. These unrecorded crimes may encompass severe harms,
including grievous bodily harm or deaths because of poverty, caused by corporate
or other offending. Changes in the recorded figures may be due not to changes
in offence levels but to fluctuations in reporting or recording, or in the rules for
counting crimes.

Very substantial steps have been taken in recent decades to alleviate these problems by developing alternative measures, above all the regular crime and victimisation surveys conducted by many jurisdictions, although all suffer from pitfalls of
their own. The creation of the British Crime Survey (BCS) in 1981 shed much
light on reporting and recording practices, allowing statistics to be interpreted more
robustly. The availability of two alternative measures of trends gives greater confidence when they point in the same direction, as they did for the first decade of
the BCS. However, in the 1990s the trends indicated by the police statistics and the
BCS began to diverge, generating a politicised debate about their relative merits.

Putting together the different sorts of data available, what can be said about the
trends since World War II? The most apparent development was the spectacular rise
in recorded crime from the late 1950s. In the early 1950s the police recorded less
than half a million offences per annum. By the mid-1970s this had risen to 2 million. The 1980s showed even more staggering rises, with recorded crime peaking
in 1992 at more than 5.5 million.

From the mid-1990s, crime began to fall as measured by both police recorded
and crime survey statistics. By 1997 police-recorded crime had fallen back to
4.5 million. Major counting rule changes introduced in 1998 and 2002 make
analysis of the subsequent figures especially fraught, but on the new rules (which
undoubtedly exaggerate the increase) just under 6 million offences were recorded

70 Social democratic criminology

by the police for 2003/4 (Reiner 2007 pp. 49–53, 63). This subsequently fell back again, to 4.95 million in 2007/8. But since 2014, police-recorded crime has once again begun to tick up. It should be noted, however, that following several serious scandals concerning the official crime statistics, as well as mounting criticism from various governmental bodies, the UK Statistics Authority in January 2014 stripped the police-recorded crime statistics of their Kitemark as officially designated National Statistics (Maguire and McVie 2017 pp. 181–185). Nonetheless, the Office for National Statistics (ONS) has continued to publish them as part of its regular bulletins on 'Crime in England and Wales', together with the results of the Crime Survey for England and Wales (CSEW).

Contrasting police-recorded statistics with victim surveys suggests a complex picture, but clearly pinpoints the reversal of the long march towards more inclusive citizenship by neoliberalism as the accelerant behind a crime explosion (Reiner 2007 Chaps. 3, 4). Three distinct phases can be distinguished on the basis of the victim survey evidence, qualifying the relentless rise in the recorded crime rate since the mid-1950s.

1955–83: recorded crime rise

Until the 1970s there was no other index of crime trends apart from police statistics. But during the 1970s the General Household Survey (GHS) began to ask about burglary victimisation. Its data showed that most of the increase in recorded burglary was due to greater reporting by victims. Between 1972 and 1983 recorded burglaries doubled, but victimisation increased by only 20%. Victims reported more burglaries mainly because of the spread of household contents insurance. This cannot be extrapolated necessarily to other crimes, or even to burglary in previous decades. Nonetheless, the GHS indicates that the increased rate for this highly significant crime was mainly a recording phenomenon, up to the early 1980s. It is plausible that this applied to volume property crimes more generally. Thus the rise of crime whilst the mixed-economy, welfarist consensus survived was probably substantially less than the recorded statistics suggested.

1983–92: crime explosion

The BCS in the 1980s showed the reverse: although recorded crime still increased more rapidly than BCS crime, the trends were similar. By both measures, crime rose at an explosive rate during the 1980s and early '90s, the Thatcher and early Major years. The decade and a half during which neoliberalism destroyed Britain's industrial base, and defined whole areas and generations out of the edifice of citizenship creating a new excluded underclass (Dahrendorf 1985; Young 1999), stimulated record growth for two industries: crime and the state agencies purporting to control it, notably police and prisons.

1993– : ambiguously falling crime

From the early 1990s the trends indicated by the police statistics and the BCS began to diverge. The BCS continued to chart a rise until 1995, but the police-recorded data fell from 1992 to 1997. Insurance companies made claiming more onerous, thus discouraging reporting by victims, and more 'businesslike' managerial accountability for policing implicitly introduced incentives to keep crime recording down.

After New Labour came to power in 1997, the two measures continued to diverge – but in the opposite direction. BCS-recorded crime has fallen continuously and by 2007/8 was below the level of the first BCS conducted in 1981.

The police-recorded statistics, however, began to rise again from 1998 up to 2004, after which they declined for another decade but rose again after 2014, as discussed previously. The earlier rise in the recorded rate was due overwhelmingly to two major changes in police procedures for counting crimes: new Home Office Counting Rules in 1998 and the 2002 National Crime Recording Standard (NCRS). These reforms boosted the recorded rate substantially compared with what would have been measured previously under the old rules (Reiner 2007 pp. 52–53, 70–71). However, the rise in crime recording since 2014 is plausibly related to the growing size of the precariat in the age of austerity (Standing 2011).

The BCS is free from the particular problems that make the police figures unreliable as a measure of trends. However, it is not (and has never claimed to be) a definitive index. It necessarily omits many offences: homicide, the supreme example of personal victimisation; crimes with individual victims who are unaware of what happened (such as successful frauds); crimes against organisations or the public at large; consensual offences such as drug-taking; and other serious examples. As an official governmental survey, it operates with a legal definition of what I referred to earlier as 'Crime', omitting any harms or wrongs that are not formally criminalised but nonetheless inflict culpable and often extremely severe suffering and loss.

Its sampling frame excludes certain highly victimised groups such as children under age 16 and the homeless. So the government's tendency to treat the BCS/CSEW as definitive is as problematic as the earlier exclusive reliance on police statistics.

The dramatic overall fall in the BCS since the mid-1990s also masks increases in some of the most alarming offences. Murder and other serious crimes of violence have increased in the past 40 years and are now a higher proportion of all crimes. During the 1960s and early '70s, the number of homicides recorded per year per million population was usually under eight, but this had more than doubled to 18 by 2003. The homicide rate then declined for a decade, until beginning to rise once more since 2014. In 1976 just 5% of recorded offences were classified as violent, but by 2007/8 this had increased to 19% (partly because the counting rule changes lowered the threshold for recording violence).

The BCS/CSEW statistics suggest a more optimistic trend of generally falling violence since the mid-1990s (though, as noted earlier, victim surveys necessarily omit homicide, which has risen for most of the period since the early 1980s).

72 Social democratic criminology

However, it is precisely in the area of violent crime that the BCS/CSEW is most problematic, as critics have pointed out from the outset. Partly this is because of the traumatic nature of such crimes, which could make women respondents reluctant to discuss their victimisation with strangers (especially if male) representing officialdom. This is especially likely in the case of domestic violence or sexual assaults, when the respondent's partner may be in the vicinity and indeed may be the perpetrator. Supporting this is the recurrent finding that surveys conducted by local or feminist organisations often uncover much higher rates of victimisation than generic crime surveys (Mooney 1994; Walby and Myhill 2001). The methodology of the BCS/CSEW has changed over time to try and mitigate these problems, but they cannot be eliminated (Percy and Mayhew 1997; Home Office 2012).

Recent research has highlighted a major flaw in the crime survey's methodology, with ramifications calling into question the established notion of an overall crime drop since the 1990s (Walby et al. 2016). The surveys have capped the number of multiple victimisations they record at five. This has resulted in a considerable undercounting since 2009, especially of domestic violence against women. When these are added in, the trend changes to increasing victimisation overall, and specifically with regard to violence, since 2009. This is plausibly related to various effects of the financial crisis and the economic downturn since 2007/8, making it harder for women to exit from violent households and get support for their plight (ibid. p. 5).

Recorded robberies have risen sharply since the early 1990s, although they then fell (erratically) until a peak in 2001/2. Since 2014, however, they have started to increase again. There has also been a highly publicised rise in the use of firearms and knives in committing crimes, including robbery and homicide. 'The volume of knife and sharp instrument offences has increased by 44% since the year ending March 2011' (ONS 2019 p. 33).

Overall, the rosy picture painted by the BCS/CSEW of falling crime since the mid-1990s has been called into question by rising serious violent crime since the advent of Conservative-led governments after 2010, with their policies of austerity. These hugely affect crime in the broader sense of culpable serious harms and wrongs, as argued earlier, calling into question the standard view of international crime decline since the mid-1990s (Kotze 2019). But this has become evident even with regard to officially recorded 'Crime', especially since 2014 as the cuts really began to bite hard.

Overall, the crime trends fit the thesis that neoliberalism has been associated with a crime explosion. This was attenuated in part by the 'third way' highly watered-down social democracy of the 1990s and early noughties. But the lid came off with the return of full-blooded neoliberal economics since 2010. The empirical association of social democracy with less crime and coercive crime control is probed further in the next section, which examines comparisons between different contemporary forms of political economy.

Political and moral economies of criminalisation: contemporary comparisons

During the twenty-first century, the volume of scholarly work on the political economy of punishment, mostly comparative, has increased. These works demonstrate clear systematic variations in patterns of punishment in contemporary systems related to their political economies (Downes 2001; Sutton 2000, 2004, 2012; Beckett and Western 2001; Cavadino and Dignan 2006; Downes and Hansen 2006; de Giorgi 2006, 2012; Reiner 2007; Lacey 2008; Wacquant 2009; Lacey et al. 2018; Melossi et al. 2018; Xenatis and Cheliotis 2018). An association between types of political economy and punishment patterns at a macro level seems clear, although interpretation of the experience of specific societies requires detailed and particularistic cultural analysis (Nelken 2010, 2017). What emerges clearly from this literature is that social democratic political economies, contrasted at the other extreme with neoliberal ones, are characterised by more harshly punitive policies, practices, and penal cultures, with more corporate capitalist societies coming in between.

Most recent research has focussed on the comparative political economy of punishment. Comparative research on crime is bedevilled by issues of comparability in the definitions and counting procedures among jurisdictions (van Dijk 2008). Nonetheless, there is evidence that the same differences in political economy underlie systematic variations in serious crime, especially homicide (Currie 1997, 1998, 2013, 2016; I. Taylor 1999; Messner and Rosenfeld 2012; Reiner 2007 pp. 103–110; Lacey 2008 p. 60; Hall and McLean 2009; Wilkinson and Pickett 2009; Gallo et al. 2018). Specifically, the higher inequality, less generous welfare, and greater social exclusion that characterises neoliberalism as opposed to social democracy is associated with more serious violent crime, including homicide (Reiner 2007 p. 106).

A heart of darkness pervades neoliberal as distinct from social democratic political economies: more serious violence *and* more cruel punishment. The immediate pain and symptom relief advocated by criminological realists (across the political spectrum) is vital, but only provided it does not become a diversionary and ultimately futile struggle to hold down the lid on what remain 'root causes' structured by different types of political economy (Matthews 2017).

Conclusion: policing, punishment or political economy? A plea for social democracy

It was seen earlier that, following the crime explosion of the first decade and a half during which neoliberalism ousted social democracy, overall recorded crime fell in the later 1990s and 2000s. This began with the Blair/Clinton era, when an attenuated 'third way' interpretation of social democracy prevailed in much of the Western world. This accepted the economic fundamentals of neoliberal globalisation,

74 Social democratic criminology

but used social policy and some *sotto voce* redistribution as sticking plasters alleviating the harshest consequences of no-holds-barred capitalism. Worrying increases in some of the most serious and frightening offences nonetheless occurred, and the simple notion of overall recorded crime reduction disguised the plausible expansion of gross harms by the powerful especially (Kotze (2018, 2019). Did this show that being tough on crime (as famously promised by Tony Blair in 1992) worked? It certainly didn't in relation to public opinion, which never accepted that crime has fallen, according to the BCS/CSEW and other surveys (Duffy et al. 2008; Hough and Roberts 2017 pp. 241–243).

The question of why crime has fallen in the UK (and even more so, in the USA) is a vexed one, and highly debated. A central part of the new tough on crime consensus since the early 1990s was that tough policing and punishment *do* work and have been instrumental in bringing crime down (Reiner 2007 Chap. 5). This hard law and order view has been doubled down on by the conservative governments elected since 2015 in the UK, USA, and several other countries, coinciding with an uptick in recorded crime and violence.

However, the bulk of the research paints a more complex picture. It is certainly widely conceded that policing and penal policy (including increased imprisonment) have played some part in bringing crime rates down, and that the 'nothing works' conclusions of the 1970s and early '80s were not warranted. The research suggests, however, that it was the 'smart' rather than the 'tough' elements of policing, prevention, and punishment changes that had the most significant impact: intelligence- and evidence-led targeting of security resources on the most vulnerable targets and most serious offenders (Tonry 2014; Farrell et al. 2014; Roeder et al. 2015; Reiner 2016 pp. 164–185). Moreover, it remains the case that criminal justice interventions of even the most effective kind play only a limited role compared with the importance of 'getting tough on the causes of crime' – the root causes in political economy and culture. A plethora of evidence indicts the key aspects of neoliberalism as causes of crime (cf. Reiner 2016 pp. 201–202 for a long list of such research). Inequality is strongly related to violent crime, and unemployment and marginal employment to property crime, and both are strongly accentuated by the egoistic and narcissistic culture of consumerism (Reiner 2007; Hall et al. 2008). In so far as crime has been suppressed by more effective security whilst the root causes of criminality – the propensity of a society to generate crime – remain virulent (Currie 2000), it is unsurprising that public anxiety is still strong. Physical security measures in particular have a double-edged effect on public confidence. They may give temporary reassurance of threats being held at bay, but at the same time they advertise the risks should they fail (Zedner 2003 p. 165).

A cruel irony is that the Blair government knew all that, but felt trapped by the wilderness years of the 1980s when Labour's espousal of the social democratic argument that the key to crime control was social and economic policy came to be seen as an electoral liability (Downes and Morgan 2007). A review by the Prime Minister's Strategy Unit concluded that 80% of the crime reduction of the decade after 1995 was due to economic factors, although this estimate was omitted from

Social democratic criminology **75**

the version of the report published on the Cabinet website, which concentrated almost entirely on criminal justice solutions (Solomon et al. 2007 p. 14). Thus, New Labour was moderately successful in reducing recorded crime, even with its very limited success in containing inequality and exclusion. But it was so locked into the politics of tough law and order that this was a success that dared not speak its name.

This chapter has shown that explosive criminalisation, in the double sense of more perceived and actually experienced crime, *and* the tough crime-control policies brought about by the politics of law and order, were consequences of the neoliberal tsunami since the 1970s. This reversed the centuries-long progress towards universal incorporation into some measure of shared social, political, and civil citizenship. The nineteenth and twentieth centuries, up to the 1960s, had witnessed the spread of social rights and greater inclusiveness. They also experienced a more benign coupling of lower crime and disorder, with more consensual and welfare-oriented policing and penality. The necessary condition of restoring that climate of greater security and less harsh criminal justice is a reversal of the neoliberalism that undermined social democracy (Reiner 2007, 2011).

The dire consequences of neoliberalism in the economic arena have become manifest since the 2007/8 financial crisis, with the return of depression on a scale unprecedented since the 1930s. The holes in the neoliberal model are widely acknowledged now even by erstwhile neoliberal economists and policy-makers. The risk society (Beck 1992) and neoliberal 'responsibilisation' (Garland 2001) were euphemisms for a massive 'risk shift' (Hacker 2006). The risks of insecurity in the shape of crime, as well as economic deprivation, were offloaded from government and corporations to the mass of the population, who could not carry the burden. The news does not seem to have penetrated most criminology as yet, but there is a growing sense amongst economic and political analysts that the state remains needed and indeed that social democracy is as necessary as the post-war generation felt it to be. The prospects for civilisation depend 'on whether the social-democratic leaders of western Europe can breathe life into the dry bones of what seemed, until recently, a dead doctrine' (Bogdanor 2009).

Tawney's statement of social democratic principles, at the start of the Great Depression of the 1930s, remains valuable for democratic and ethical politics, policing and crime control:

> Its fundamental criticism of capitalism is not merely that it impoverishes the mass of mankind – poverty is an ancient evil – but that it makes riches a god . . . Socialism accepts . . . the principles which are the cornerstones of democracy, that authority, to justify its title, must rest on consent; that power is tolerable only so far as it is accountable to the public; and that differences of character and capacity between human beings, however important on their own plane, are of minor significance compared with the capital fact of their common humanity.
>
> *(Tawney 1931 p. 197)*

76 Social democratic criminology

Contrary to popular mythology and much recent criminology, even the most effective policing and punishment (public and/or private) cannot provide the foundations of security. But if these foundations *are* once more reproduced by inclusive economic and social policies, then criminal justice can offer what it is capable of: legitimate and effective responses to specific individual crimes.

The next chapter analyses the character and context of the changes towards harsher crime control policies following in the wake of neoliberalism. As with social and economic strategy (discussed in Chapter 1), the question is how to account for a casting aside of what seemed to be working well in the heyday of social democracy. The concluding Chapter 4 then probes the prospects of the revival of social democratic criminology, now that the failures of neoliberal approaches are increasingly manifest.

References

Albertson, K. and Fox, C. (2012) *Crime and Economics* Abingdon: Routledge.

Aldred, J. (2010) *The Sceptical Economist* Abingdon: Routledge.

Aldred, J. (2019) *Licence to Be Bad: How Economics Corrupted Us* London: Allen Lane.

Baker, A., Epstein, G. and Montecino, J. (2019) 'The UK's Finance Curse University of Sheffield: Speri' https://pdfs.semanticscholar.org/c334/992ab49a32780e1a73f577d2299 67c9fd5a1.pdf

Bauman, Z. (1989) *Legislators and Interpreters* Cambridge: Polity.

Beck, U. (1992) *Risk Society* London: Sage.

Becker, G. (1968) 'Crime and Punishment: An Economic Approach' *Journal of Political Economy* 76: 175–209.

Beckett, K. and Western, B. (2001) 'Governing Social Marginality: Welfare, Incarceration and the Transformation of State Policy' *Punishment and Society* 3/1: 43–59.

Beirne, P. (1993) *Inventing Criminology* Albany: SUNY Press.

Bernard, T., Snipes, J. and Gerould, A. (2015) *Vold's Theoretical Criminology* 7th ed. Oxford: Oxford University Press.

Bittle, S., Snider, L., Tombs, S. and Whyte, D. (Eds.) (2018) *Revisiting Crimes of the Powerful* Abingdon: Routledge.

Bogdanor, V. (2009) 'Loosening Labour's Golden Straitjacket' *New Statesman* 19 March.

Bonger, W. (1943) *Race and Crime* New York: Columbia University Press.

Bonger, W. (1916/1969) *Criminality and Economic Conditions* Bloomington: Indiana University Press.

Bonnell, V. and Hunt, L. (Eds.) (1999) *Beyond the Cultural Turn* Berkeley: University of California Press.

Boukli, A. and Kotze, J. (Eds.) (2018) *Zemiology* London: Macmillan.

Bourdieu, P. (1990) *The Logic of Practice* Cambridge: Polity.

Bowling, B., Reiner, R. and Sheptycki, J. (2019) *The Politics of the Police* 5th ed. Oxford: Oxford University Press.

Braithwaite, J. (1997) 'Charles Tittle's Control Balance and Criminological Theory' *Theoretical Criminology* 1/1: 77–97.

Bratton, W. (1998) 'Crime is Down: Blame the Police' in N. Dennis (Ed.) *Zero Tolerance: Policing A Free Society* 2nd ed. London: Institute of Economic Affairs.

Brisman, A. and South, N. (2017) 'Green criminology' in A. Brisman, E. Carrabine and N. South (Eds.) *The Routledge Companion to Criminological Theory and Concepts* Abingdon: Routledge.

Social democratic criminology 77

Brooks, R. (2014) *The Great Tax Robbery* London: Oneworld.

Bullough, O. (2018) *Moneyland* London: Profile.

Case, A. and Deaton, A. (2020) *Deaths of Despair and the Future of Capitalism* Princeton: Princeton University Press.

Cavadino, M. and Dignan, J. (2006) *Penal Systems: A Comparative Approach* London: Sage.

Chakrabortty, A. (2017) 'Over 170 Years after Engels, Britain is Still a Country that Murders its Poor' www.theguardian.com/commentisfree/2017/jun/20/engels-britain-murders-poor-grenfell-tower

Chandler, R. (1953/1977) *The Long Goodbye* London: Heinemann.

Chang, H.-J. (2011) *23 Things They Don't Tell You About Capitalism* London: Penguin.

Chernomas, R. and Hudson, I. (2008) *Social Murder* Winnipeg: Arbeiter Books.

Clark, T. and Heath, A. (2015) *Hard Times* New Haven: Yale University Press.

Clarke, R. (2012) 'Opportunity Makes the Thief. Really? And so What?' *Crime Science* 1/3: 1–9.

Cloward, R. and Ohlin, L. (1960) *Delinquency and Opportunity* Abingdon: Routledge.

Coleman, C. and Moynihan, J. (1996) *Understanding Crime Data* Buckingham: Open University Press.

Colquhoun, P. (1797) *Treatise on the Police of the Metropolis* London: Bye and Law.

Colquhoun, P. (1800) *Treatise on the Commerce and Police of the River Thames* London: J. Mowman.

Colquhoun, P. (1806) *A New and Appropriate System of Education for the Labouring People* London: Hatchard.

Cooper, V. and Whyte, D. (Eds.) (2017) *The Violence of Austerity* London: Pluto.

Cornish, D. and Clarke, R. (Eds.) (1986) *The Reasoning Criminal* New York: Springer-Verlag.

Cowling, M. (2008) *Marxism and Criminological Theory* London: Palgrave.

Curran, K., Dale, M., Edmunds, M., Hough, M., Millie, A. and Wagstaff, M. (2005) *Street Crime in London* London: Government Office for London.

Currie, E. (1997) 'Market, Crime and Community: Toward a Mid-range Theory of Post-industrial Violence' *Theoretical Criminology* 1/1: 147–172.

Currie, E. (1998) 'Crime and Market Society: Lessons From the United States' in P. Walton and J. Young (Eds.) *The New Criminology Revisited* London: Macmillan.

Currie, E. (2000) 'Reflections on Crime and Criminology at the Millennium' *Western Criminology Review* 2(1), 1–15.

Currie, E. (2013) *Crime and Punishment in America* New York: Picador.

Currie, E. (2016) *The Roots of Danger* New York: Oxford University Press.

Dahrendorf, R. (1985) *Law and Order* London: Sweet and Maxwell.

De Giorgi, A. (2006) *Rethinking the Political Economy of Punishment* Aldershot: Ashgate.

De Giorgi, A. (2012) 'Punishment and Political Economy' in J. Simon and R. Sparks (Eds.) *Handbook of Punishment and Society* London: Sage.

Devlin, P. (1959/1965) *The Enforcement of Morals* Oxford: Oxford University Press.

Downes, D. (2001) 'The Macho Penal Economy' *Punishment and Society* 3/1: 61–80.

Downes, D. and Hansen, K. (2006) 'Welfare and Punishment in Comparative Perspective' in S. Armstrong and L. McAra (Eds.) *Perspectives on Punishment* Oxford: Oxford University Press.

Downes, D. and Morgan, R. (2007) 'No Turning Back: The Politics of Law and Order into the Millennium', in M. Maguire, R. Morgan and R. Reiner (Eds.) *The Oxford Handbook of Criminology* 4th ed. Oxford: Oxford University Press.

Downes, D. and Newburn, T. (2020) *The Politics of Law and Order* Abingdon: Routledge, forthcoming.

Dragiewicz, M. (Ed.) (2014) *Global Human Trafficking* Abingdon: Routledge.

Dubber, M. (2005) *The Police Power* New York: Columbia University Press.

78 Social democratic criminology

Dubber, M. and Valverde, M. (Eds.) (2006) *The New Police Science* Palo Alto: Stanford University Press.

Duffy, B., Wake, R., Burrows, T. and Bremner, P. (2008) 'Closing the Gaps – Crime and Public Perceptions' *International Review of Law, Computers and Technology* 22: 1.

Durkheim, E. (1897/1951) *Suicide* London: Routledge.

Durkheim, E. (1893/1973) *The Division of Labour in Society* Glencoe: Free Press.

Earle, J., Moran, C. and Ward-Perkins, Z. (2017) *The Econocracy* Manchester: Manchester University Press.

Ekblom, P. (2018) 'Technology, Opportunity, Crime and Crime Prevention: Current and Evolutionary Perspectives' in B. LeClerc and E. Savona (Eds.) *Crime Prevention in the 21st Century* Charn: Springer.

Ekblom, P. and Tilley, N. (2000) 'Going Equipped: Criminology, Situational Crime Prevention and the Resourceful Offender' *British Journal of Criminology* 40/3: 376–398.

Elias, N. (1939/1994) *The Civilising Process* Oxford: Blackwell.

Engels, F. (1844/2009) *The Condition of the Working Class in England* London: Penguin.

Farrell, G., Tilley, N., and Tseloni, A. (2014) 'Why the Crime Drop?' in M. Tonry (Ed.) *Why Crime Rates Fall and Why They Don't* Chicago: University of Chicago Press.

Farrell, G., Tseloni, A., Mailley, J. and Tilley, N. (2011) 'The Crime Drop and the Security Hypothesis' *Journal of Research on Crime and Delinquency* 48/2: 147–175.

Felson, M. and Clarke, R. (1998) *Opportunity Makes the Thief: Practical Theory for Crime Prevention* London: Home Office.

Ferrell, J. (2007) 'For a Ruthless Cultural Criticism of Everything Existing' *Crime, Media, Culture* 3/1: 101–109.

Ferrell, J., Hayward, K., Morrison, W. and Presdee, M. (Eds.) (2004) *Cultural Criminology Unleashed* Abingdon: Routledge.

Ferrell, J., Hayward, K. and Young, J. (2015) *Cultural Criminology: An Invitation* 2nd ed. London: Sage.

Findlay, M., Boon Kijo, L. and Si Wei, L. (2013) *International and Comparative Criminal Justice* Abingdon: Routledge.

Fleming, P. (2017) *The Death of Homo Economicus* London: Pluto.

Fleming, P. (2019) *The Worst is Yet to Come* London: Repeater.

Franko, K. (2017) 'Criminology, Punishment and the State in a Globalised Society' in A. Liebling, S. Maruna and L. McAra (Eds.) *The Oxford Handbook of Criminology* 6th ed. Oxford: Oxford University Press.

Franko, K. (2019) *Globalisation and Crime* 3rd ed. London: Sage.

Fullbrook, E. (Ed.) (2007) *Real World Economics* London: Anthem.

Gallo, Z., Lacey, N. and Soskice, D. (2018) 'Comparing Serious Violent Crime in the US and England and Wales' in K. Reitz (Ed.) *American Exceptionalism in Crime and Punishment* New York: Oxford University Press.

Garland, D. (1985) *Punishment and Welfare* Aldershot: Gower.

Garland, D. (2001) *The Culture of Control* Oxford: Oxford University Press.

Garland, D. (2019) 'Punishment and Welfare Revisited' *Punishment and Society* 21/3: 267–274.

Garrett, B. (2014) *Too Big to Jail* Cambridge: Harvard University Press.

Gatrell, V. (1980) 'The Decline of Theft and Violence in Victorian and Edwardian England' in V. Gatrell, B. Lenman and G. Parker (Eds.) *Crime and the Law* London: Europa.

Geary, R. (1985) *Policing Industrial Disputes* Cambridge: Cambridge University Press.

Gill, M. (2005) 'Reducing the Capacity to Offend' in N. Tilley (Ed.) *Handbook of Crime Prevention and Community Safety* Cullompton: Willan.

Gilligan, J. (2011) *Why Some Politicians are More Dangerous Than Others* Cambridge: Polity.

Glenny, M. (2017) *McMafia* London: Vintage.

Gottfredson, M. and Hirschi, T. (1990) *A General Theory of Crime* Stanford: Stanford University Press.

Green, P. and Ward, T. (2017) 'Understanding State Crime' in A. Liebling, S. Maruna and L. McAra (Eds.) *The Oxford Handbook of Criminology* 6th ed. Oxford: Oxford University Press.

Greer, C. and Reiner, R. (2012) 'Mediated Mayhem: Media, Crime, Criminal Justice' in M. Maguire, R. Morgan and R. Reiner (Eds.) *The Oxford Handbook of Criminology* 5th ed. Oxford: Oxford University Press.

Grover, C. (2018) 'Violent Proletarianisation: Social Murder, the Reserve Army of Labour and Social Security "austerity" in Britain' *Critical Social Policy* 39/3: 335–355.

Habermas, J. (1996) *Between Facts and Values* Cambridge: Polity.

Hacker, J. (2006) *The Great Risk Shift* New York: Oxford University Press.

Hall, S. (2007) 'The Emergence and Breakdown of the Pseudo-Pacification Process', in K. Watson (Ed.) *Assaulting the Past: Violence and Civilization in Historical Context* Newcastle upon Tyne: Cambridge Scholars Press.

Hall, S. (2012) *Theorizing Crime and Deviance* London: Sage.

Hall, S., Critcher, C., Jefferson, T., Clarke, J. and Roberts, B. (1978) *Policing the Crisis* London: Macmillan.

Hall, S. and McLean, C. (2009) 'A Tale of Two Capitalisms: Preliminary Spatial and Historical Comparisons of Homicide Rates in Western Europe and the USA' *Theoretical Criminology* 13/3: 313–339.

Hall, S. and Winlow, S. (2003) 'Rehabilitating Leviathan: Reflections on the State, Economic Regulation and Violence Reduction' *Theoretical Criminology* 7: 139–162.

Hall, S. and Winlow, S. (2004) 'Barbarians at the Gates: Crime and Violence in the Breakdown of the Pseudo-pacification Process' in J. Ferrell, K. Hayward, W. Morrison and M. Presdee (Eds.) *Cultural Criminology Unleashed* London: Glasshouse.

Hall, S. and Winlow, S. (2007) 'Cultural Criminology and Primitive Accumulation' *Crime, Media, Culture* 3/1: 82–90.

Hall, S., Winlow, S. and Ancrum, C. (2008) *Criminal Identities and Consumer Culture* Cullompton: Willan.

Haring, N. and Douglas, N. (2012) *Economists and the Powerful* London: Anthem.

Harrington, B. (2016) *Capital Without Borders* Cambridge: Harvard University Press.

Hart, H. (1961) *The Concept of Law* Oxford: Oxford University Press.

Hart, H. (1963) *Law, Liberty, and Morality* Stanford: Stanford University Press.

Hayward, K. (2004) *City Limits* London: Glasshouse.

Henry, S. and Lanier, M. (Eds.) (2001) *What is Crime?* Lanham, MD: Rowman and Littlefield.

Hillyard, P., Pantazis, C., Tombs, S. and Gordon, D. (Eds.) (2004) *Beyond Criminology* London: Pluto.

Hillyard, P. and Tombs, S. (2017) 'Social Harm and Zemiology' in A. Liebling, S. Maruna and L. McAra (Eds.) *Oxford Handbook of Criminology* 6th ed. Oxford: Oxford University Press.

Hinton, E. (2016) *From the War on Poverty to the War on Crime* Cambridge: Harvard University Press.

Hirschi, T. (1969) *Causes of Delinquency* Berkeley: University of California Press.

Home Office (2012) 'British Crime Survey: Methodology' www.gov.uk/government/statistics/british-crime-survey-methodology

80 Social democratic criminology

Hopkins Burke, R. (2018) *An Introduction to Criminological Theory* 5th ed. Abingdon: Routledge.

Horsley, M., Kotze, J. and Hall, S. (2015) 'The Maintenance of Orderly Disorder: Modernity, Markets and the Pseudo-pacification Process' *Journal of European History of Law* 6/1: 18–29.

Hough, M. and Roberts, J. (2017) 'Public Opinion, Crime, and Criminal Justice' in A. Liebling, S. Maruna and L. McAra (Eds.) *Oxford Handbook of Criminology* 6th ed. Oxford: Oxford University Press.

Jameson, F. (1991) *Postmodernism* Durham, NC: Duke University Press.

Jameson, F. (1998) *The Cultural Turn* London: Verso.

Jewkes, Y. and Yar, M. (Eds.) (2009) *Handbook of Internet Crime* Cullompton: Willan.

Karstedt, S. and Farrall, S. (2006) 'The Moral Economy of Everyday Crime: Markets, Consumers and Citizens' *British Journal of Criminology* 46/6: 1011–1036.

Katz, J. (1988) *Seductions of Crime* New York: Basic Books.

Keen, S. (2011) *Debunking Economics* London: Zed Books.

Kotze, J. (2018) 'Criminology or Zemiology?' in A. Boukli and J. Kotze (Eds.) *Zemiology* London: Macmillan.

Kotze, J. (2019) *The Myth of the "Crime Decline"* Abingdon: Routledge.

Lacey, N. (2008) *The Prisoners' Dilemma: Political Economy and Punishment in Contemporary Democracies* Cambridge: Cambridge University Press.

Lacey, N., Soskice, D. and Hope, D. (2018) 'Understanding the Determinants of Penal Policy: Crime, Culture, and Comparative Political Economy' *Annual Review of Criminology* 1: 195–217.

Lacey, N. and Zedner, L. (2017) 'Criminalisation: Historical, Legal, and Criminological Perspectives' in A. Liebling, S. Maruna and L. McAra (Eds.) *Oxford Handbook of Criminology* 6th ed. Oxford: Oxford University Press.

Lasko-Skinner, R., Glover, B. and Lockey, A. (2019) *Value Added: How Better Government Procurement can Build a Fairer Britain* London: Demos.

Lea, J. (2002) *Crime and Modernity* London: Sage.

Lea, J. and Young, J. (1984) *What is to be Done About Law and Order?* Harmondsworth: Penguin.

Levi, M. and Lord, N. (2017) 'White-Collar and Corporate Crime' in A. Liebling, S. Maruna and L. McAra (Eds.) *Oxford Handbook of Criminology* 6th ed. Oxford: Oxford University Press.

Lilly, J., Cullen, F. and Ball, R. (2018) *Criminological Theory* 7th ed. London: Sage.

Loader, I. (2006) 'Fall of the "Platonic Guardians": Liberalism, Criminology and Political Responses to Crime in England and Wales' *British Journal of Criminology* 46/4: 561–586.

Maguire, M. and McVie, S. (2017) 'Crime Data and Criminal Statistics: A Critical Reflection' in A. Liebling, S. Maruna and L. McAra (Eds.) *Oxford Handbook of Criminology* 6th ed. Oxford: Oxford University Press.

Mannheim, H. (1946) *Criminal Justice and Social Reconstruction* London: Routledge.

Mannheim, H. (Ed.) (1960) *Pioneers in Criminology* London: Stevens.

Mannheim, H. (1965) *Comparative Criminology* Abingdon: Routledge.

Marenin, O. (1982) 'Parking Tickets and Class Repression: The Concept of Policing in Critical Theories of Criminal Justice' *Contemporary Crises* 6/3: 241–266.

Marshall, T.H. (1950) *Citizenship and Social Class* Cambridge: Cambridge University Press.

Matthews, R. (2017) *Realist Criminology* London: Macmillan.

Mayhew, P., Sturan, A. and Hough, M. (1976) *Crime As Opportunity* London: Home Office.

McDonnell, J. (Ed.) (2018) *Economics for the Many* London: Verso.

Social democratic criminology 81

McGuire, M. and Dowling, S. (2013) *Cybercrime: A Review of the Evidence* London: Home Office.

McLaughlin, E. and Newburn, T. (Eds.) (2013) *The Sage Handbook of Criminological Theory* London: Sage.

Melossi, D., Sozzo, M. and Brandariz, J. (Eds.) (2018) *The Political Economy of Punishment Today* Abingdon: Routledge.

Merton, R. (1938) 'Social Structure and Anomie' *American Sociological Review* 3/5: 672–682.

Messner, S. and Rosenfeld, R. (2012) *Crime and the American Dream* 5th ed. Belmont, CA: Wadsworth.

Mill, J.S. (1859/1998) *On Liberty* Oxford: Oxford University Press.

Milovanovich, D. (2018) 'Postmodern Criminology' in W. DeKeseredy and M. Dragiewicz (Eds.) *The Routledge Handbook of Critical Criminology* 2nd ed. Abingdon: Routledge.

Mooney, J. (1994) *The Prevalence and Social Distribution of Domestic Violence: An Analysis of Theory and Method* PhD thesis. London: Middlesex University.

Morris, R. (2001) ' "Lies, Damned Lies and Criminal Statistics": Reinterpreting the Criminal Statistics in England and Wales' *Crime, History and Societies* 5/1: 111–127.

Muzzatti, S. and Smith, E. (2018) 'Cultural Criminology' in W. DeKeseredy and M. Dragiewicz (Eds.) *The Routledge Handbook of Critical Criminology* 2nd ed. Abingdon: Routledge.

Natarajan, M. (Ed.) (2011) *Crime Opportunity Theories* Abingdon: Routledge.

Nelken, D. (2010) *Comparative Criminal Justice* London: Sage.

Nelken, D. (2012) 'White-Collar and Corporate Crime' in M. Maguire, R. Morgan and R. Reiner (Eds.) *The Oxford Handbook of Criminology* 5th ed. Oxford: Oxford University Press.

Nelken, D. (2017) 'Rethinking Comparative Criminal Justice' in A. Liebling, S. Maruna and L. McAra (Eds.) *The Oxford Handbook of Criminology* 5th ed. Oxford: Oxford University Press.

Neocleous, M. (2000) *The Fabrication of Social Order* London: Pluto.

Newburn, T., Cooper, K., Deacon, R. and Diski, R. (2015) 'Shopping for Free'? Looting, Consumerism and the 2011 Riots' *British Journal of Criminology* 55/1: 39–64.

O'Hara, M. (2015) 'Life and Death Under Austerity' *Mosaic* https://mosaicscience.com/story/life-and-death-austerity/

ONS (2019) 'Knife Crime in London' www.ons.gov.uk/aboutus/transparencyandgovernance/freedomofinformationfoi/knifecrimeinlondon

Pasquino, P. (1978) 'Theatrum Politicum: The Genealogy of Capital – Police and the State of Prosperity' *Ideology and Consciousness* 4/1: 41–54.

Pemberton, S. (2016) *Harmful Societies* Bristol: Policy Press.

Percy, A. and Mayhew, P. (1997) 'Estimating Sexual Victimisation in a National Crime Survey: A New Approach' *Studies on Crime and Crime Prevention* 6/2: 125–150.

Pinker, S. (2011) *The Better Angels of Our Nature* London: Allen Lane.

Presdee, M. (2000) *Cultural Criminology and the Carnival of Crime* Abingdon: Routledge.

Radzinowicz, L. (1956) *A History of the English Criminal Law and its Administration from 1750* Vol. III. London: Stevens.

Radzinowicz, L. and Hood, R. (1986) *A History of English Criminal Law and its Administration* Vol. VI. London: Stevens.

Raworth, K. (2018) *Doughnut Economics* London: Random House.

Reiman, J. and Leighton, P. (2012) *The Rich Get Richer and the Poor Get Prison* 10th ed. New York: Routledge.

Reiner, R. (1988) 'British Criminology and the State' *British Journal of Criminology* 28/2: 138–158.

82 Social democratic criminology

Reiner, R. (2007) *Law and Order: An Honest Citizen's Guide to Crime and Control* Cambridge: Polity.

Reiner, R. (2010) *The Politics of the Police* 4th ed. Oxford: Oxford University Press.

Reiner, R. (2011) *Policing, Popular Culture and Political Economy* Farnham: Ashgate.

Reiner, R. (2012a) 'Casino Capital's Crimes: Political Economy, Crime, and Criminal Justice', in M. Maguire, R. Morgan and R. Reiner (Eds.) *The Oxford Handbook of Criminology* 5th ed. Oxford: Oxford University Press.

Reiner, R. (2012b) 'Political Economy and Criminology: The Return of the Repressed' in S. Hall and S. Winlow (Eds.) *New Directions in Criminological Theory* Abingdon: Routledge.

Reiner, R. (2016) *Crime: The Mystery of the Common-Sense Concept* Cambridge: Polity.

Reiner, R. (2018) 'Critical Political Economy, Crime and Justice' in W. DeKeseredy and M. Dragiewicz (Eds.) *The Routledge Handbook of Critical Criminology* 2nd ed. Abingdon: Routledge.

Rock, P. (2019) *The Official History of Criminal Justice in England and Wales: Volume I: The "Liberal Hour"* Abingdon: Routledge.

Roeder, O., Eisen, L.-B., and Bowling, J. (2015) *What Caused the Crime Decline?* New York: Brennan Center for Justice, NYU Law School.

Rogan, T. (2018) *The Moral Economists* Princeton: Princeton University Press.

Rosenfeld, R. and Messner, S. (2013) *Crime and the Economy* London: Sage.

Rusche, G. and Kirchheimer, O. (1939/2003) *Punishment and Social Structure* Piscataway, NJ: Transaction Books.

Ryan, K. (2019) *Crippled: Austerity and the Demonisation of Disabled People* London: Verso.

Shaxson, N. (2012) *Treasure Islands* London: Vintage.

Shaxson, N. (2018) 'The Finance Curse: How the Outsized Power of the City of London Makes Britain Poorer' www.theguardian.com/news/2018/oct/05/the-finance-curse-how-the-outsized-power-of-the-city-of-london-makes-britain-poorer

Shaxson, N. (2019) *The Finance Curse* London: Vintage.

Sheptycki, J. and Wardak, A. (Eds.) (2005) *Transnational and Comparative Criminology* London: Glasshouse.

Smith, A. (1763/1978) *Lectures on Jurisprudence* Oxford: Oxford University Press.

Solomon, E., Eades, C. and Garside, R. (2007) *Ten Years of Criminal Justice Under Labour: An Independent Audit, Kings College* London: Centre for Crime and Justice Studies.

Standing, G. (2011) *The Precariat: The New Dangerous Class* London: Bloomsbury.

Stead, P.J. (Ed.) (1977) *Pioneers in Policing* Montclair, NJ: Patterson Smith Publishing.

Stuckler, D. and Basu, S. (2013) *The Body Economic: Why Austerity Kills* New York: Basic Books.

Surette, R. (2014) *Media, Crime, and Criminal Justice* 5th ed. Belmont: Wadsworth.

Sutton, J.R. (2000) 'Imprisonment and Social Classification in Five Common-Law Democracies, 1955–1985' *American Journal of Sociology* 106/8: 350–386.

Sutton, J.R. (2004) 'The Political Economy of Imprisonment in Affluent Western Democracies, 1960–1990' *American Sociological Review* 69/1: 170–189.

Sutton, J.R. (2012) 'Imprisonment and Opportunity Structures' *European Sociological Review* 38/1: 12–27.

Sykes, G. and Matza, D. (1957) 'Techniques of Neutralisation' *American Sociological Review* 33: 46–62.

Tawney, R.H. (1931) *Equality* London: Unwin (1964 reprint).

Taylor, I. (1999) *Crime in Context* Cambridge: Polity.

Taylor, I. (1981a) *Law and Order – Arguments for Socialism* London: Macmillan.

Taylor, I. (1981b) *Social Democracy and the Crime Question in Britain: 1945–1980* PhD thesis. University of Sheffield: Centre for Criminological and Socio-Legal Studies http://etheses.whiterose.ac.uk/1885/1/DX171455_1.pdf

Taylor, C. (2004) *Modern Social Imaginaries* Durham, NC: Duke University Press.

Taylor, H. (1998a) 'The Politics of the Rising Crime Statistics of England and Wales,1914–1960' *Crime, History and Societies* 2/1: 5–28.

Taylor, H. (1998b) 'Rising Crime: The Political Economy of Criminal Statistics Since the 1850s' Economic History Review LI: 569–590.

Taylor, H. (1999) 'Forging the Job: A Crisis of "Modernisation" or Redundancy for the Police in England and Wales 1900–39' *British Journal of Criminology* 39/1: 113–135.

Taylor, I., Walton, P. and Young, J. (1973) *The New Criminology* London: Routledge.

Tilley, N. and Farrell, G. (Eds.) (2011) *The Reasoning Criminal* Abingdon: Routledge.

Tittle, C. (1995/2019) *Control Balance: Towards a General Theory of Deviance* Abingdon: Routledge.

Tonry, M. (Ed.) (2014) *Why Crime Rates Fall and Why They Don't* Chicago: Chicago University Press.

Tooze, A. (2018) *Crashed* London: Allen Lane.

Van Dijk, J. (2008) *The World of Crime* London: Sage.

Wacquant, L. (2009) *Punishing the Poor: The Neoliberal Government of Social Insecurity* Durham, NC: Duke University Press.

Walby, S. and Myhill, A. (2001) 'New Survey Methodologies in Researching Violence Against Women' *British Journal of Criminology* 41/3: 502–522.

Walby, S., Towers, J. and Francis, B. (2016) 'Is Violent Crime Increasing or Decreasing? A New Methodology to Measure Repeat Attacks Making Visible the Significance of Gender and Domestic Relations' *British Journal of Criminology* 56/6: 1203–1234.

Wall, D. (2007) *Cybercrime* Cambridge: Polity.

Weingast, B. and Whitman, D. (Eds.) (2008) *The Oxford Handbook of Political Economy* Oxford: Oxford University Press.

Wilkinson, R. and Pickett, K. (2009) *The Spirit Level: Why More Equal Societies Almost Always Do Better* London: Allen Lane.

Williams, G. (1955) 'The Definition of Crime' *Current Legal Problems* 8: 107.

Wilson, J.Q. (1975) *Thinking About Crime* New York: Basic Books.

Winlow, S., Hall, S., Treadwell, J. and Briggs, D. (Eds) (2015) *Riots and Political Protest* Abingdon: Routledge.

Wootton, B. (1959) *Social Science and Social Pathology* London: Allen and Unwin.

Wootton, B. (1981/1992) *Selected Writings: Crime and the Penal System* edited by V. Seal and P. Bean. London: Macmillan.

Xenatis, S. and Cheliotis, L. (2018) 'Neoliberalism and the Politics of Imprisonment' in W. DeKeseredy and M. Dragiewicz (Eds.) *Routledge Handbook of Critical Criminology* 2nd ed. Abingdon: Routledge.

Yar, M. and Steinmetz, K. (2019) *Cybercrime and Society* 3rd ed. London: Sage.

Young, J. (1986) 'The Failure of Criminology: The Need for a Radical Realism' in R. Matthews and J. Young (Eds.) *Confronting Crime* London: Sage.

Young, J. (1999) *The Exclusive Society* London: Sage.

Young, J. (2003) 'Merton With Energy, Katz With Structure: The Sociology of Vindictiveness and the Criminology of Transgression' *Theoretical Criminology* 7/3: 389–414.

Zedner, L. (2003) 'Too Much Security?' *International Journal of the Sociology of Law* 31/1: 155–184.

Zucman, G. (2016) *The Hidden Wealth of Nations* Chicago: University of Chicago Press.

3

THE STRANGE DEATH OF SOCIAL DEMOCRATIC CRIMINOLOGY

Social democratic criminology: the success that dared not speak its name

The title of this chapter echoes Dangerfield's classic study of liberal England (Dangerfield 1935). It poses a similar question: how was it that a sensibility about political economy, crime and criminal justice, and a mode of policy and practice informed by it, should suddenly disappear, even though it had been a widely shared aspect of national pride and identity, and a relative success?

Dangerfield's thesis was that liberal England's strange death occurred in just four years: 1910–14. The eclipse of social democratic criminology (SDC), in Britain and around the world, was somewhat more drawn out: just over a decade between the late 1960s and early 1980s. But it was a parallel process of unexpected, and yet seemingly decisive, decline and fall. It was, of course, an aspect of the broader, brutal dispatch of the post-war social democratic consensus by neoliberalism since the 1970s (analysed in the first half of Chapter 1). This chapter focuses on the specific form and sources of that transition in relation to crime and criminal justice, stressing how profound a break it marked from a long-term trajectory towards greater social equality, inclusiveness, and peace.

La longue duree: the history and achievements of SDC

The previous chapter detailed the substantial historical achievements of social democratic sensibilities about crime, disorder, and criminal justice. The idea of a long-term trajectory in the modern world towards greater social justice and political-economic inclusion has been widespread since the eighteenth-century Enlightenment. As an ideal it was most dramatically emblazoned in the French

The strange death of SDC **85**

Revolutionary slogan 'liberty, equality, fraternity' (the sexist innuendo of the latter ideal was recognised by some contemporaries, although a gender-neutral alternative remains to be coined). Analytically, the thesis of a long march towards gradual incorporation of most members of society into the institutions of liberal (and perhaps social) democratic citizenship has been proposed not only by the 'Whig' interpretation of history that was once pervasive (and remains influential, at least in popular culture). It is also found in sociological accounts of the 'institutionalisation' of class conflict (Dahrendorf 1959), celebrated by some social democratic sociologists (Marshall 1950) but lamented by other left critics of parliamentary democracy as frustrating socialism (Miliband 1961, 1969).

The previous chapter assembled data showing that the long-term incorporation of class conflict and citizenship was associated with a decline of crime in the everyday sense, as well as industrial and political violence, and a liberal humanisation of criminal justice. There were, however, distinct reversals in this trajectory along the way, and a deepening one since the 1970s. These can be associated with particular phases in the history of capitalist political economies – 'long waves' of development and decline. These are often called 'Kondatrieff cycles' after the Soviet economist who postulated them during the 1920s, whose work became known in Western economics through its influence over Kuznets and Schumpeter (Kuznets 1930; Schumpeter 1939).

There has been considerable argument about the very existence of such waves, as well as their length, causes, and impact. Nonetheless, the basic notion is still turned to regularly in attempts to explain and predict the trajectory of capitalist economies (Rostow 1975; Nevin 1983/2013; Bernard et al. 2014; Grinin et al. 2016). Most commonly, endogenous waves are said to be associated with the boost provided by the introduction of new technologies, markets, or productive resources, and the eventual playing down of the impetus to growth as these innovations become absorbed and routinised. In addition, of course, economic fluctuations can be caused by exogenous events such as wars or natural disasters. This implies that there isn't necessary any fixed amplitude to economic fluctuations, nor any necessary recovery.

The broad phases of capitalist development that most analysts agree upon are discussed next; each represented huge shifts in politics, social formations, and culture. As part of this, there are ensuing criminological consequences for what is labelled as crime, and for patterns of criminal justice.

Long waves of capitalist political economy

Mid-eighteenth century–1979

Origins and primitive accumulation   Markets for goods and labour have existed since ancient times, and proliferated during the late Middle Ages and early modernity. Although often loosely regarded as synonymous with the spread of

86 The strange death of SDC

'free' markets, capitalism is a much more specific phenomenon, a particular mode of production emerging in modern times:

> Capitalism is a system in which goods and services, down to the most basic necessities of life, are produced for profitable exchange, where even human labour-power is a commodity for sale in the market, and where all economic actors are dependent on the market. . . . The basic objective of the capitalist system . . . is the production and self-expansion of capital.
>
> *(Wood 2017 pp. 2–3)*

For all the familiar talk about 'free' markets, capitalism is characterised by compulsion, as is indeed implied by the term market 'forces' (ibid. p. 6–7). Actors at all levels of the class structure, capitalists as much as workers, are driven by the system's structural requirements of reproducing and growing profits.

The exact dating of the origins of capitalism as the primary mode of production and exchange is disputed (ibid.). But there is no doubt that, in England at any rate, capitalist industrialisation was well under way by the mid-eighteenth century. The early stages were harshly brutal in their impact on most people, and were fiercely contested. So too was the expansion of capitalist relations around the globe, necessitated by capitalism's built-in drive to seek new markets and resources. 'The original sin of simple robbery, which centuries ago had made possible "the original accumulation of capital" (Marx) and had started all further accumulation, had eventually to be repeated lest the motor of accumulation suddenly die down' (Arendt 1968 p. 28; Marx 1867/1976 Pt. 8).

Capitalist growth has always been attended by major political conflict, in seventeenth-century England, eighteenth-century France and the USA, revolutions and civil war in the nineteenth and early twentieth centuries in the USA and many parts of Europe. During these centuries there was also a gradual achievement of civil, legal, and political rights, at least in principle, for most citizens. Extensive debate about the impact of industrial capitalism on the economic welfare of the mass of the population has taken place, and material benefits are hard to discern up to the mid-nineteenth century (A'Hearn 2014; Clark and Cummins 2014; Floud et al. 2014). Thereafter, there is clear evidence of an overall (but bumpy) trajectory of general material improvement up to 2010 (Fazeley 2014; Floud et al. 2014). Nonetheless, the economic benefits of industrial growth remained highly concentrated amongst a small upper class and expanding middle class, and progress was punctuated by depression, especially in the 1870s and the interwar years.

Capitalism was created by a long and harsh 'so-called primitive accumulation' process (Marx 1867/1967 Pt. 8; Wood 1999 pp. 36–37). What this entails is not so much the accumulation of capital as a physical means of production, but a qualitative transformation of relations of production. Accomplishing this was 'a wide range of processes', including

> the commodification and privatisation of land and the forceful expulsion of peasant populations; the conversion of various forms of property rights

(common, collective, state, etc.) into exclusive private property rights; the suppression of rights to the commons; the commodification of labour power; . . . the slave trade; and usury, the national debt, and ultimately the credit system as radical means of primitive accumulation.

(Harvey 2005 p. 145)

Class incorporation and citizenship   Even during the period of early capitalism, a slow incorporation of the whole of British society into a broad notion of citizenship occurred, in three sub-phases (Marshall 1950). This was not an inevitable 'Whig' march of progress but carried by conflicts, and pockmarked by reversions. Legal and civil rights spread in principle to all citizens after the civil war and 'Glorious Revolution' in the second half of the seventeenth century. Political rights were advanced through struggles and concessions during the nineteenth and early twentieth centuries. Economic and social rights expanded after the late nineteenth century, culminating after much conflict, in the 'New Jerusalem' of social democratic incorporation and welfarism discussed in Chapter 1.

Neo-liberal counter-revolution: 1979–2008

The reassertion of free market utopian ideals against the post-war social democratic consensus was analysed in Chapter 1. In the political sphere the triumph of neoliberalism was signified most sharply by the elections of Margaret Thatcher (1979) in Britain and Ronald Reagan (1980) in the USA, although its roots lie earlier. It can be divided into two broad phases, and as we will see, these have quite distinct implications for the politics of law and order:

1979–1992: contested neoliberalism   In the early years, neoliberal governments were confronted by a considerable measure of resistance to their policies of cutting public expenditure and workers' rights, and the unemployment and inequality generated by their monetarist economic policies. In Britain there were urban riots on a scale not experienced for a century (Scarman 1981; Benyon 1984), and a huge increase in violence during clashes between striking trade unionists and the police, primarily because of a militarisation of public-order policing (Geary 1985 Chap. 7), especially in the 1984/5 Miners' Strike (Beckett and Hencke 2009; Milne 2014). The strength of the labour movement was crippled sharply after the defeat of the miners, and parliamentary opposition was split hopelessly when the 'Gang of 4' leading MPs left the Labour Party to set up the Social Democratic Party in 1981, and later merged with the Liberals (King and Crewe 1995). There was also an explosion of recorded crime.

1992–2008: hegemonic neoliberalism   After a final flurry of anti-government militancy during the popular campaign against the Poll Tax (Waddington 1994 pp. 15–16, 52–64), during the early 1990s a new consensus around neoliberal hegemony developed in Western countries. There were two primary sources of this.

88 The strange death of SDC

A major background stimulus was the fall of the USSR, widely interpreted at the time in triumphalist mode as signifying that liberal democracy was the only viable mode of governance, and marked the 'end of history' (Fukuyama 1992). Second, the Left was chastened by successive election defeats after 1979 (and the defeat of French Socialist president Mitterand's attempt to implement a left-wing programme in the early 1980s, because of opposition from financial markets cf. Bell 2005 Chap. 6). This led erstwhile political opponents (British Labour, US Democrats, etc.) to convert to the belief that there was no alternative to neoliberal economics (Mrs Thatcher's TINA formula). To be sure, the 'new' *soi-disant* social democratic parties of the 'third way' embraced social policies that were far more liberal in the realms of personal freedom than their right-wing predecessors, but there was at best only tinkering around the edges with *sotto voce* attacks on poverty and inequality (Seldon 2007).

2008–'Zombie' neoliberalism   Chapter 1 analysed how the 2007/8 financial crash, and the ensuing seemingly permanent economic crisis, fatally challenged the intellectual basis of neoliberalism (Streeck 2014; Tooze 2018; Blakeley 2019). Nonetheless, it remains the dominant form of economic structure and policy (Crouch 2011; Mirowski 2014). Its signature policy response to the crisis ('austerity') remains in place throughout much of the Western world, although some populist right-wing politicians elected since 2016 have begun to question it rhetorically. New left-wing political challenges have also arisen in recent years, although so far without electoral success. Whether this must remain the case is probed in the book's conclusion.

Long waves of criminalisation

Each of the long waves of capitalist development correspond to specific phases of crime and criminal justice policy. As discussed in the previous chapter, the long movement towards more inclusive citizenship was associated both with a pacification of crime and disorder, and more humane criminal justice policies. These were reversed in the early stages of neoliberalism, as crime and disorder rocketed, and criminal justice rhetoric and policy became ever tougher. As neoliberal hegemony bedded in, there was a decline in the levels of mainstream recorded crime and an attenuation of law and order rhetoric. But since 2015/6, rising rates of violent crime have returned, as well as a harshening of tough crime control policy declarations and practice.

The next section reviews recent trends through a contrast between two ideal types of criminal justice policy and rhetoric, and their fluctuating dominance. These are related to the rise and fall of inclusive citizenship.

From SDC to the politics of law and order

The long-term project of inclusive citizenship

Since at least the middle of the eighteenth century, and its Enlightenment or Enlightenments (Israel 2011; Robertson 2015), there has been a discernible motif of progress towards social justice and inclusion, in thought and action, for all sections of societies. Nonetheless, despite incremental improvements, contemporary societies remain riven by divisions of class, power, status, gender, race, and sexuality, and there are continuing threats of regression. Panglossian, Pollyannish narratives of inevitable improvement through the power of reason (a la Pinker 2018) are highly debatable. But there has been a complex, contested, and chequered forward march halted, and then reversed, by the crushing hegemony of neoliberalism (as suggested by Eric Hobsbawm's influential 1978 lecture cf. Jacques 1981). The long-term egalitarian trend was apparent even to those who were ambivalent or hostile to it. In 1888 the Liberal politician Sir William Harcourt declared to Parliament 'We are all socialists now'. Even though he was the chancellor of the exchequer who introduced death duties in the 1894 budget, he was a staunch Liberal, not a socialist sympathiser.

The *locus classicus* for much debate about citizenship in the last half-century has been Marshall's seminal 1949 lecture 'Citizenship and Social Class', delivered in Cambridge in honour of his illustrious (unrelated) namesake Alfred Marshall, the dominant figure in the articulation of the neoclassical synthesis in economics. These 60 pages of text have generated debate that continues to flourish (Turner 1993, 2016; Bulmer and Rees 1996; Shafir 1998; Isin et al. 2008). Marshall's analysis is a quintessential embodiment of an ethical socialist perspective (Dennis and Halsey 1988 Chap. 6), and its fortunes have ebbed and flowed with the vicissitudes of social democracy, although it has remained a lodestar even for many critics. The most striking aspects of Marshall's work are the threefold categorisation of citizenship into civil, political, and social rights, and the evolutionary sequence in which he traces their historical development in the British case. In essence, he suggested, civil rights were the achievement of the eighteenth century, political rights of the nineteenth, and social rights an ongoing process (in 1949 when he was writing).

Marshall's conceptual and historical schema has attracted criticism from a variety of positions. The most common criticisms among those broadly sympathetic to Marshall's political values have been accusations of Anglocentrism, and a focus on class inequality (implicit in his title) that neglects other dimensions of diversity – primarily gender, ethnicity, and sexual preference. Critics have emphasised the variety of ways in which citizenship rights have developed in the Western industrial world, through many different routes, stages, and forms. They have also questioned Marshall's historical account of the British case, especially an implicit Whiggish perspective, with its apparent assumptions of steady and smooth progress towards an inevitable crowning achievement of the welfare state, mixed-economy consensus that prevailed for a time after the Second World War. These criticisms are not fundamental rebuttals of Marshall's position but they are extensions and developments of it. 'Citizenship and Social Class' is, after all, a relatively brief sketch rather than an attempt at a comprehensive analysis.

The focus on the British experience is as a case study without any suggestion that it offers a universal template. Marshall would no doubt have welcomed research on the variety of forms of development of citizenship in different places that has taken place since he gave his lecture (Mann 1996; Isin and Turner 2002;

90 The strange death of SDC

Isin and Nyers 2014). Although Marshall does indeed suggest a clear long-term trajectory of the extension of citizenship, he does not claim its inevitability, and is aware of how its development was uneven and achieved by many conflicts. Whereas he focused on class inequality rather than ethnicity, gender, or other divisions, the struggles to extend citizenship rights to all people is fully in line with his position (he does e.g. look favourably at Catholic emancipation, and the struggle for women's suffrage).

The claim that Marshall was primarily concerned with economic redistribution rather than cultural recognition is questionable. One of his central arguments is that quantitative economic differences are not problematic unless they threaten a fundamentally shared status of citizenship, as achieved (he believed) by the welfare state. This has plausibly been interpreted as making the crucial problem of class not material difference in itself, but emotional resentment if financial inequalities signify qualitative differences of status (Barbalet 1993).

More fundamental criticism of Marshall has always come from the political Right. The increasing purchase of this conservative critique in political discourse and practice since the 1970s threatened to eclipse the contemporary relevance of his work altogether. The central conservative claim is that Marshall's interpretation of citizenship stresses rights at the expense of responsibilities, promulgating a welfare state that has exacerbated the problems it purported to remedy. It is said to have undermined the compulsion to work and the duty to contribute to society as a core concomitant of citizenship.

In fact, Marshall anticipated this issue in the conclusion of his essay, citing the eighteenth century arguments of Colquhoun and Mandeville that labourers' wages must remain low enough to act as a goad to work, and to prevent poverty from sliding into indigence. He wrote explicitly that it was 'no easy matter to revive the sense of the personal obligation to work in a new form in which it is attached to the status of citizenship', and especially to maintain the duty 'to put one's heart into one's job and work hard' (Marshall 1950 p. 124). As he grew older, this problem vexed him more and more. It has been suggested that Marshall ultimately abandoned the more socialist 1949 version of his theory and came to see citizenship rights as primarily civil and political, with economic welfare predicated on performance of responsibilities rather than an absolute right (Rees 1995).

The most crucial issue in assessing Marshall and the social democratic notion of citizenship he advanced in 1949 is thus whether it has any relevance today. After four decades in which the tide of history has moved very much in the opposite direction, does the idea of a march of citizenship towards greater civil, political, economic, and social inclusion still have plausibility or purchase?

Marshall did not portray the progress of citizenship as inevitable, automatic, or irreversible. But he did convey a sense that the consolidation and further extension of the most controversial social dimension of citizenship was going with the grain of history. This comes out most forcefully in his opening remarks, which at the time probably would have been seen as perfunctory pleasantries. The lectures were part of an annual series in commemoration of Alfred Marshall, and Tom Marshall harked back to a paper Alfred had delivered in 1873 to the Cambridge Reform Club on 'The Future of the Working Classes'.

Alfred Marshall posed the question, 'whether there be valid ground for the opinion that the amelioration of the working classes has limits beyond which it cannot pass'. And Marshall, the doyen of neoclassical economics, argued that there were no such limits:

> The question is not whether all men will ultimately be equal – that they certainly will not – but whether progress may not go on steadily, if slowly, till, by occupation at least, every man is a gentleman. I hold that it may, and that it will.

He supported this conclusion primarily by an analysis of trends in the occupational structure that were reducing the proportion of unskilled labouring jobs in favour of skilled and non-manual ones, with a concomitant reduction in economic inequality. This would continue, he forecast, but Alfred Marshall also advocated some forms of state intervention, in particular compulsory education, to facilitate the trend. He was at pains to distance this from socialism, although he acknowledged that

> [t]he picture . . . will resemble in some respects those which have been shown to us by the Socialists, that noble set of untutored enthusiasts who attributed to all men an unlimited capacity for those self-forgetting virtues that they found in their own breasts.

Tom Marshall notes further that the published version of Alfred Marshall's lecture notes toned down this already rather sympathetic critique of the 'socialists' (by removing the distancing capital 'S' and omitting the phrase 'untutored enthusiasts' [Marshall 1950 p. 70, fn. 3]).

Tom Marshall built his 1949 lectures around the same question as Alfred Marshall's 1873 paper: whether 'there were limits beyond which the amelioration of the working classes could not pass'. And he adopts the same sociological hypothesis: that some quantitative economic inequalities were not incompatible with a fundamental equality of status as citizens. But he stressed that the progress towards the realisation of social rights of citizenship in the 75 years that separated the Cambridge lectures by the two Marshalls had (rightly, in his view) involved a degree of state interference in the market that the leading architect of neoclassical economics would have condemned. 'Our modern system is frankly a Socialist system, not one whose authors are, as [Alfred] Marshall was, eager to distinguish it from socialism', although 'the market still functions – within limits' (op.cit.).

So Tom Marshall's 1949 lectures do convey a strong sense that further consolidation of citizenship in this social democratic mould, through the welfare state and mixed economy, was likely although not inevitable, and certainly desirable. But what is striking some 70 years later, and after five decades of reversal of this equalising trend, is how deeply embedded it then was, in discourse and policy.

92 The strange death of SDC

Tom Marshall's reference back to Alfred Marshall's lecture shows that the belief that growing economic and social equality was progressive, in the double sense that it went with the grain of history *and* represented a desirable advance, was not merely a reflection of the high point of Labourism during the post-war Attlee government. It was a perspective that had long been accepted across a broad sweep of the political spectrum, including even the leading figure in the formulation of neoclassical economics, a vigorous champion of the virtues of markets.

So does Tom Marshall's analysis still have any relevance? After all, his optimistic view of the advance of citizenship in his sense has been reversed, first by the 1980s neoliberal blitzkrieg under its arch enthusiasts Margaret Thatcher and Ronald Reagan. This was consolidated in the 1990s through the acceptance of neoliberalism's fundamentals by the erstwhile parties of the democratic Left, born again in 'new' market-embracing versions. It has been reinforced with a vengeance by the Conservative governments in the UK since 2010, and the right-wing populist regimes elected in much of the world since 2015.

I regard the core themes of Marshall's work as still valid. Above all, his basic theoretical and normative position remains relevant. The two terms in the title of his lectures, 'citizenship' and 'social class', represent 'opposing principles', the former tending towards equality, the latter being 'a system of inequality'. As he declares, 'in the twentieth century, citizenship and the capitalist class system have been at war' (op.cit. p. 87). It is this conception of a fundamental war between the principles of class and the market, on the one hand, and citizenship on the other, that is Marshall's primary point, underlying the evolutionary schema that occupies most of the essay. The salience of this 'war' between the principles of capitalism and citizenship runs through the historical narrative. It shows that the extension of civil and political rights from the eighteenth century onward, desirable as it was, remained largely formal and empty until the development of social rights in the twentieth century. For example, the advance of state education and legal aid after 1945 was necessary to breathe life and substance into civil and political rights. Much of this is indeed reminiscent of Marx, but the crucial differences are Marshall's unremitting assumption that only peaceful democratic means are acceptable, and that a good enough measure of citizenship is compatible with some room for markets to operate, though it entails a degree of economic inequality. Marshall does not develop these theoretical assumptions except by placing them in a historical narrative. But the work of explicating and justifying them has been done by other theorists of social democracy and welfarism whose positions are very similar (e.g. Polanyi 1944; Barry 2005), as well as by welfarist liberals (above all, Rawls 1971). And the values of ethical, democratic socialism underpinning Marshall's lectures remain inspirational to many.

Marshall's social democratic analysis and principles help to understand long-term developments in criminalisation, in the double sense of the occurrence of criminalised conduct, and the labelling and punishment of this by criminal law and criminal justice. This is a specific but crucial aspect of Marshall's general depiction of a war between citizenship and capitalist markets. Erosion of the social and economic dimensions of citizenship vitiates the realisation of civil and political rights, even if these remain formally intact. Beyond that, growing inequality poses a threat to formal civil rights too (as made explicit recently by Trump and Boris Johnson).

For all the defeats suffered by social democracy since the 1970s, its ideals continue to resonate and inspire. Martin Luther King completed his speech at the end of the third 1965 march from Selma to Montgomery with the rousing words: 'the arc of the moral universe is long, but it bends toward justice' (King used the phrase several times in his writings and speeches cf. King 1991). Scarcely three years later King was assassinated, during the momentous year 1968 which culminated in the election of Richard Nixon on a law and order ticket, and the beginning of the end of the post-war social democratic consensus. But as has often been pointed out, King's stirring words were derived from an essay by a nineteenth-century white theologian, whose original text was rather less confident, although still fired with hope:

> Look at the facts of the world. You see a continual and progressive triumph of the right. I do not pretend to understand the moral universe, the arc is a long one, my eye reaches but little ways. I cannot calculate the curve and complete the figure by the experience of sight; I can divine it by conscience. But from what I see I am sure it bends towards justice.
>
> *(Parker 1855)*

The achievements of the abolitionist Theodore Parker were largely vitiated by post-Civil War Reconstruction and Jim Crow. Martin Luther King's trusted that the civil rights anthem 'We Shall Overcome' would soon be replaced by the 'cosmic past tense' of 'We Have Overcome' (in a 1967 speech in Atlanta, which repeated the arc of the moral universe assertion). King's famous dream seemed to have triumphed in a swathe of 1960s civil rights legislation. But his vision has been frustrated more recently by increasing racism, perhaps most evidently in the sphere of criminal 'justice' (despite the 2008 election of the first black US president, who often quoted King's moral universe trope).

From social democratic criminology to 'law and order'

A social democratic sensibility in thinking about crime and criminal justice prevailed for most of the twentieth century but has largely been destroyed during the neoliberal hegemony that became embedded since the 1970s. This constituted a profound rupture in culture, political economy, crime, and criminal justice. The sources and consequences of this seismic shift are analysed and evaluated in this section, which formulates an ideal type of social democratic criminology. This is contrasted it with the law and order perspective which displaced it after the 1970s.

The concluding chapter considers the prospects of a revival of the social democratic perspective in criminological thinking, following the fracturing of the last half-century of neoliberal hegemony in the wake of the 2007/8 financial crash.

94 The strange death of SDC

Two quotes in search of an analysis

The contrast between social democratic criminology and the politics of law and order is sharply highlighted by the following two quotes from US police chiefs, just 22 years apart:

i   'We are not letting the public in on our era's dirty little secret; that those who commit the crime which worries citizens most – violent street crime – are, for the most part, the products of poverty, unemployment, broken homes, rotten education, drug addiction, and alcoholism, and other social and economic ills about which the police can do little, if anything.

   Rather than speaking up, most of us stand silent and let politicians get away with law and order rhetoric that reinforces the mistaken notion that the police – in ever greater numbers and with ever more gadgetry – can alone control crime'. (Di Grazia 1976)

ii 'Crime is down: blame the police'. (Bratton 1998)

The 1976 quote encapsulates social democratic sensibility about crime. We will analyse its subsequent suppression by the law and order toughness captured in 1998 by Bratton's boast.

Social democratic criminology: an ideal type

There has never been an explicit school of social democratic criminology (SDC). But a recognisably social democratic analysis of crime and its causes was a widespread sensibility amongst academic criminologists, opinion-formers, criminal justice practitioners, and policy-makers before the 1970s. This was especially so during the heyday of the post-war consensus, but stretched back a long way before. It was not restricted to overt social democrats but was the tacit conventional wisdom across the political spectrum (as illustrated by the quote by the then Boston police chief Robert di Grazia which heads this section).

'Criminology' here is not restricted to the academic discipline or professionals espousing the label, but connotes a broader social imaginary or sensibility in thinking about crime and control. It encompasses policy-makers, practitioners, the mass media, and the public in general. The essence of SDC, as with social democracy in general, is a tacit assumption of the fundamental equality of all individuals, who should be treated with equal concern and respect. The specifically criminological implication is that those convicted of crime are not a qualitatively different species of humanity. If some people deviate in behaviour, transgressing social norms, there must be special causes or reasons, which it is the task of research to probe. And if penal sanctions are applied, they should be for restitution, reform, and reintegration, a restoration of ruptured social relations, not total or permanent exclusion from society.

The strange death of SDC **95**

Durkheim postulated a century ago that restitutive sanctions were characteristic of modern diverse societies (Durkheim 1893/1973), but the repressive punitiveness that he saw as being superseded has returned with a vengeance since the 1970s (Pratt et al. 2005). Early on during this tilt to tough law and order, John Braithwaite inspiringly mapped out how reintegrative approaches were both more effective and ethical than exclusionary ones, influencing a burgeoning restorative justice movement (Braithwaite 1989). Although this peace-making perspective and practice has considerable impact on academic criminology and amongst some practitioners, the dominant trends in Western criminal justice policy have been towards tough exclusionary law and order, and away from social democratic inclusiveness.

Five elements can be analysed as constituting an ideal type model of social democratic sensibility on crime.

Crime in its place

There is much misunderstanding and talking at cross purposes in discussions about crime, at every level of society, from everyday chats to the mass media, political and professional debate, and in academia (Reiner 2016). However, in all these spheres, when referring to 'crime' without qualification, the meaning is very specific but usually not explicitly spelled out. The most explicit statement of the tacit commonsense notion of crime underpinning most everyday discourse is James Q. Wilson, the doyen of conservative criminology, who led the charge against social democratic (or as he would call it in the US sense, liberal) criminology. 'Unless otherwise stated or clearly implied, the word "crime" when used in this book refers to predatory crime for gain, the most common forms of which are robbery, burglary, larceny, and auto theft' (Wilson 1975, p. xx). He argues that this is because such 'predatory street crimes are a more serious matter than consumer fraud, antitrust violations or gambling, because predatory crime . . . makes difficult or impossible the maintenance of meaningful human communities' (ibid.). He also claims that this 'is the conviction of most citizens' (ibid.). It is true that such crimes are the overwhelming majority of those which are recorded in any way, and constitute the bulk of the work of criminal justice institutions. It is not at all obvious, however, that these crimes are the most 'serious', although this is clearly a rather slippery term. Most people rate criminal homicide the most serious offence, although it is fairly rare compared with those on Wilson's list, even in the USA. And the low-level anti-social behaviours and 'vice' offences that he also casts as less serious can wreak havoc for community life, as he later spelled out in his influential 'broken windows' thesis (Wilson and Kelling 1982). Above all, however, the white collar and 'victimless' offences, that he explicitly and airily dismisses, inflict far more physical and property harm than predatory street crime, as critical criminologists and zemiologists have long demonstrated (Hillyard et al. 2004; DeKeseredy and Dragiewicz 2017).

Although social democratic and other critical criminologists are and have been well aware of these points, nevertheless most research, public debate, and policy

96 The strange death of SDC

concentrates on Wilson's street crimes rather than suite crimes. Without sharing Wilson's conservative politics, they do so because this is the officially recorded and formally processed part of the spectrum of problematic behaviours that could potentially be called crimes.

Recorded crime does indeed often involve acts that inflict serious harm on vulnerable and innocent people, causing great alarm and distress, which are morally repugnant. This is the germ of the left realist criminology that developed at roughly the same time as Wilson's conservative realism (Taylor 1981a; Lea and Young 1984).

But most recorded crimes pale into relative insignificance compared with the many other serious problems facing the world: economic depression, inequality, poverty, war, health, housing, education. To take a vivid and tragic contemporary example, it has been estimated that 80 people per month die after being declared fit for work and thus denied benefits (https://www.theguardian.com/commen tisfree/2015/aug/27/death-britains-benefits-system-fit-for-work-safety-net; cf. also: Lansley and Mack 2015; Alston 2018; Ryan 2019). An article in the British medical journal *Open* reported that 'Cuts to public spending on healthcare and social care are linked to around 120000 excess deaths from 2010 to 2017' and predicted this could rise to 200,000 by 2020 unless policies change (doi: https://doi. org/10.1136/bmj.j5332, 16 November 2017).

Similar conclusions have been reached about 'deaths of despair' and have been documented in the USA:

> For those aged 45–54, if the white mortality rate had held at its 1998 value, 96,000 deaths would have been avoided from 1999 to 2013, 7,000 in 2013 alone. If it had continued to fall at its previous (1979-1998) rate of decline of 1.8% per year, 488,500 deaths would have been avoided in the period 1999-2013, 54,000 in 2013.
>
> *(Case and Deaton 2015 p. 1, 2020)*

Such 'social murder' (Engels 1844) takes many more lives than the homicides recorded in criminal statistics. It has been estimated that '"social murder" kills thousands each year' (https://www.crimeandjustice.org.uk/news/social-murder-kills-thousands-each-year, citing Tombs 2016). By contrast, criminal statistics have recorded between 600 and 800 homicides per annum in England and Wales during the twenty-first century (https://www.ons.gov.uk/peoplepopulationand community/crimeandjustice/articles/homicideinenglandandwales/yearending march 2017).

Until the late 1960s, criminal justice policy was not a partisan political matter. In Britain it did not feature in any party's election manifesto between the Second World War and 1970, and only became prominent from the late 1970s (Downes and Morgan 1994, 2012). Although in the USA the 1964 Republican candidate Barry Goldwater attempted to make law and order a central issue, he suffered a landslide defeat at the hands of Lyndon Johnson. However, only four years later

Richard Nixon rode to victory with law and order as a central theme of his campaign (Harris 1970; Scheingold 1984; Flamm 2005). In the hands of the political Right, the demand for law and order condensed a number of specific meanings – above all, that law could and should produce order – but that it failed to do so because of weak formulation and enforcement. Law's purpose was crime control, but it was said to be shackled by excessive due process restraints. The law and its frontline troops, the police, should be unleashed to restore order. Law and order became a code word for race, culture, and generational backlash in Nixon's 1968 campaign.

Crime was not an important political issue to the British public until the 1970s, at least as registered by opinion polls (Duffy et al. 2008), although it has been a favourite theme in popular entertainment for centuries (Greer and Reiner 2012; Reiner 2016 Chap. 6). In the USA there is considerable difference of opinion amongst scholars about the origins of the rising public concern about law and order. Some argue that public concern was stoked by mass media and politicians' highlighting of the issue (Beckett 1997). Others, using somewhat different data sources and methodological interpretations, claim that the line of causation runs the other way: public concern influenced political and mass media focus on law and order (Enns 2016). Yet others suggest that law and order did not feature prominently in public priorities until much later (Cheliotis 2019). And, of course, the broader issue of 'disorder' represented by the urban riots and political protests of the 1960s (together with their often brutal suppression), were the background to both public concern and policy debates. Disorder, as well as rising recorded crime, and by the late 1970s widespread experience of victimisation by predatory crime, were at the core of anxieties about law and order (Flamm 2005; Miller 2015, 2016).

Some specific aspects of criminal justice policy have been perennially controversial, notably capital punishment, and competing penal policy lobbies campaigned vigorously over it (Ryan 1983, 2003; Bailey 2000; Logan 2017; Rock 2019 Chaps. 2,3). Particularly spectacular or salacious crimes have always been regular topics of popular fascination (Biressi 2001; Rowbotham et al. 2013), part of a perennial tendency for middle-aged respectable opinion to bewail the supposedly declining moral standards of young people (Pearson 1983). But the overall state of crime was not a widespread cause of concern, nor was criminal justice policy subject to political controversy and conflict, until the 1960s in the USA and the 1970s in the UK.

The politicisation of law and order was heralded in Britain in the 1970 general election, when the Conservative Party manifesto (which anticipated the overall neoliberal agenda) said that 'the Labour Government cannot entirely shrug off responsibility' for rising 'crime and violence' (Downes and Morgan 2002 p. 288). It also linked crime with industrial disputes as instances of 'the age of demonstration and disruption'. Labour replied by attacking the Conservatives' attempt 'to exploit for Party political ends the issue of crime and law enforcement', but the genie was out of the bottle.

The politicisation of law and order really accelerated under Margaret Thatcher's leadership of the Conservative Party (Reiner 2007 Chap. 5). During the late 1970s,

98 The strange death of SDC

in the build-up to her election victory in 1979, Mrs Thatcher blamed the Labour government head on for rising crime and disorder, pledging a 'ring of steel' to protect people against lawlessness. She promised to boost the resources and powers of the police to tackle crime, and to toughen penal policy, reversing the 'softness' on crime that was attributed to Labour. The Tories' law and order campaign was greatly helped by the emergence of the police as a political lobby, backing the Conservatives' agenda in a series of advertisements and speeches (Reiner 1980; Bowling et al. 2019 p. 87). The issue was a major factor in Thatcher's 1979 election victory.

The party political gulf on law and order reached its widest point in Britain during the mid-1980s. The key conflicts were over the policing of urban disorders and of the 1984/5 Miners' Strike (both results of the economic and social dislocation engendered by the Thatcher government's monetarist policies), the Police and Criminal Evidence Act 1984, and campaigns for democratic police accountability (Bowling et al. 2019 pp. 84–87). On all these issues, Labour took a civil libertarian stance, attacking the Conservative government for violating the principles of the rule of law. Labour also attacked Conservative law and order policies for being counter-productive in increasing social divisions and aggravating rather than reforming the root causes of crime in social inequality and relative deprivation (Farrall and Jennings 2012; Farrall and Hay 2014). Whilst this position may have had the support of the majority of criminologists, it was an electoral liability for Labour, holding many 'hostages to fortune' (Downes and Morgan 2002). In the 1984 and 1987 general elections the Tories redoubled their attack on Labour for being 'soft' on crime because of the latter's concerns about civil liberties, 'permissiveness', links with trade unionism (aggravating disorder according to the Conservatives), and failure to develop tough short-term solutions to bolster public protection. Ultimately, Labour, especially in its 'New Labour' guise, came to shift towards the Conservative stance on law and order. But during the heyday of post-war social democratic consensus, crime as an issue was firmly in its place as a serious but non-partisan matter.

Social **and** *individual explanation*

What most clearly marked out SDC from later right-wing law and order crime control discourse was its highlighting of aetiology as a central question. The commission of acts that were labelled as criminal was caused by a complex mix of social and individual processes. The overall level of crime at different times and places was a function of political economy and culture, as explained by 'root causes' theories such as Robert Merton's (1938) influential anomie theory, for example. But individual offenders had a degree of autonomy, and hence responsibility, that to most criminologists justified the imposition of punishment, although the primary purpose of this was to rehabilitate. Whilst penal policy was important in relation to the conduct of identified offenders and the achievement of justice in specific cases, the overall control of crime was primarily a function of social, economic, and cultural processes.

This perspective can be illustrated by many criminologists working in the era of social democratic consensus. Some could be described as 'actually existing' social democratic criminologists, as they did identify with social democratic politics. Nonetheless, all claimed their criminological conclusions were based on hard evidence, research, and analysis. We shall focus on Willem Bonger, Herman Mannheim, and Barbara Wootton, Robert Merton, and the Presidential Crime and Violence Commissions of the 1960s.

Willem Bonger (1876–1940)

Bonger is generally regarded as the first avowedly Marxist academic criminologist – although not the first Marxist to write seriously about crime (Greenberg 1981 p. 11). He is a key exemplar of social democratic criminology (Moxon 2014). Bonger's career was

> marked by honesty, doubt and marginality. In politics as he moved from the doctrinal Marxism of the Second International to social democracy, he found himself in conflict with his fellow party members for being too 'soft', not orthodox enough. . . . But in the 1930s . . . the journal he edited (*De Socialistiche Gids*) was *too* Marxist for his social democratic friends and was closed down. His academic life was also marked by controversy; he was never afraid to choose subjects and express thoughts that ran against the current of the time.
>
> *(Cohen 1998 p. 99)*

In the words of a Dutch intellectual biography: 'Bonger lived in two worlds: the world of social-democratic politics and the world of social-scientific research. On both sides he was considered by many as a marginal man . . . professor in the party, socialist at the university' (van Heerikhuizen 1987 p. 322, cited in Cohen ibid.; van Swaaningen 1997 pp. 50–51). In the end, his intellectual and ethical integrity made Bonger marginal to the orthodoxies of both institutions to which he devoted his life. He committed suicide in 1940, driven to despair by the Nazi subjugation of the Netherlands, which ruthlessly crushed the Jewish, gay, and other minority populations that he sought to champion.

Bonger's criminology exemplifies all the features of the ideal type of social democracy distinguished in Chapter 1. He was the compleat social democratic criminologist, developing over his academic and political careers a systematic analysis of crime and its control (van Swaaningen 1997 op.cit). Bonger took very seriously the problems of defining crime, the precondition of the criminological enterprise, although it is usually glossed over. He analysed crime explicitly as a social, not natural construction (Bonger 1916/1969 pp. 22–23, Bonger 1936/2015 pp. 1–19). The behaviours that are regarded as crimes are not abnormal or condemned in themselves: in certain contexts they may even be celebrated (e.g. killing by soldiers or police). The essence of crime is behaviour deemed seriously immoral

100 The strange death of SDC

and/or harmful by certain groups of people (Bonger ibid. pp. 22–24). However, such acts only become formally criminalised if regarded as such by the powerful. Bonger recognised the de facto force of the legal formulation of crime, but in any unequal society criminalisation is linked inextricably to injustice:

> Power then is the necessary condition for those who wish to class a certain act as a crime. It follows that in every society which is divided into a ruling class and a class ruled penal law has been principally constituted according to the will of the former. We must at once add . . . that most of them (the present legal prescriptions) are directed against acts that are prejudicial to the interests of both classes equally (for example, homicide, rape, etc.) . . . . However, in every existing penal code hardly any act is punished if it does injure the interests of the dominant class.
>
> *(Bonger 1916/1969 p. 24)*

Most of Bonger's voluminous writings were taken up with a detailed analysis of the aetiology of crime. This was conducted both at a macro level, tracing the sources of varying levels of crime over time and space, between and within societies, *and* at a micro level, seeking to drill down the social factors that caused people to commit crimes. Bonger's is the epitome of the 'root cause' theories that attracted the venom of James Q. Wilson and other conservative criminologists (Wilson 1975). Summing up a detailed analysis of evidence about the sources of crime of different types, Bonger concludes, 'Upon the basis of what has gone before, we have a right to say that the part played by economic conditions in criminality is preponderant, even decisive' (Bonger ibid. p. 197). However, this is far from the simple economic determinism that he has been attacked for by some more recent radical criminologists (notably Taylor et al. 1973 Chap. 7). True, to Bonger a prime source of crime of all kinds is the injustice and oppression inherent in capitalism as a mode of production. But the relationship is not directly determined. Indeed, even more fundamental than the political economy of capitalism is its moral (or more specifically, immoral) economy. The root cause of crime is egoism, the drive or willingness to 'do acts injurious to the interests of those with whom he forms a social unit' (Bonger ibid. p. 26). The connection between political economy and crime is mediated by the propensity of different modes of production, and their diverse economic circumstances, to encourage more egoistic or more altruistic consciousness and action. Capitalism in particular was prone to extreme individualism:

> The present economic system and its consequences weaken the social feelings. . . . Its principal characteristic is that the means of production are in the hands of a few, and most men are altogether deprived of them. This state of things especially stifle men's social instincts; it develops on the part of those with power, the spirit of domination, and of insensibility to the ills of others, whilst it awakens jealousy and servility on the part of those who depend

upon them. Further the contrary interests of those who have property, and the idle and luxurious life of some of them, also contribute to the weakening of the social instincts.

(Bonger ibid. pp. 194–195)

Capitalism not only shapes the egoistic culture that makes criminal (i.e. egoistic) acts in general more likely. It also underlies the pattern of formal criminalisation, with the anti-social egoistic conduct of the less powerful and the economically deprived much more likely to fall foul of penal sanctions. Bonger was well aware of the depredations of the wealthy, and that these were often at least as harmful as those of labelled criminals who tended to be poor. But it was only the latter that came to be seen as *the* problem of crime. This was not to minimise the serious wrongs of conventionally defined crime, but to put it in its place compared with the serious economic and physical suffering caused by the egoistic acts of the powerful:

> The great speculator who, by manipulating the market, forces thousands of people to pay more for the necessities of life . . . is not less egoistic than the robber-baron of the middle ages. . . . Capitalism is a system of exploitation in which, in place of the exploited person's being robbed he is compelled by poverty to use all his powers for the benefit of the exploiter.
>
> *(Bonger ibid. p. 28)*

Bonger analysed many of the social mediating processes that structured differences within societies as well as between them, and how these changed over time. He examined the roles of education, religion, and family patterns and traced other dimensions of social inequality that intersected with economic class, notably gender, ethnicity, and sexuality (Bonger 1913, 1939/1943, 1916/1969 Part C; Hebberecht 2010 pp. 60–61). Bonger deployed exhaustive analysis of available statistical data to reject biological and individualistic explanations of criminal and other behaviour, in favour of sociological accounts based on political and moral economy.

Bonger's Marxism was clearly social democratic rather than revolutionary. He attached moral importance to democratic and peaceful strategies for achieving social justice. He committed suicide when the Nazis occupied the Netherlands, rather than 'bow to this scum which will now overmaster us' (ibid. p. 62). Nevertheless, he remained confident that ultimately social democracy and justice would prevail. Shortly before Bonger's suicide, the young writer Ettie Hillesum (who was subsequently murdered in Auschwitz) asked him: 'Do you believe that democracy will win?' To which Bonger replied 'It surely will win, but it will be at the expense of some generations' (https://www.astro.com/astro-databank/ Bonger,_Willem_Adriaan).

This confidence in the ultimate achievement of social democratic justice, and the ensuing disappearance of all but very rare crimes caused by individual

102 The strange death of SDC

psychopathology, is embodied in the conclusions of his major criminological work. They constitute a stirring rallying cry for SDC. He argues for

> the optimistic conclusion . . . that where crime is the consequence of economic and social conditions, we can combat it by changing those conditions. . . . In a society based upon the community of the means of production, great contrasts of fortune would like commercial capital be lacking and thus cupidity would find no food. These (economic) crimes will not totally disappear so long as there has not been a redistribution of property according to the maxim, "to each according to his needs", something that will probably be realised, but not in the immediate future. The changes in the position of women which are taking place in our present society, will lead, under this future mode of production, to her economic independence, and consequently to her social independence. . . . The final result will be the disappearance of the harmful effects of the economic and social preponderance of man. . . . In such a society there can be no question of crime properly so called. . . . There will be crime committed by pathological individuals, but this will come rather within the sphere of the physician than that of the judge. . . . "It is society that prepares the crime", says the true adage of Quetelet. For all those who have reached this conclusion, and are not insensible to the sufferings of humanity, this statement is sad, but contains a ground of hope. It is sad, because society punishes severely those who commit the crime which she has herself prepared. It contains a ground of hope, since it promises to humanity the possibility of someday delivering itself from one of its most terrible scourges.
> *(Bonger 1916/1969 pp. 197–200)*

This is a clear expression of the 'left idealism' found in the closing pages of the central text of 1970s radical criminology (Taylor et al. 1973), later repudiated by its authors in favour of 'left realism'. However, Bonger devoted most of his analytic and empirical attention to the aetiology of specific types of crime, and how the harms they inflicted could be mitigated, not the longer-term dream of overcoming capitalism itself with its egoism and criminality. His early writing in particular, from which the foregoing quotes are drawn, was composed at a time when both revolutionary and evolutionary social democracy were powerful, growing forces, seen as likely to triumph by supporters and opponents alike. Bonger didn't lose faith in the ultimate bending of the 'arc of history' towards justice, even as he prepared to commit suicide in the face of the dark age of Nazism. Whether this remains justified in the present dark age of growing authoritarianism is explored in the concluding chapter.

British SDC: Mannheim and Wootton

Bonger was the most comprehensive and explicit example of a social democratic criminologist. But his emphasis on the social causation of crime, and its root cause in social injustice, can be widely found in criminological research and official reports published during the post-war heyday of the social democratic consensus.

The most detailed account of British social democratic criminological analysis and policy in its heyday is Ian Taylor's PhD thesis on the topic, only partly available in published form (Taylor 1981a, 1981b). It was only during this period that British criminology was transformed from 'the part-time activity of a few practitioners and enthusiasts . . . into an established academic discipline' (Garland 2002 p. 39). A key but fortuitous impetus for this was 'the rise of Nazism in Germany, and the appointment of three distinguished European emigres, Hermann Mannheim, Max Grunhut, and Leon Radzinowicz, to academic posts at elite British universities' (Morris 1989; Hood 2004). The development of criminology in Britain was intimately inter-related with the post-war project of social reconstruction, initiated during the wartime coalition and put into practice under the Labour government elected in 1945. This gave it a strong policy-oriented and practical character, tied in with the agendas of the governments of the day. Labour or Conservative, these were all clearly within the broad social democratic consensus of the period until 1970, despite differences in emphasis.

They were thus primarily concerned with detailed research on the aetiology of different crimes and their variation between groups and individuals, as well as the evaluation of particular penal strategies. But all saw the root causes and fundamental solutions to crime in broader political and moral economy, and were optimistic about their alleviation by the advance of social security and justice through Keynesian economics and the welfare state. They also saw the key purpose of penal intervention as reform and rehabilitation. In the words of an article by the leading penal reformer Margery Fry (Logan 2017), which introduces a key text on which all the leading social democratic criminologists of the day collaborated: 'Treatment not Punishment' (Fry 1947 Chap. I).

Two prolific and influential criminologists of the social democratic era were Hermann Mannheim and Barbara Wootton. As mentioned earlier, Mannheim was one of the founders of academic criminology in Britain. His major works include a book analysing crime patterns in the inter-war years (Mannheim 1940), another on the problems facing criminal justice during the post-war project of social reconstruction (Mannheim 1946), and a two-volume text on comparative criminology (Mannheim 1965). Most of his work comprises painstaking reviews of research on specific sorts of crime and offender and the various theories proposed to explain them. He also conducted several evaluative studies of particular penal measures (e.g. Mannheim and Wilkins 1955). Whilst treating individualistic explanations, whether biological or psychological, with meticulous care, he is ultimately sceptical of their value, if only because those who are caught are likely to be atypical of all offenders (Mannheim 1965 p. 279). He was also well aware of the significance of middle- and upper-class 'white-collar' and business crime to which he devoted considerable attention (Mannheim 1940 Chap. 7; Mannheim 1946 Chaps. 7, 8; Mannheim 1965 Chap. 21). For all the detail on specific types of offending, however, Mannheim's conclusions on the fundamental causes are rooted in social

104 The strange death of SDC

democratic political and moral economy. 'The criminologist who tries to lay bare the principal driving forces making for crime in a given society cannot fail to place a rather heavy responsibility at the door of this "acquisitive society" itself' (Mannheim 1940 p. 186, drawing on the terminology of his LSE colleague Tawney 1921). He spells out the implications of this in his detailed probing of the problems of 'economic crime' in post-war reconstruction (again reflecting the social critiques of Tawney and other socialists):

> The weakening of the *moral* and *social* elements in the institution of property . . . is the result of the growing inequality of its distribution and of the concentration of wealth in the hands of a comparatively small number of individuals and giant corporations.
>
> *(Mannheim 1946 p. 101)*

By the time of his final major work (Mannheim 1965), the continuous rise of recorded crime over the previous decade had stimulated increasing political concern about how to tackle it (Rock 2019; Downes and Newburn forthcoming). The liberal Conservative Home Secretary R.A.B. Butler (the 'But' of Butskellism) met this with considerable backing for the expansion of criminological research and a fundamentally social democratic consensus approach to the causes of crime. But he faced considerable criticism from Tory backbenchers and right-wing commentators, who attributed rising crime to erosion of discipline induced by excessive liberalisation and welfare.

The Home Office White Paper in which Butler set out his stall (Home Office 1959) opened by stating the problem thus:

> It is a disquieting feature of our society that, in the years since the war, rising standards in material prosperity, education and social welfare have brought no decrease in the high rate of crime . . . on the contrary crime has increased and is still increasing.
>
> *(ibid. p. 1)*

This apparent paradox of rising crime in a supposed age of affluence was subsequently dubbed the 'aetiological crisis' of SDC, which was seen (misleadingly) as primarily attributing crime to absolute deprivation. Mannheim would have none of this argument. He cited several sources demonstrating the continuing salience of poverty and insecurity, despite their diminution by Keynesian economics and the welfare state (e.g. Titmuss 1958, 1962; Galbraith 1958; Shanks 1962). More fundamentally, he again drew on Tawney's 1921 critique of 'The Acquisitive Society' to argue that it was relative deprivation rather than absolute that nurtured crime. The growth of 'affluence' fed this by stimulating aspirations beyond attainment. This same analysis underpinned the 1964 Labour Party study group report, intended to inform the Wilson government's criminal justice agenda (Clarke 1980 pp. 79–95).

They attributed rising crime to Conservative economic policies, which prioritised materialistic success and the 'get rich quick ethos' of a mass consumer society. These led to a

> weakening moral fibre. . . . If men and women are brought up . . . to regard personal advancement and ruthless self-interest as the main considerations, material success will certainly not train them in social responsibility, and worldly failure may lead to . . . a resentful sense of inferiority.
>
> *(Labour Party 1964 pp. 4–5)*

A cornerstone of analysis of crime causation by British criminologists in the era of the social democratic consensus is the work of Barbara Wootton (1897–1988). The first woman to become a life peer, she was a major figure in the development of feminism, social democracy, and social science in Britain (Bean and Whynes 1986; Oakley 2011). She was a paradigm of the public intellectual, a magistrate for more than 50 years, member and chair of numerous public committees, and a regular commentator on public policy issues in print and broadcast media. Her most ambitious criminological work (Wootton 1959) was an 'exhaustive analysis' (Downes 1986 p. 196) of empirical studies pertaining to what she saw as the 12 predominant explanations of crime, and which satisfied her very tough methodological requirements. Although in the end none quite met her rigorous tests, she argued for more and better criminological research. But what attracted most controversy was her conclusion about criminal responsibility and penal policy (developed further in Wootton 1963/1992). She advocated an extreme determinism, leaving no room for individual responsibility, and proposed a medical model for the criminal justice process. The purpose of courts would be only to ascertain the factual causation of criminal acts. The question of the appropriate disposal of offenders was a matter for medical and penal experts, who had to decide the most appropriate course of treatment to achieve rehabilitation (if possible). This attracted considerable criticism from jurisprudential and penological opinion, including other social democratic lawyers and criminologists (Hart 1965, 1968; Bean and Whynes 1986 Part II; Matravers and Cocoru 2014).

Wootton's overall perspective on crime causation was characteristically expressive of social democratic values and analysis. In her 'Reflections on Fifty Years' Experience' as a magistrate she concluded, 'In short, the causes of crime (and here the Marxist is, in my view, at least three-quarters right) lie deep in the whole economic and social structure of contemporary society' (Wootton 1978 p. 245). And in her controversial 1963 Hamlyn lectures, she channelled the Tawney-Galbraith perspective typical of SDC:

> The "affluent" society is not affluent. It derives that name rather from its esteem of affluence; and the prizes which it offers, though unequally distributed, are nevertheless not wholly unattainable. . . . A highly competitive,

106 The strange death of SDC

socially hierarchical, acquisitive society offers in fact an ideal breeding-ground for crimes against property; just as a mechanistic, speed-besotted age is a standing invitation to motorised violence.

(Wootton 1963/1992 pp. 16–17)

US SDC: Merton and the 1960s presidential commissions

Similar social democratic analyses of crime causation also typify US criminology and official reports in the New Deal to Great Society era 'between the late 1930s and 1968'. The classic text of this is Robert Merton's seminal analysis of anomie and social structure (Merton 1938). Despite the ritual slaying of caricatures of Merton's analysis in countless textbooks and exam answers over the decades, it remains an illuminating structural social theory of crime. Contemporary American versions frequently reduce Merton's structural political economy to 'strain' theory, a social psychology attributing deviance to a psychic gap between individual aspirations and achievement (Agnew 2006). But Merton's paper is a classic analysis of how macro-social structures of political and moral economy affect variations in motivations to commit crime among cultures and over time. It has been dubbed 'filleted Marxism' (Downes 1998 p. 108), recognising its politically social democratic implications, which were toned down, especially in its later elaborations during the McCarthyite climate of the late 1940s and early 1950s, when Merton himself was suspected of being a Communist agent (Keen 2004 p. 125). Merton's analysis was first developed in the 1930s to explain why the USA was then the Western world's crime capital. Legitimate opportunities to gain wealth were structurally limited, generating pressures for crime in a culture that encourages widespread wealth aspirations for all. This was epitomised by the 'American Dream' of the open possibility of rising from rags to riches. Cultures which prioritise material and monetary success generate strains towards deviance to achieve these aspirations at *all* levels of society, not least – indeed, perhaps above all – among elites, although it is the lower strata that tend to be criminalised.

There is no terminal point for monetary aspirations, and success breeds desire rather than satisfaction. Winning is all that counts. Conceptions of legitimate means get pushed aside: nice guys or gals finish last; losers are zeroes. Cutting corners, coming first, is all that matters, at all levels of society and all times.

These arguments have been used widely to understand contemporary crime patterns (e.g. Reiner 1980, 2007 pp. 14–15, 84–85, 92, 109; Young 2003; Messner and Rosenfeld 2012), testimony to the power of this 80-year-old theory. Mediated through its reformulation to emphasise illegal opportunity structures by Cloward and Ohlin (1960), Merton's analysis became a key input into John F. Kennedy's attempt to tackle juvenile delinquency and Lyndon Johnson's 'Great Society' programme (Flamm 2005 pp. 24–28; Hinton 2016 pp. 20, 35–40, 52).

During the 1960s there was increasing political and public concern about 'law and order' in the USA (first formulated as an issue by Barry Goldwater's unsuccessful 1964 presidential campaign). This rose in resonance, partly because of rising crime statistics. Crucially, middle American concern was fanned by the urban riots and protest movements concerned with advancing civil rights and against the Vietnam War, which often involved violent clashes with the police. A series of presidential commissions were appointed, the key ones being the Crime Commission (1965–67), the Kerner Commission on Violence and Civil Disorders (1967/8), and the National Violence Commission (1968/9). There is a considerable and still growing literature with conflicting interpretations of these reports. To what extent did they stimulate, as opposed to just respond to, the growth of public concern? What is clear is that in 1968 anxieties about crime and disorder produced Richard Nixon's electoral victory on a law and order platform (Clark 1970; Harris 1970; Scheingold 1984; Beckett 1997; Flamm 2005; Murakawa 2014; Hinton 2016; Enns 2016; Miller 2016; Cheliotis 2019).

Some recent scholarship has challenged the conventional view (presented in this book) that the triumph of law and order politics represented by Nixon's 1968 victory was a break with a more liberal (or in European terms, social democratic) agenda, pursued from the New Deal to the Great Society and its War on Poverty. Critics suggest that the Democrats' acceptance of the idea that 'the first civil right' is 'Safety and Security of the Person' (as postulated by President Harry Truman in 1947) meant that 'Liberals Built Prison America', albeit unintentionally (Murakawa op.cit.). On this account, the War on Poverty paradoxically paved the way for mass incarceration via its links with the 'War on Crime' (Hinton op.cit.). However, these books themselves seem to document a social democratic analysis of crime underpinning all the 1960s presidential reports on crime, disorder, and violence instituted by Lyndon Johnson. When President Truman spoke of the right to safety and security, he specifically meant *from* mob violence or police brutality against black people (cited in Murakawa op.cit. p. 1), not the subsequent code whereby law and order connoted white backlash. The 1965 Crime Commission declared that 'Warring on poverty, inadequate housing, and unemployment is warring on crime. A civil rights law is a law against crime. . . . More broadly and more importantly every effort to improve life in America's "inner cities" is an effort against crime' (cited by Hinton op.cit. pp. 100–101). Nonetheless she suggests the report 'advanced the punitive turn' (ibid. p. 100) as it promoted 'strengthening law enforcement' as well. Although Kerner adopted a clear social democratic aetiology of crime and disorder, declaring 'the problem is white racism compounded by poverty', Hinton concludes 'Beneath its liberal rhetoric . . . the Kerner Commission supported a massive War on Crime' (Hinton op.cit. pp. 124–131). The Eisenhower Report on Violence, set up by President Johnson after the assassinations of Martin Luther King Jr. and Robert Kennedy in 1968, but reporting to President Nixon in 1969, was also predicated on a clear social democratic analysis:

> To be a young, poor male; to be undereducated and without means of escape from an oppressive urban environment; to want what the society claims is available (but mostly to others); to see around oneself illegitimate and often violent methods being used to achieve material success; and to observe

108 The strange death of SDC

others using these means with impunity – all this is to be burdened with an enormous set of influences that pull many towards crime and delinquency. To be also a Negro, Mexican or Puerto Rican American and subject to discrimination and segregation adds considerably to the pull of these other criminogenic forces.

(Eisenhower 1969 pp. xxi–xxii)

The golden thread running through many articulations of SDC, across an expanse of time and space, is this emphasis on locating the 'root causes' of crime and control in the wider structures of political and moral economy. This was combined in diverse ways with detailed empirical research into the social and psychological aetiology linking these macro structures to the more immediate sources of different types of offence, and the penal and remedial techniques for handling them.

Concern for offenders and victims

The significance of this aspect of SDC can only really be appreciated by contrast with the law and order perspective. The latter interprets concern for offenders (even in order to understand them) as inimical to the plight and interests of victims, conceived largely as desire for retribution. SDC, by contrast, was of course not only concerned with the plight of victims, but also that of offenders. However, concern for victims often was not expressed explicitly. To Bonger, for example, the very essence of crime was egoism, that is, doing 'acts injurious to the interests of others with whom he forms a social unit' (Bonger 1916/1969 p. 26). However, when enumerating the costs of crime, he lists only in passing 'the damage and grief suffered by the victims of crime' (Bonger 1936/2015 p. 6). Sympathy for the suffering of victims, especially of unjustified violence, was taken for granted and hardly needed spelling out (see e.g. the media stories analysed in Reiner 2007 pp. 143–151). But concern was not a zero-sum game; concern for victims did not preclude offenders from also being subjects of concern. The core intellectual puzzle was how and why someone (presumed to be of the same common human stock as non-offenders) had done wrong by harming others.

Morally and practically there was the question how offenders' behaviour could be reformed and future wrongdoing averted, for their sake as well as for potential victims. This required research into the sources of crime by probing the circumstances and perspectives of offenders, not at the expense of concern for victims, but to minimise future suffering for victims as well as offenders.

Nonetheless, a tendency to overlook the significance and needs of victims was a lacuna of criminologists, whatever their political identifications, in the period up to the 1970s. This was built into the general acceptance of definitions of crime and criminals, and the statistics purporting to measure them, taken over from the criminal law and formal justice system. Social democratic criminologists explicitly recognised the biases and limitations of these official conceptions (e.g. Bonger op.cit. pp. 12–14; Mannheim 1965 pp. 109–118; Wootton 1963/1992 Chap. 1), with

The strange death of SDC **109**

damaging consequences not only for justice but also for theorisation about causes based on official data. But in the absence of alternatives, and wedded to humane concerns about those caught up in penal processes, most of their detailed research and policy work operated with the categories of state criminal justice. These had a built-in tendency to marginalise victims.

Criminal laws in all modern societies are deemed to be offences against the public realm, as distinct from private interests, even if there is also harm to specific individuals as well. Many offences are 'crimes without victims' (cf. Schur 1965), although some of these have been decriminalised in recent decades, and for several types of crimes the 'victim' is the public at large. The legislative and judicial arms of the state have the authority to determine what is to be seen as criminal – that is, subject to state-organised punishment rather than private redress or revenge. This is symbolised clearly by the way criminal cases are named, as (in the UK) the Crown against the defendant, *R. v. X*, with the name of the victim (if any) not featuring.

This was the culmination of a long set of processes by which state agencies became responsible for the investigation of offences and the prosecution of offenders, which had hitherto been left to private initiatives (Godfrey and Lawrence 2014 Chap. 3). Proceedings in the criminal courts are concerned with establishing whether a defendant has committed an offence against a universally framed and state-defined rule of law (Lacey 2013).

Establishing the authority of an apparently impersonal, universalistic law involved protracted and often violent conflict, for example, over redefining as theft what had hitherto been seen as customary perquisites of the poor (like gleaning crops or gathering fallen wood cf. Linebaugh 1976). Theft itself was a highly disputed category, constructed slowly over centuries (Hall 1952; Lacey et al. 2003 Chap. 4). It only became established as a general offence during the eighteenth century, as capitalist relations became dominant. Until then, in the absence of violence (making it robbery) or physical trespass, taking something claimed by another was widely seen as a civil issue to be settled between the parties, as late as in Blackstone's *Commentaries on the Laws of England*, published in the 1760s (Palmer 1977).

The proliferation of capital punishment for minor property offences during the eighteenth century paradoxically underlines the severity of the struggle over definition (Thompson 1975). It reflected the tighter conception of property rights in capitalist market relations, which displaced the 'moral economy' embedded in traditional networks of obligation and entitlement. The process of appropriating the 'commons', resources for public benefit, for private ownership, remains a site of struggle (Standing 2019). A never fully submerged sense of some crime as 'social' – defiance of the power of the privileged orders – survived in subterranean fashion (Thompson 1971, 2009; Hobsbawm 1972; Linebaugh 1976, 2014; Lea 1999).

Victims featured in criminal cases technically as witnesses rather than principals, although there has been some movement in recent decades to alleviate their marginality to proceedings. More generally there has been progress in policy and practice in many jurisdictions around the world since the 1970s, developing public support to alleviate the suffering of victims of crime (Rock 1987, 1991, 2004).

110 The strange death of SDC

Academic interest in understanding victimisation began to develop in the 1940s, with some advocating a parallel discipline of victimology. This has become an integral part of the broader discipline of criminology, with a huge impact on theorising and measuring crime (Hoyle and Zedner 2007; Davies et al. 2016; Walklate 2017). In particular, because of evidence that the socio-economic characteristics of those deemed to be perpetrators and victims of the most common volume crimes are largely isomorphic (stressed by feminist and left-realist criminologists since the 1970s cf. Lea and Young 1984), analysis and policy formulation concerning victimisation is now a major part of critical criminology in particular (DeKeseredy and Schwartz 2018 pp. 35–36).

The growth of policy and critical theoretical focus on the position of victims is salutary. However, in the public arena it has largely been overshadowed by the law and order construction of an idealised and decontextualised figure of 'the victim' (Garland 2001; Reiner 2007 Chap. 5; Simon 2007 Chap. 3). This has become central to the cultural characterisation of crime as a zero-sum battle between demonised and depraved perpetrators and the qualitatively distinct species of (ideal typically) white, respectable, young, female targets. The social democratic conception of both victims and offenders as hewn from the same rough timber of humanity, so that respect and concern do not form a zero-sum game, is intellectually, practically and morally preferable. 'The artificial distinction between one human being and another implicit in a class hierarchy are to me outrageous blemishes upon professedly democratic society' (Wootton 1992 p. xvii).

Limits of criminal justice

Criminalisation has serious moral and practical limitations. SDC (in common with liberalism) saw punishment as inherently problematic because it involved the infliction of pain. Penal sanctions were justifiable only if necessary and proportionate, and to some (e.g. Wootton 1959) they should only be adopted for rehabilitation and prevention, using a medical model of expertise.

So the reach of criminal law and sanctions should be restricted to occasions where it prevented greater harm to innocent victims or social welfare. Debates have flourished since the mid-nineteenth century (Reiner 2016 pp. 39–57) between the conservative view that criminal law should prohibit behaviour commonly deemed immoral (Devlin 1965 p. 10 – moot point by whom, general consensus or the powerful?) vs. the liberal contention that punishment is only justified to prevent 'harm to others' (Mill 1859/1998 p. 322; Hart 1968). The victory in the 1960s of the Mill/Hart view, officially articulated in the British Report of the Committee on Homosexual Offences and Prostitution (Wolfenden 1957), resulted in a wave of decriminalising legislation during the 1960s in many jurisdictions, celebrated or reviled as 'the permissive society' (Newburn 1991). The legitimate ambit of criminal law remains acutely controversial, with liberal condemnation of 'over-criminalisation' (Husak 2008) coexisting with radical calls for 'pro-minority' criminalisation to protect vulnerable people from violence and hate crime (Aharonson

2010, 2014). Both have been outstripped by the march of punitiveness under the law and order banner.

SDC not only advocated normative boundaries to criminal law, but also emphasised its practical limits. Indeed, this followed from the core social democratic analysis of the aetiology of crime. Criminal law, policing, and penal policy were not the major elements in public protection, because they did not and could not reach the root causes of criminality. Ultimately, crime levels were shaped by deep social, economic, and cultural processes, and could be reduced only by broader policy reforms beyond the ambit of courts, codes, and constables.

This did not mean that the criminal justice process was unimportant. The cases it dealt with vary in significance, of course, but were often serious, sometimes life trashing, to victims and suspects. Most criminologists in the social democratic era were deeply involved in criminal justice policy and practice in a variety of ways. But implicitly at least, a distinction could be drawn between the micro issues of everyday criminal justice practice and the macro level of crime and public safety overall. Given that only a small proportion of crimes ever get recorded by the police, and that an even tinier number get cleared up in any way, and yet fewer result in formal sanctions, even the most effective rehabilitation programmes can have miniscule effects on overall crime levels. And high recidivism rates in all jurisdictions mean that penal sanctions generally have had little impact on offending totals.

Barbara Wootton cites Sir Thomas More's sixteenth-century warning that 'if you do not remedy the conditions which produced thieves, the vigorous execution of justice in punishing them will be in vain' (Wootton 1963/1992 p. 17). Pondering the lack of impact of the reforms she had so assiduously promoted, she herself later agonised that:

> I have been increasingly haunted by the image . . . of the whole penal system as in a sense a gigantic irrelevance – wholly misconceived as a method of controlling phenomena the origins of which are inextricably rooted in the structure of our society.
>
> *(ibid. p. 76)*

Keep calm: crime under control

The slogan 'Keep Calm and Carry On' became ubiquitous on posters, mugs, T-shirts, and all sorts of consumer ephemera in the wake of the 2008 financial crash (Hatherley 2017). This was the first time the rallying cry was widely displayed, as Owen Hatherley's incisive deconstruction of its use in propping up the Cameron government's unnecessary and hugely damaging choice of austerity policies in 2010 shows (ibid. Chap. 1). When tested by the Ministry of Information in 1939, only a few posters were ever printed, as the message irritated rather than calmed the public – perhaps because those sheltering from the Luftwaffe's bombs during the Blitz had no option but to carry on, calm or not. Its use as 'austerity nostalgia' (ibid.) by Conservative governments to legitimate imposing cuts by choice – masquerading

112 The strange death of SDC

as necessity – required the co-option of the heroic wartime spirit of sacrifice, a process taken to its apogee in the campaign for Brexit after 2016.

However, the keep calm slogan does conjure up criminological and public policy discussions of crime from the mid-nineteenth century to the last quarter of the twentieth. Although many (but far from all) recorded offences inflicted harm on individual victims, the overall state of crime was not generally regarded as problematic. This ceased to be true as the recorded statistics rose remorselessly for some four decades after the mid-1950s (Reiner 2007 Chaps. 3, 4). Whilst spectacular crimes and court cases have always aroused huge popular interest, and were staples of the mass media, the state of crime overall was not a matter of concern, and was not seen as a threat to the social order as such. As discussed earlier in the section 'Crime in its place', law and order did not register high in public anxieties, as indicated by opinion polls and political debate. Especially gory or salacious individual cases could cause temporary, often localised, anxieties and prurience. But the general pattern, trends, and level of crime did not excite great alarm or moral panics – a term only introduced in the early 1970s as the cultural climate changed.

Specific policy issues were highly controversial, notably capital punishment. However, criminal justice matters hardly figured in the news media or in the political arena, until the late 1960s in the USA and slightly later in the UK. And they were largely discussed in a non-partisan and calm manner (Downes and Morgan 2002; Ryan 2003; Loader 2006; Rock 2019; Downes and Newburn forthcoming). Criminologists in the social democratic era were heavily involved in research and practice on particular aspects of crime and criminal justice policy and practice. But these were always seen as important but relatively minor issues compared with major concerns in political economy and keeping international peace.

Repression of social democratic criminology: how and why

The gradual and uneven spread of social citizenship from the mid-nineteenth century to the 1970s saw a growth of increasingly shared prosperity, security, and inclusion. Measured crime rates were low and stable from the 1860s until the First World War, and despite some increase in the inter-war period there was little general alarm (Mannheim 1940). Policing of public order also became more pacific, shifting from a 'battle' to a 'match' (Geary 1985).

Recorded crime began a seemingly inexorable rise from the mid-1950s up to the mid-1990s. This was stimulated by the advent of consumerism (it is symbolic that the beginning of the crime rise coincided with the 1955 launch of commercial television in Britain, with its fueling of acquisitive aspirations). Mass affluence brought significant changes in the nature of property, and in attitudes and practices concerning it. There was a proliferation of big-ticket consumer durables (such as cars, transistor radios, and television sets), which were highly tempting and vulnerable to theft. They were also much more likely to be insured and thus reported if stolen. Rising crime rates from the 1950s to the 1970s were in large part a result of a greater propensity for crime to be recorded (Reiner 2007 pp. 64–65). Consumerist culture no doubt stimulated 'criminality' – 'the tendency of our society to produce criminals' (Currie 2000 p. 6; Hall et al. 2008). Aspirations were heightened faster than legitimate opportunities to acquire the tempting goodies, exacerbating Tawneyesque acquisitiveness and Mertonian anomie. But until the neoliberal counter-revolution of the late 1970s, the crime rise was as much a recording phenomenon as a problem of enhanced criminality.

The spread of inclusive citizenship from the seventeenth century on ultimately ameliorated crime and disorder after the mid-nineteenth century. It also underlay a civilising transformation of criminal justice. During the century between the 1850s and 1950s, 'policing by consent' became established at least as an ideal in jurisdictions claiming the mantle 'democratic' (Bowling et al. 2019 Part II). Police legitimacy in the sense of growing public acceptance did not mean legitimate policing practices prevailed. There was undoubtedly much corruption *sub rosa* and brutal treatment of powerless 'police property' groups, disguised by cosy *Dixon of Dock Green* and 'Officer Friendly' images (ibid.). During the same period, 'penal welfarism' became the prevailing response to apprehended offenders, again with its own failings and abuses, but with an aspiration of benign rehabilitation (Clarke 1980; Garland 1985, 2001, 2019; Bailey 1987). Although it had complex conditions of existence, the underlying context was the gradual incorporation of the mass of the population into social as well as civil and political citizenship (Reiner 2010). The heyday of SDC was an era of greater justice and greater peace. And the reversal of the trend towards greater inclusion with the advent of neoliberalism since the 1970s generated crime and disorder explosions, and the harsher politics of law and order of recent times.

During the 1970s the post-war Keynesian, mixed-economy, welfarist consensus rapidly became displaced by a neoliberal hegemony in economic and social policy. In criminology, the social democratic sensibility was attacked head-on by a new right-wing politicisation of 'law and order'. Social democratic analysis of crime and criminal justice became an electoral 'hostage to fortune' for the parties of the Left, castigated as 'soft and flabby' or even as actively encouraging crime and disorder (Downes and Morgan 2012).

The new law and order consensus

In the early 1990s the Clinton Democrats and Tony Blair's New Labour sought to shed this electoral liability by declaring they were at least as 'tough on crime and tough on the causes of crime' as their right-wing opponents. A new consensus on 'tough' law and order rapidly emerged. It reversed the five elements of SDC with a new model, ideal typically based on these core propositions (Reiner 2007 Chap. 5):

Crime is public enemy no. 1

Crime came to be seen as a major threat to society. It is a significant (often *the* No. 1) concern named in public opinion polls, and is in the forefront of party political debate, which became an auction of toughness.

114 The strange death of SDC

Crime is caused by criminals

Crime is the result purely of the *individual* pathology or choice of offenders. To discuss social causes of crime is not only wrong analytically, but also it insults the law-abiding majority, and encourages offenders by mitigating their guilt.

The victim is iconically central to criminal justice

Criminal justice policy discussions become a zero-sum game of victim vs. offender. Any concern, analytic or *a fortiori* sympathy, for offenders is demeaning and insensitive to the plight of victims. The victim's main interest is taken to be the punishment of offenders.

Criminal justice works

After a period in the 1970s and '80s when evaluation research questioned the efficacy of traditional criminal justice tactics, conducive to a climate of 'nothing works', there was a resurgence of can-do confidence among criminal justice agencies, supported by positive research evaluations of new tactics. Policing, prevention, and punishment came to be taken as panaceas for crime, provided they were tough and/or smart enough.

The conquering 'culture of control' (Garland 2001)

Crime and its control become the focal points of popular culture and practices. Fear, risk, and insecurity govern daily life, from the design of homes and cars, to the journey to school and work, and their layout and organisation. A self-generating loop develops between fear and visible measures intended to contain risk (Zedner 2003, 2009). Supposed security devices symbolise and express the fears they are intended to alleviate, thus exacerbating underlying anxieties. Even if they succeed in suppressing the actual occurrence of crime, they testify to the underlying persistence of criminality, so public fear survives despite the statistical drop in offending.

How the law and order consensus developed

During the 1980s, Margaret Thatcher's Tories pledged a 'ring of steel' against crime and disorder. But despite the tough rhetoric, this was largely a phoney 'war on crime' (except in the sphere of public order where there was a clear espousal of militaristic policing tactics). One reason for this was the continuing commitment of Labour to a social democratic analysis of crime as socially caused. As crime rates rose rapidly to record levels as a result of monetarist economic policies that exacerbated the causes of crime, and as the inner cities broke out in unprecedented rioting, there was a constant threat that the social democratic analysis might become widely plausible.

New Labour's espousal of tough law and order rhetoric from 1992 defused this debate, and ensured the hegemony of tougher penal policies in practice. On gaining office in 1997, New Labour initially adopted a 'third way' combination of toughness plus smartness. The flagship 1998 Crime and Disorder Act encouraged evidence-led policy and partnership (embodied in the ensuing Crime Reduction Programme) but also minimum mandatory sentences, anti-social behaviour orders, curfews, and prison privatisation. Over time, 'tough on crime' eclipsed 'tough on the causes of crime': there was a remorseless growth of police powers (without concern for balancing safeguards as in PACE [Police and Criminal Evidence Act 1984], which were watered down), and record increases in prison numbers – despite falling crime rates.

Explaining the new law and order consensus

How can the development of the post-1992 law and order consensus be explained?

Truth will out?

This is the account favoured by conservatives. Mrs Thatcher said she hadn't made law and order an issue; the British public had. In this view, law and order is simply the only solution to soaring crime rates. But in Britain crime rates had increased for 20 years before law and order began to be politicised; it remains in place despite crime falling for nearly two decades. In the USA it has been shown that the politicisation of law and order tracks political and media campaigning but not crime (Beckett 1997).

Blame it on The Sun?

To what extent is the dominance of the law and order perspective due to the huge exaggeration of the threat of crime by most of the media, which has been documented by countless studies? Certainly the media have played a major role in recurrent moral panics, amplifying fear and insecurity.

There have been quantitative and qualitative shifts in media discourse, paralleling the rise of law and order politics. Increasing media focus on crime is an important trend of recent decades (see Reiner et al. 2003). Narrative structures in media crime stories have also changed in ways conducive to the law and order frame. These changes include: a) *accentuate the negative*: bad news drives out good; crime is depicted as ever more heinous and threatening; b) *victim culture*: media narratives construct a zero-sum game of victim vs. offender; c) *individualism and decontextualisation*: offenders and victims are not depicted as part of social relations and structures, but purely as individually evil or innocent; and d) *desubordination*: crime is constructed as bad by media narratives because it hurts and traumatises sympathetic individuals, not as an offence against an authoritative structure of law and morality.

116 The strange death of SDC

These transformations in the pattern of media narratives frame the issue in law and order terms. However, the media shifts developed dialectically with the politicisation of criminal justice discourse and policy, rather than as a prior and independent cause.

New times, new crime, and control?

The transformation of the politics of law and order is fundamentally related to the deep ruptures in political economy, culture, and social relations associated with the hegemony of neoliberalism since the 1970s. This involved a corruption of 1960s liberalism, which had been associated with an ethic of reciprocal individualism concerned with peace and justice as well as freedom, summed up by the slogan 'make love, *not* war'.

Neoliberalism generated hugely greater inequality and social exclusion, producing more crime and wider insecurities. It also undermined the efficacy of, and belief in, social tools for alleviating these problems. Neoliberalism spawned a narcissistic, consumerist, cool culture of aggressively egoistic individualism (Hall et al. 2008). 'Make love, *and* war. . . *and* loadsamoney'.

Coalition criminal justice

When David Cameron became Conservative leader at the end of 2005, he embarked on a series of much-publicised stunts signalling the ambition of detoxifying the Tory brand. Embracing the mantle of compassionate conservatism, Cameron sought to become 'heir to Blair' by identifying with green and liberal issues, suggesting an image of cool modernity. Cameron even entertained a social analysis of crime, in his so-called hug-a-hoodie speech in July 2006, suggesting that without an understanding of crime's 'root causes' criminal justice policies were just a sticking plaster.

The Conservative-Liberal Democrat Coalition elected in 2010 at first stirred some hopes of change to the culture of control. Its early statements and policies suggested a return to the 'smart' consensus that prevailed briefly around 1990 (embodied in the 1991 Criminal Justice Act), based on the premise that prison was an 'expensive way of making bad people worse'. Many liberal and even radical criminologists welcomed the Coalition's early moves on criminal justice. In particular, there was a warm reception for a landmark speech by Justice Secretary Kenneth Clarke on 30 June 2010 at the Centre for Crime and Justice Studies, trumpeting a promised 'rehabilitation revolution'.

Initially too, the Coalition government appeared as if it might reverse the trend towards remorseless expansion of police powers. Home Secretary Theresa May announced on 8 July 2010 that s. 44 of the Terrorism Act 2000, empowering officers to stop and search anyone in a designated area without having to show reasonable suspicion, was suspended. This followed a ruling by the European Court of Human Rights that the powers were unlawful because they were too broadly drawn and lacked sufficient safeguards. However, the ensuing Terrorism Act 2000 (Remedial) Order March 2011 merely tightened the procedure and criteria for declaring a designated area, retaining the power to stop/search in the absence of reasonable suspicion.

After a few brief salad days during which the Coalition appeared to burnish its liberal criminal justice credentials, there was a rapid return to form as the government reverted to tough law and order (for a detailed analysis of Coalition penal policy, see Skinns 2016). Fundamentally, this represented the predictable unfolding of the consequences of its quintessentially neoliberal economic strategy. It was sadly predictable that the Coalition's liberal pretensions would be frustrated in practice by increasing crime and disorder flowing from the austerity cuts to welfare and the global economic downturn. What was somewhat less predictable was the speed and savagery with which David Cameron squashed Kenneth Clarke's reforms, buckling under to tabloid fury. This was hugely accentuated by the rise of right-wing populist governments since 2015, symbolised above all by the victory of the Brexit campaign in the 2016 UK referendum and the election of Donald Trump as US president.

New Right populist vigilantism

The British Conservative-led Coalition government tilted back towards a harder line on law and order in 2012, with the appointment of Chris Grayling as justice secretary. He part-privatised the probation system, instituting a 'payment by results' system that is universally seen as a disaster, leading to spiralling rates of recidivism (https://www.theguardian.com/politics/2019/jun/30/chris-grayling-probation-privatisation-disaster). He banned books being sent to prisoners to read, a step widely condemned as especially vindictive and counter-productive, overturned in 2015 by the High Court. He severely cut the legal aid budget, denying most poor defendants access to representation. His record was summed up by Shadow Justice Minister Sadiq Khan as the worse in 342 years (https://www.independent.co.uk/news/uk/politics/andy-mcsmiths-diary-chris-grayling-the-worst-lord-chancellor-for-342-years-no-worse-10114748.html).

The return to tough law and order by the Tories was signalled even more clearly when Boris Johnson appointed right-winger Priti Patel as home secretary in 2019. The tougher than tough line was announced by her in her first interview in her new role:

> I fundamentally think the Conservative party is the party of law and order. Full stop. . . . My focus now is restating our commitment to law and order and restating our commitment to the people on the frontline, the police. I've always felt the Conservative party is the party of the police and police officers . . . quite frankly, with more police officers out there and greater police

118 The strange death of SDC

presence, I want [criminals] to literally feel terror at the thought of committing offences.

(https://www.theguardian.com/politics/2019/aug/03/
priti-patel-home-secretary-wants-criminals-to-literally-feel-terror)

President Trump has also pursued redoubled tough law and order rhetoric and policies, explicitly reversing what he castigated as liberal steps under Obama (https://edition.cnn.com/2017/08/29/politics/trump-law-order-jeff-sessions/index.html). This has included a renewed militarisation of police equipment, and pardoning Sheriff Joe Arpaio, who was convicted of contempt in a case alleging racial profiling. Trump supported Sheriff Joe's unrelenting crackdowns on alleged illegal immigration. He instructed prosecutors to file the most serious available charges, disregarding Obama administration concerns over the massive growth of incarceration. Altogether, tough law enforcement and punishment are back in vogue under Trump, coupled with disdain for issues of human rights or the rule of law. During the 2020 election, he cast himself as the 'law and order president' (https://www.independent.co.uk/us-election-2020/trump-white-house-us-election-2020-george-floyd-protests-washington-dc-a9543176.html). Trump doubled down on tough law and order, especially after widespread demonstrations in the wake of the killing of George Floyd, an African American, by white police in Minneapolis on 25 May 2020.

The concluding chapter examines the prospects of countering this trend.

References

Aaronson, E. (2010) '"Pro-Minority" Criminalization and the Transformation of Visions of Citizenship in Contemporary Liberal Democracies: A Critique' *New Criminal Law Review* 13/2: 286–308.

Aaronson, E. (2014) *From Slave Abuse to Hate Crime: The Criminalization of Racial Violence in American History* New York: Cambridge University Press.

Agnew, R. (2006) *Pressured Into Crime* New York: Oxford University Press.

A'Hearn, B. (2014) 'The British Industrial Revolution in a European Mirror' in R. Floud, J. Humphries and P. Johnson (Eds.) *The Cambridge Economic History of Modern Britain* Vol. 1. Cambridge: CUP, 1–52.

Alston, P. (2018) 'Statement on Visit to the United Kingdom, by Professor Philip Alston, United Nations Special Rapporteur on Extreme Poverty and Human Rights' www.ohchr.org/documents/issues/poverty/eom_gb_16nov2018.pdf

Arendt, H. (1968) *Imperialism* New York: Harcourt Brace.

Bailey, V. (1987) *Delinquency and Citizenship* Oxford: Oxford University Press.

Bailey, V. (2000) 'The Death Penalty in British History' *Punishment and Society* 2/1: 106–113.

Barbalet, J. (1993) 'Citizenship, Class Inequality and Resentment' in B. Turner (Ed.) *Citizenship and Social Theory* London: Sage.

Barry, B. (2005) *Why Social Justice Matters* Cambridge: Polity.

Bean, P. and Whynes, D. (Eds.) (1986) *Barbara Wootton: Social Science and Public Policy* Abingdon: Routledge.

Beckett, K. (1997) *Making Crime Pay* Oxford: Oxford University Press.

Beckett, F. and Hencke, D. (2009) *Marching to the Faultline* London: Constable and Robinson.

Bell, D. (2005) *Francois Mitterand* Cambridge: Polity.

Benyon, J. (Ed.) (1984) *Scarman and After* Oxford: Pergamon.

Bernard, L., Gevorkyan, A., Palley, T. and Semmler, W. (2014) *Time Scales and Mechanisms of Economic Cycles: A Review of Theories of Long Waves* University of Massachusetts Amherst: Political Economy Research Unit.

Biressi, A. (2001) *Crime, Fear and the Law in True Crime Stories* Basingstoke: Palgrave.

Blakeley, G. (2019) *Stolen* London: Repeater Books.

Bonger, W. (1913) *Religion and Crime* Leiden: Brill.

Bonger, W. (1939/1943) *Race and Crime* New York: Columbia University Press.

Bonger, W. (1916/1969) *Criminality and Economic Conditions* Bloomington: Indiana University Press.

Bonger, W. (1936/2015) *An Introduction to Criminology* Abibgdon: Routledge.

Bowling, B., Reiner, R. and Sheptycki, J. (2019) *The Politics of the Police* 5th ed. Oxford: Oxford University Press.

Braithwaite, J. (1989) *Crime, Shame and Reintegration* Cambridge: Cambridge University Press.

Bratton, W. (1998) 'Crime is Down: Blame the Police' in N. Dennis (Ed.) *Zero Tolerance: Policing A Free Society* 2nd ed. London: Institute of Economic Affairs.

Bulmer, M. and Rees, A. (Eds.) (1996) *Citizenship Today* London: Routledge.

Case, A. and Deaton, A. (2015) 'Rising Morbidity and Mortality in Midlife Among White Non-Hispanic Americans in the 21st Century' *Proceedings of the National Academy of the Sciences* 112/49: 15078–15083.

Case, A. and Deaton, A. (2020) *Deaths of Despair and the Future of Capitalism* Princeton: Princeton University Press.

Cheliotis, L. (2019) 'Neither Dupes, nor Pipers: Violent Crime, Public Sentiment and the Political Origins of Mass Incarceration in the United States' *Current Issues in Criminal Justice* 32/1: 1–21.

Clark, G. and Cummins, N. (2014) 'Inequality and Social Mobility in the Era of the Industrial Revolution' in R. Floud and J. Humphries (Eds.) *The Cambridge Economic History of Modern England, Volume 1: Industrialisation, 1700–1870* Cambridge: Cambridge University Press, pp. 211–236.

Clark, R. (1970) *Crime in America* New York: Simon and Schuster.

Clarke, J. (1980) 'Social Democratic Delinquents and Fabian Families' in National Deviancy Conference (Ed.) *Permissiveness and Control* London: Macmillan.

Cloward, R. and Ohlin, L. (1960) *Delinquency and Opportunity* Abingdon: Routledge.

Cohen, S. (1998) 'Intellectual Scepticism and Political Commitment' in P. Walton and J. Young (Eds.) *The New Criminology Revisited* London: Macmillan.

Crouch, C. (2011) *The Strange Non-Death of Neoliberalism* Cambridge: Polity.

Currie, E. (2000) 'Reflections on Crime and Criminology at the Millennium' *Western Criminology Review* 2(1), 1–15.

Dahrendorf, R. (1959) *Class and Class Conflict in Industrial Society* Stanford: Stanford University Press.

Dangerfield, G. (1935/2017) *The Strange Death of Liberal England* Abingdon: Routledge.

Davies, P., Francis, P. and Greer, C. (Eds.) (2016) *Victims, Crime and Society* 2nd ed. London: Sage.

DeKeseredy, W. and Dragiewicz, M. (Eds.) (2017) *Routledge Handbook of Critical Criminology* 2nd ed. Abingdon: Routledge.

DeKeseredy, W. and Schwartz, M. (2018) 'Left Realism: A New Look' in W. DeKeseredy and M. Dragiewicz (Eds.) *Routledge Handbook of Critical Criminology* 2nd ed. Abingdon: Routledge.

Dennis, N. and Halsey, A.H. (1988) *English Ethical Socialism* Oxford: Oxford University Press.

120 The strange death of SDC

Devlin, P. (1959/1965) *The Enforcement of Morals* Oxford: Oxford University Press.

Di Grazia, R. (1976) 'What's Wrong with America's Police Leadership?' *Police*, May, 24.

Downes, D. (1986) 'Back to Basics: Reflections on Barbara Wootton's "Twelve Criminological Hypotheses"' in P. Bean and D. Whynes (Eds.) *Barbara Wootton: Social Science and Public Policy* London: Tavistock.

Downes, D. (1998) 'Back to the Future: The Predictive Value of Social Theories of Delinquency' in S. Holdaway and P. Rock (Eds.) *Thinking About Criminology* London: UCL Press.

Downes, D. and Morgan, R. (1994) 'Hostages to Fortune'? The Politics of Law and Order in Post-War Britain' in M. Maguire, R. Morgan and R. Reiner (Eds.) *The Oxford Handbook of Criminology* Oxford: Oxford University Press.

Downes, D. and Morgan, R. (2002) 'The Skeletons in the Cupboard: The Politics of Law and Order at the Turn of the Millennium' in M. Maguire, R. Morgan and R. Reiner (Eds.) *The Oxford Handbook of Criminology* 3rd ed. Oxford: Oxford University Press.

Downes, D. and Morgan, R. (2012) 'Overtaking on the Left? The Politics of Law and Order in the "Big Society"' in M. Maguire, R. Morgan and R. Reiner (Eds.) *The Oxford Handbook of Criminology* 5th ed. Oxford: Oxford University Press.

Downes, D. and Newburn, T. (2020) *The Politics of Law and Order* Abingdon: Routledge, forthcoming.

Duffy, B., Wake, R., Burrows, T. and Bremner, P. (2008) 'Closing the Gaps – Crime and Public Perceptions' *International Review of Law, Computers and Technology* 22: 1.

Durkheim, E. (1893/1973) *The Division of Labour in Society* Glencoe: Free Press.

Eisenhower, M. (1969) *National Commission on the Causes and Prevention of Violence Final Report* Washington, DC: U.S. Government Printing Office.

Engels, F. (1844/2009) *The Condition of the Working Class in England* London: Penguin.

Enns, P. (2016) *Incarceration Nation* Cambridge: Cambridge University Press.

Farrall, S. and Jennings, W. (2012) 'Policy Feedback and the Criminal Justice Agenda: An Analysis of the Economy, Crime Rates, Politics and Public Opinion in Post-War Britain' *Contemporary British History* 26/4: 467–488.

Farrall, S. and Hay, C. (Eds.) (2014) *The Legacy of Thatcherism* Oxford: Oxford University Press.

Flamm, M. (2005) *Law and Order* New York: Columbia University Press.

Floud, R., Humphries, J. and Johnson, P. (Eds.) (2014) *The Cambridge Economic History of Modern Britain* Vols. 1 and II. Cambridge: Cambridge University Press.

Fry, M. (1947) *Lawless Youth* London: Allen and Unwin.

Fukuyama, F. (1992) *The End of History and the Last Man* London: Penguin.

Galbraith, J.K. (1958) *The Affluent Society* London: Penguin.

Garland, D. (1985) *Punishment and Welfare* Aldershot: Gower.

Garland, D. (2001) *The Culture of Control* Oxford: Oxford University Press.

Garland, D. (2002) 'Of Crime and Criminals: The Development of Criminology in Britain' in M. Maguire, R. Morgan and R. Reiner (Eds.) *The Oxford Handbook of Criminology* 3rd ed. Oxford: Oxford University Press.

Garland, D. (2019) 'Punishment and Welfare Revisited' *Punishment and Society* 21/3: 267–274.

Geary, R. (1985) *Policing Industrial Disputes* Cambridge: Cambridge University Press.

Godfrey, B. and Lawrence, P. (2014) *Crime and Justice Since 1750* 2nd ed. Abingdon: Routledge.

Greenberg, D. (1981) *Crime and Capitalism* Palo Alto: Mayfield.

Greer, C. and Reiner, R. (2012) 'Mediated Mayhem: Media, Crime, Criminal Justice' in M. Maguire, R. Morgan and R. Reiner (Eds.) *The Oxford Handbook of Criminology* 5th ed. Oxford: Oxford University Press.

Grinin, L., Korotayev, A., and Tausch, A. (2016) *Economic Cycles, Crises, and the Global Periphery* New York: Springer.

Hall, J. (1935/1952) *Theft, Law and Society* 2nd ed. Indianapolis: Bobbs-Merrill.

Hall, S., Winlow, S. and Ancrum, C. (2008) *Criminal Identities and Consumer Culture* Cullompton: Willan.

Harris, R. (1970) *Justice* New York: Dutton.

Hart, H. (1965) 'Review of Crime and the Criminal Law by Barbara Wootton' *Yale Law Journal* 74: 1325–1331.

Hart, H. (1968) *Law, Liberty and Morality* Oxford: Oxford University Press.

Harvey, D. (2005) *The New Imperialism* Oxford: Oxford University Press.

Hatherley, O. (2017) *The Ministry of Nostalgia* London: Verso.

Hebberecht, P. (2010) 'Willem Bonger' in K. Hayward, S. Maruna and J. Mooney (Eds.) *Fifty Key Thinkers in Criminology* Abingdon: Routledge.

Hillyard, P., Pantazis, C., Tombs, S. and Gordon, D. (Eds.) (2004) *Beyond Criminology* London: Pluto.

Hinton, E. (2016) *From the War on Poverty to the War on Crime* Cambridge: Harvard University Press.

Hobsbawm, E. (1972) 'Social Criminality: Distinctions between Socio-political and other Forms of Crime' *Bulletin of the Society for the Study of Labour History* (25): 5–6.

Home Office (1959) *Penal Practice in a Changing Society White Paper* London: HMSO.

Hood, R. (2004) 'Hermann Mannheim and Max Grunhut: Criminological Pioneers in London and Oxford' *British Journal of Criminology* 44/4: 469–495.

Hoyle, C. and Zedner, L. (2007) 'Victims, Victimization and Criminal Justice' in M. Maguire, R. Morgan and R. Reiner (Eds.) *The Oxford Handbook of Criminology* 4th ed. Oxford: Oxford University Press.

Husak, D. (2008) *Overcriminalization: The Limits of the Criminal Law* New York: Oxford University Press.

Isin, E. and Nyers, P. (Eds.) (2014) *Routledge Handbook of Global Citizenship Studies* Abingdon: Routledge.

Isin, E., Nyers, P. and Turner, B. (Eds.) (2008) *Citizenship Between Past and Future* Abingdon: Routledge.

Isin, E. and Turner, B. (Eds.) (2002) *Handbook of Citizenship Studies* London: Sage.

Israel, J. (2011) *A Revolution of the Mind* Princeton: Princeton University Press.

Jacques, M. (Ed.) (1981) *The Forward March of Labour Halted?* London: Verso.

Keen, M. (2004/2017) *Stalking Sociologists* Abingdon: Routledge.

King, A. and Crewe, I. (1995) *SDP* Oxford: Oxford University Press.

King, M.L. (1991) *Testament of Hope* New York: Harper Collins.

Kuznets, S. (1930) *Secular Movements in Production and Prices* New York: Houghton Mifflin.

Labour Party (1964) *Crime: A Challenge to Us All* London: Labour Party.

Lacey, N. (2013) 'The Rule of Law and the Political Economy of Criminalisation' *Punishment and Society* 15/4: 349–366.

Lacey, N., Wells, C. and Quick, O. (2003) *Reconstructing Criminal Law* 3rd ed. London: Butterworths.

Lansley, S. and Mack, J. (2015) *Breadline Britain* London: Oneworld.

Lea, J. (1999) 'Social Crime Revisited' *Theoretical Criminology* 3/3: 307–325.

Lea, J. and Young, J. (1984) *What is to be Done About Law and Order?* Harmondsworth: Penguin.

Linebaugh, P. (1976) 'Karl Marx, the Theft of Wood, and Working-Class Composition: A Contribution to the Current Debate' *Crime and Social Justice* 6: 5–16.

Linebaugh, P. (2014) *Stop, Thief! The Commons, Enclosures, and Resistance* Oakland: PM Press.

122 The strange death of SDC

Loader, I. (2006) 'Fall of the "Platonic Guardians": Liberalism, Criminology and Political Responses to Crime in England and Wales' *British Journal of Criminology* 46/4: 561–586.

Logan, A. (2017) *The Politics of Penal Reform: Margery Fry and the Howard League* Abingdon: Routledge.

Mann, M. (1996) 'Ruling Class Strategies and Citizenship' in M. Bulmer and A. Rees (Eds.) *Citizenship Today* Abingdon: Routledge.

Mannheim, H. (1940) *Social Aspects of Crime in England Between the Wars* London: Allen and Unwin.

Mannheim, H. (1946) *Criminal Justice and Social Reconstruction* London: Routledge.

Mannheim, H. (1965) *Comparative Criminology* Abingdon: Routledge.

Mannheim, H. and Wilkins, L. (1955) *Prediction Methods in Relation to Borstal Training* London: HMSO.

Marshall, T.H. (1950) *Citizenship and Social Class* Cambridge: Cambridge University Press.

Marx, K. (1867/1976) *Capital* Vol. 1. London: Penguin.

Matravers, M. and Cocoru, A. (2014) 'Revisiting the Hart/Wootton Debate on Responsibility' in C. Pulman (Ed.) *Hart on Responsibility* New York: Springer.

Merton, R. (1938) 'Social Structure and Anomie' *American Sociological Review* 3/5: 672–682.

Messner, S. and Rosenfeld, R. (2012) *Crime and the American Dream* 5th ed. Belmont, CA: Wadsworth.

Miliband, R. (1961) *Parliamentary Socialism* London: Allen and Unwin.

Miliband, R. (1969) *The State in Capitalist Society* London: Weidenfeld.

Mill, J.S. (1859/1998) *On Liberty* Oxford: Oxford University Press.

Miller, L. (2015) 'What's Violence Got to do with it? Inequality, Punishment, and State Failure in US Politics' *Punishment and Society* 17/2: 184–210.

Miller, L. (2016) *The Myth of Mob Rule: Violent Crime and Democratic Politics* Oxford: Oxford University Press.

Milne, S. (2014) *The Enemy Within* London: Verso.

Mirowski, P. (2014) *Never Let A Serious Crisis Go to Waste* London: Verso.

Morris, T. (1989) *Crime and Criminal Justice Since 1945* Oxford: Blackwell.

Moxon, D. (2014) 'Willem Bonger' in J.M. Miller (Ed.) *The Encyclopedia of Theoretical Criminology* Oxford: Blackwell.

Murakawa, N. (2014) *The First Civil Right* Oxford: Oxford University Press.

Newburn, T. (1991) *Permission and Regulation* London: Routledge.

Oakley, A. (2011) *A Critical Woman: Barbara Wootton, Social Science and Public Policy in the Twentieth Century* London: Bloomsbury.

Palmer, J. (1977) 'Evils Merely Prohibited' *British Journal of Law and Society* 3(1): 1–16.

Parker, T. (1855) *Ten Sermons of Religion* Boston: Little, Brown.

Pearson, G. (1983) *Hooligan* London: Macmillan.

Pinker, S. (2018) *Enlightenment Now* London: Penguin.

Polanyi, K. (1944/2001) *The Great Transformation* Boston: Beacon.

Pratt, J., Brown, D., Brown, M., Hallsworth, S. and Morrison, W. (Eds.) (2005) *The New Punitiveness* Cullompton: Willan.

Rawls, J. (1971) *A Theory of Justice* Cambridge: Harvard University Press.

Rees, A. (1995) 'The Other T.H. Marshall' *Journal of Social Policy* 24: 341–362.

Reiner, R. (1980) 'Fuzzy Thoughts: The Police and "Law and Order" Politics' *Sociological Review* 28/2: 377–413.

Reiner, R. (2007) *Law and Order: An Honest Citizen's Guide to Crime and Control* Cambridge: Polity.

Reiner, R. (2010) *The Politics of the Police* 4th ed. Oxford: Oxford University Press.

Reiner, R. (2016) *Crime: The Mystery of the Common-Sense Concept* Cambridge: Polity.

Reiner, R., Livingstone, S. and Allen, J. (2003) 'From Law and Order to Lynch Mobs: Crime News Since the Second World War' in P. Mason (Ed.) *Criminal Visions* Cullompton: Willan.

Robertson, J. (2015) *The Enlightenment* Oxford: Oxford University Press.

Rock, P. (1987) *A View From the Shadows* Oxford: Oxford University Press.

Rock, P. (1991) *Helping Victims of Crime: The Home Office and the Rise of Victim Support in England and Wales* Oxford: Oxford University Press.

Rock, P. (2004) *Constructing Victims' Rights* Oxford: Oxford University Press.

Rock, P. (2019) *The Official History of Criminal Justice in England and Wales: Volume I: The "Liberal Hour"* Abingdon: Routledge.

Rostow, W.W. (1975) 'Kondratieff, Schumpeter, Kuznets: Trend Periods Revisited' *Journal of Economic History* 35/4: 719–753.

Rowbotham, J., Stevenson, K. and Pegg, S. (2013) *Crime News in Modern Britain: Press Reporting and Responsibility, 1820–2010* London: Palgrave.

Ryan, K. (2019) *Crippled: Austerity and the Demonisation of Disabled People* London: Verso.

Ryan, M. (1983) *The Politics of Penal Reform* London: Longman.

Ryan, M. (2003) *Penal Policy and Political Culture in England and Wales* Winchester: Waterside.

Scarman, Lord. (1981) *The Brixton Disorders* London: HMSO.

Scheingold, S. (1984) *The Politics of Law and Order* London: Longman.

Schumpeter, J. (1939) *Business Cycles* New York: McGraw Hill.

Schur, E. (1965) *Crimes Without Victims* Englewood Cliffs: Prentice Hall.

Seldon, A. (Ed.) (2007) *Blair's Britain* Cambridge: Cambridge University Press.

Shafir, G. (1998) *The Citizenship Debates* Minneapolis: University of Minnesota Press.

Shanks, M. (1962) *The Stagnant Society* London: Penguin.

Simon, J. (2007) *Governing Through Crime* Oxford: Oxford University Press.

Skinns, D. (2016) *Coalition Government Penal Policy 2010–2015* London: Macmillan.

Standing, G. (2019) *Plunder of the Commons* London: Pelican.

Streeck, W. (2014) *Buying Time* London: Verso.

Tawney, R.H. (1921) *The Acquisitive Society* London: Bell.

Taylor, I. (1981a) *Law and Order – Arguments for Socialism* London: Macmillan.

Taylor, I. (1981b) *Social Democracy and the Crime Question in Britain: 1945–1980* PhD thesis. University of Sheffield: Centre for Criminological and Socio-Legal Studies http://ethe ses.whiterose.ac.uk/1885/1/DX171455_1.pdf

Taylor, I., Walton, P. and Young, J. (1973) *The New Criminology* London: Routledge.

Thompson, E.P. (1971) 'The Moral Economy of the English Crowd in the Eighteenth Century' *Past & Present* 50/1: 76–136.

Thompson, E.P. (1975) *Whigs and Hunters* London: Penguin.

Thompson, E.P. (2009) *Customs in Common* London: Merlin.

Titmuss, R. (1958) *Essays on the Welfare State* London: Allen and Unwin.

Titmuss, R. (1962) *Income Distribution and Social Change* London: Allen and Unwin.

Tombs, S. (2016) *"Better Regulation": Better for whom?* London: Centre for Crime and Justice Studies.

Tooze, A. (2018) *Crashed* London: Allen Lane.

Turner, B. (Ed.) (1993) *Citizenship and Social Theory* London: Sage.

Turner, B. (2016) *Citizenship and Capitalism* Abingdon: Routledge.

van Heerikhuizen, B. (1987) *W.A. Bonger: Sociologist and Socialist (in Dutch; Summarised in Cohen 1998)* Groningen: Wolters Noordhoff.

van Swaaningen, R. (1997) *Critical Criminology* London: Sage.

Waddington, P.A.J. (1994) *Order and Liberty* London: UCL Press.

Walklate, S. (Ed.) (2017) *Handbook of Victims and Victimology* Abingdon: Routledge.

Wilson, J.Q. (1975) *Thinking About Crime* New York: Basic Books.

Wilson, J.Q. and Kelling, G. (1982) 'Broken Windows' *The Atlantic* 249: 29–38.

Wolfenden, J. (1957) *Report of the Committee on Homosexual Offences and Prostitution* London: Her Majesty's Stationery Office.

Wood, E.M. (1999) *The Origin of Capitalism* New York: Monthly Review Press.

Wood, E.M. (2017) *The Origin of Capitalism: A Longer View* London: Verso.

Wootton, B. (1959) *Social Science and Social Pathology* London: Allen and Unwin.

Wootton, B. (1978) *Crime and Penal Policy* London: Allen and Unwin.

Wootton, B. (1963/1992) 'Crime and the Criminal Law reprinted' in V. Seal and P. Bean (Eds.) *Barbara Wootton Selected Writings* London: Macmillan.

Wootton, B. (1981/1992) *Selected Writings: Crime and the Penal System* edited by V. Seal and P. Bean. London: Macmillan.

Young, J. (2003) 'Merton With Energy, Katz With Structure: The Sociology of Vindictiveness and the Criminology of Transgression' *Theoretical Criminology* 7/3: 389–414.

Zedner, L. (2003) 'Too Much Security?' *International Journal of the Sociology of Law* 31/1: 155–184.

Zedner, L. (2009) *Security* Abingdon: Routledge.

4

CONCLUSION

Born-again social democratic criminology

Good things can come from bad things, though they cannot compensate for them. I am writing from lockdown in the face of the 2020 coronavirus pandemic and fear to read the latest figures on COVID-19 fatalities. We should mourn each death not as a statistic but as if it were one of our own loved ones. Yet there are also hints of hope, in a genuine change of public mood. We experience and hear of reverence for the NHS and 'the science', after years lampooning 'experts'; neighbourliness and a new spirit of mutuality; a huge expansion of public spending to cope with the emergency; and the command and control closedown of the market 'for the duration'. Failure to heed the lessons of the 2007/8 financial crisis may have unleashed truly apocalyptic consequences, but surely, *now*, the neoliberal narrative has been falsified. A new wave of thinkers stands ready to take forward the grand tradition of social democracy. I have suggested how this is rooted in the biblical golden rule of 'Love your neighbour as yourself'' and conceptions of social justice through the ages. When applied in the *trente glorieuses* post-war years before neoliberalism took hold, it provided widely shared rising living standards, inclusion, and greater security and social justice. The twenty-first century has brought to the forefront existential challenges of climate change, pandemic disease, antibiotic resistance, and food insecurity, exacerbating the key social inequalities and tensions of all kinds that generate crime. The ambitious but vitally necessary aim of countering these threats has been brilliantly captured by Kate Raworth in her inspiring image of the doughnut. This posits 'a safe and just space for all', between the inner ring of 'a social foundation of well-being that no one should fall below' and the outer curve of the doughnut representing 'an ecological ceiling of planetary pressure that we should not go beyond' (Raworth 2018 p. 11). This homely metaphor captures and synthesises the growing critique by a new generation of political, moral, green economists questioning established economic analysis. Conventional economic theory and policy rests on an unexamined notion of ever greater growth

126 Conclusion

as the ideal, measured by the notoriously inadequate index of GDP (gross domestic product). It disregards the (often literally) burning issues of fairness within and among populations, and the threats to the foundational ecological infrastructure of our existence created by unfettered growth. This chapter charts the necessity of reviving social democracy implied by the growing critiques of establishment economics. It then suggests ways forward, bringing together the achievements of a growing number of younger political economists, critical criminologists, and political activists. I dearly hope the virus doesn't get me, but if it does, I will go with hope in my heart, because of the remarkable effluence of newly multiplying radical thinkers and doers, even though they have suffered severe setbacks in the 2019/20 elections.

'America will never be a socialist country'. Trump's 2019 State of the Union war cry is echoed daily by right-wing chat shows and phone-ins, op eds, blogs, and comments. The attempt to introduce 'socialism' results inevitably, they say, in oppression.

After restraining myself from smashing the TV or radio, I usually shout out: 'but what about the British NHS? What about the achievements of the post-war consensus, the New Deal, the welfare states around the West (threadbare as they are after half a century of neoliberalism)? What about growth in which all shared during the post-war decades? Welfare state security against the vicissitudes of capitalist fluctuations and natural misfortunes, from "cradle to grave"' (as detailed in Chapter 1)?

And as for freedom from tyranny, what about the post-war British ideal of – in the words of Britain's most successful social democratic prime minister – a police service that is 'the protector not the oppressor of society' (Attlee 1955, p. v; Bowling et al. 2019 critically probes the kernel of truth in this patriotic claim).

The right-wing governments, in place for most of the last half-century of neoliberal hegemony, may still be promising to 'Make America Great Again' or 'Take Back Control'. But they have delivered comparatively miniscule overall economic growth, almost all of which has been snatched by the billionaires whose numbers and wealth proliferate obscenely. Meanwhile, general life expectancy declines, and social murder and public squalor spread apace. The toughening of law and order policing, and the 'new punitiveness' of penality, have failed ultimately to keep the lid down on a maelstrom of crime, violence, and injustice (in all senses).

The right-wing commentators who declare socialism has never worked might retort (as indeed would many on the Left) that what I am invoking is not socialism. Both Right and Left alike tend to define socialism primarily, if not exclusively, in terms of state ownership of the means of production. This cannot be attained or maintained, it is commonly argued, without insurrectionary violence and subsequent oppression of dissidence. The latter, neoliberals argue (in the wake of Hayek 1944/2001), is also true of evolutionary or parliamentary socialism, depicted as the first slippery step on 'The Road to Serfdom'.

This common rejection of post-war social democracy (exemplified by the 1945–51 Attlee governments) as a form of socialism is deeply problematic, in principle and practice. Until its Blairite remodelling after 1995, even the British Labour Party, supposedly the acme of moderation and gradualism, was pledged by Clause Four of its 1918 Constitution to pursue 'the common ownership of the means of production, distribution and exchange'. Post-war social democratic governments were widely seen by contemporaries as on a trajectory towards realising socialist ideals and aspirations, whether this was welcomed or castigated. The Attlee government did indeed nationalise several major industries (coal, railways, road haulage, Thomas Cook, iron and steel, telecommunications), as well as the Bank of England. Others such as gas were taken into public ownership under local government auspices. This amounted to some 20% of the British economy. Although the private sector remained much larger, it is arguable that there was at least a considerable step towards controlling the 'commanding heights' (in Lenin's phrase) of industrial and transport infrastructure, and of finance. Little of this was returned to private ownership when the Conservatives returned to power in 1951. It was only three decades later, after neoliberalism had become firmly embedded, that Margaret Thatcher undertook a controversial privatisation programme, including the railways and telecommunications. And it was only after the 2007/8 financial crisis offered a fig leaf for further shrinkage of the state sector under the mantra of austerity that the Cameron government resumed this ideologically motivated assault on the public realm, selling off the Royal Mail in 2013.

Certainly the post-war British Labour government did not achieve socialism in the sense of implementing its own Clause Four in full. But if we define socialism not as a specific set of institutions but as a cluster of ethical principles based on equality, liberty, and the public interest (as was done in the first two chapters of this book), then the Attlee government made giant steps towards these ideals, by democratic means. And it was largely successful in this, in common with many Western governments in the post-war decades, even if they did not espouse socialism in name. A wealth of evidence supports the view that this was demonstrably to the benefit of the security and prosperity of the whole population (Piketty 2020 is a magisterial analysis of the data supporting this proposition).

The foregoing chapters have demonstrated that the development of social democracy was associated with a trajectory of increasing civil, political, and socio-economic justice and inclusiveness, resulting in greater domestic security, peace, and relatively humane crime control. All this was set into precipitous decline with the neoliberal blitzkrieg since the 1970s, with only very limited and partial deceleration during the 'third way' era of the later 1990s and early 2000s.

This concluding chapter seeks to find nuggets of comfort and hope in the rubble. What possibilities of reviving the pursuit of the values of fairness and social democracy remain? Almost certainly not in terms of resuscitating the previous modes of implementation. Rather by finding new feasible ways of realising the ancient and modern virtues of liberty, equality, and reciprocity. We begin by identifying from the earlier chapters' exploration of the undermining of social democracy what are the principal barriers (some old, some new), before suggesting ways forward to overcoming them.

128 Conclusion

Reviving SDC? Problems and prospects

As postulated in earlier chapters, the essential tenets of social democratic criminology (SDC) are a political and moral economy informed by the ideals and analysis of social democracy more broadly (as outlined in Chapter 1). Crime, and the character of the control systems for handling it, are moulded ultimately by root causes stemming from capitalism. Social democrats see capitalism as an economic structure based on the relentless, remorseless pursuit of individual profit, with an elective affinity for ruthless egoism. The bulk of intellectual and practical work within SDC involved drilling down through labyrinthine institutional, social, and cultural layers to understand, minimise, and redress the harms caused by specific acts deemed criminal. But the root causes were seen as the macroeconomic and cultural ills that were the targets of social democracy more broadly. Thus the prospects of reviving SDC resolve in the end into the question of whether social democracy itself can be resuscitated.

This does not signify the anachronistic project of revivifying the institutional forms in which social democracy once was garbed. It means identifying and developing new strategies for realising the fundamental moral economy of egalitarian liberty and justice. This is not just desirable but also an absolute imperative if humanity, indeed perhaps our planet itself, are to survive much longer, as argued long ago by many prominent socialist thinkers.

Social democracy or barbarism

A century ago, Rosa Luxemburg, the justly celebrated and influential Marxist thinker and political activist, famously declared that 'society stands at the crossroads, either transition to socialism or regression into barbarism' (Luxemburg 1915/2010 p. 204). Luxemburg herself condensed this into the pithy rallying cry 'socialism or barbarism', in her last writings before her 1919 murder by the right-wing paramilitary Freikorps (www.marxists.org/archive/luxemburg/1918/12/14. htm). The origins of Luxemburg's inspirational warning have been much debated – she herself attributed it to Engels. However, this is now generally recognised as incorrect. Luxemburg was writing whilst imprisoned for campaigning against the First World War, without access to books. The author of her quote probably was Karl Kautsky, co-founder and leader of the Social Democratic Party, whose support of the War was bitterly opposed by Luxemburg (https://climateandcapital ism.com/2014/10/22/origin-rosa-luxemburgs-slogan-socialism-barbarism/). The context was partly the basic socialist contention that capitalism had built-in tendencies to ever greater inequality, material and moral alienation, injustice, mass powerlessness, and insecurity. All these issues were aggravated by inevitable economic and financial cycles.

The desperation articulated by the cry 'socialism or barbarism' was doubtless accentuated by the grim horrors of the war. The suffering of the interwar decades – the Great Depression and the ensuing rise of fascism, ultimately culminating in the yet more bloody and destructive agonies of the Second World War – was not specifically prophesied by Luxemburg. But she would have envisaged that, in the absence of the socialist revolution she advocated, such a nightmare scenario would ensue – hence 'socialism or barbarism'.

For three decades after the Second World War there was a practical (and to a lesser extent ideological) consensus that economic and social policy should be directed at ensuring such tragedies never again recurred. And there did ensue an unprecedented period of social democratic policy consensus that succeeded in improving mass living standards and security. This was accompanied by efforts to establish an international order based on peace and human rights, albeit constantly threatened by the Cold War between the USSR and other Communist regimes on the one hand, and the USA and its NATO allies on the other. However, for reasons also probed in Chapter 1, this halcyon period was increasingly undermined during the 1970s and replaced by a neoliberal hegemony. Neoliberalism still dominates economic, social, and criminal justice policy despite increasing challenge since the 2007/8 financial crash.

Luxemburg's cry was '*socialism* or barbarism', but I advocate rewording it as 'social democracy or barbarism'. By this I do not mean the decaffeinated and anaemic version associated since the 1980s with the party that took that name in Britain in 1981. This de-gutted its meaning to slightly left of centre liberalism. Nor do I mean the 1990s 'third way' parties, including 'New' Labour, which accepted the basics of neoliberal political economy (although with some welcome, but mild and largely covert redistribution). When Rosa Luxemburg coined her slogan, she remained a member of the Social Democratic Party. She split from the party because of its support for the war and in 1915 co-founded the Spartacus League (later the German Communist Party). But for most of her life she would have identified with social democracy and socialism, although she was a revolutionary critic of Bernstein's evolutionary, reformist version (Tudor and Tudor 1988; Luxemburg 1899/2006).

To me the social democratic or democratic socialist labels are preferable, because they emphasise, first, that as a target socialism means the realisation of democracy in the fullest substantive sense. Formal democratic institutions are frequently undermined by plutocracy, becoming dominated by those with the greatest material resources, as the twenty-first century underlines to an increasing extent. Second, they indicate that whilst recourse to violence cannot be ruled out – especially if defensive – it must be governed by ethical criteria, along the lines set out in just war theory (Walzer 2015; J.T. Reiner 2018, 2019). Premature or disproportionate violence is unjust, and arguably counter-productive in most cases, losing the democratic element of social democracy. As Luxemburg put it in her (sympathetic) critique of the Russian Revolution:

> Socialist democracy is not something which begins only in the promised land after the foundations of socialist economy are created; it does not come as

130 Conclusion

some sort of Christmas present for the worthy people who, in the interim, have loyally supported a handful of socialist dictators.

(Luxemburg 1918/2006 Chap. 6)

Her interpretation of democracy included several elements of the parliamentary version, as checks on autocracy:

Without general elections, without unrestricted freedom of press and assembly, without a free struggle of opinion, life dies out in every public institution, becomes a mere semblance of life, in which only the bureaucracy remains as the active element. Public life gradually falls asleep.

(ibid.)

The version of social democracy I am arguing for is based on ethics, as Chapter 1 emphasised. Social democratic ethics pivots on justice, in the sense of the maximum possible expression of equality, liberty, and common humanity. This was pursued by the prophets of the Bible, rebels throughout history from ancient times to the present day, and justified most compellingly by John Rawls (1971).

A standard revolutionary critique of the primacy of ethics claim is the one articulated by Marx and Engels in their attacks on 'utopian socialism'. However, my rebuttal would be the demonstration of the achievements for the welfare and safety of people accomplished by the social democratic consensus era. Social democracy, as embodied best to date by the post-war Attlee government, can be characterised as the utopia that worked. The problem is, it only worked for a time. As detailed in Chapter 1, its achievements were undermined by the neoliberal counter-revolution, developing from the 1970s.

The task of this chapter is to probe the prospects of reviving the pursuit of social democracy and its values. The first step is to recognise that social democracy is *necessary* to avert the barbarisms of massive inequality, in terms of political power, class, race, gender, sexuality, and generation, which blight capitalism. This is also the first step to combatting the excessive crime, and repressive control, that flow from the deeper evils of inequality and injustice (Reiner 2007; Hall 2012). If there is no reversal of these drivers of egoism and exclusion, the 'high crime' society and cultures of control will worsen.

The vaunted intelligence-led, actuarial, risk-based tactics for preventing crime succeeded in reducing recorded crime throughout the Western world for some two decades after the mid-1990s, the heyday of 'third way' *soi-disant* social democracy. This was in part because 'third way' governments did attenuate the galloping inequality and social exclusion of the 1980s. But these crime control techniques worked through 'liddism' (Rogers 2010), the suppression of everyday crime and disorder by smart situational opportunity reduction and problem solving (Farrell et al. 2014; Roeder et al. 2015; Reiner 2016 pp. 164–185). These symptom alleviation approaches turn criminology from intellectual analysis of the concepts and causes of crime to 'liddology', the technical design of better-fitting lids with which to hold down social tensions. In so far as they are targeted pre-emptively against officially identified potential offenders, they increase the exclusion of those predicted to be risky, exacerbating the fundamental causes of crime. The gathering of data on which to base these predictions becomes a sinister aspect of 'surveillance capitalism' (Zuboff 2019; Foroohar 2019), safeguarding a regime of accumulation in which a small but expanding layer of billionaires soar away from the increasingly immiserated masses. The latter are controlled by qualitatively more subtle and penetrating ubiquitous intelligence technology.

And beyond legally defined crime, 'zemiologists' remind us, there lurks the multiplicity of harmful wrongs and cruelties perpetrated by the powerful, by corporations and states (Hillyard et al. 2004; Hillyard and Tombs 2017). The respectable 'killing fields' of pollution, dangerous work conditions, destruction of public health and welfare in the name of fiscal prudence and private profitability, and wars of choice, are all also fuelled by rampant neoliberalism (Tombs and Whyte 2015; Cooper and Whyte 2017; Green and Ward 2017; Bittle et al. 2018).

If the curbing of neoliberalism and a restoration of the social democratic project are necessary to avert the spiralling harms and evils of capitalism on steroids, what can be done? There are formidable barriers to any prospect of social democracy redux, partly in terms of whether it is at all feasible. More crucially still, where will the agency for supporting it come from? This has become especially problematic with the sharp electoral lurch to a populist – arguably neo-fascist – Right, in recent years. To make matters even more bleak, the twenty-first century has laid bare the significance of new world-threatening challenges that had largely been ignored before. The most formidable of these are climate change, pandemics coupled with antibiotic resistance, and the qualitative leaps in information technology and artificial intelligence – altogether, an ambiguous, complex package of both hope for redemption and threat of destruction.

Reviving social democracy: key barriers

The obstacles to a successful revival of social democracy derive from: a) political economy, b) moral economy, and c) the problem of agency. All raise issues that are far from new, but have taken much deeper, complexly twisting, roots since the1970s. It is commonly claimed now that neoliberal political and moral economy has rendered impossible the once highly successful social democratic mixed economies of the Keynesian/welfare state heyday. Some of these arguments turn on politico-economic issues posed by globalisation (especially in its neoliberal version associated with financial deregulation). Others invoke changes in moral economy, social values, and culture. These point to a supposed breakdown of support for communal engagement, altruism, and public concerns, in favour of egoistic hedonism, competitive consumerism, and individual or family material aspirations. Finally, these trends in political and moral economy reinforce the perennial problem of agency – what social forces are credible bearers of the struggle to achieve a society based on socialist values of equality, liberty, and reciprocal fellow feeling and

132 Conclusion

solidarity. And the flip side of this also needs to be addressed. What are the fundamental interests and forces that will oppose the success of such values? Are these really in the end just the 1%, the few and not the many, even though a very powerful few? Are there any prospects at all of dominant elites coming to accept at least the inevitability, perhaps even the desirability, of fairer forms of social organisation? Arguably this was a key factor in the social democratic consensus after World War II, and is a crucial issue for the chances of peaceful transition to socialism. These are the questions that are addressed in these final sections.

Political economy barriers

It is often claimed that social democracy has been rendered unattainable by neoliberal globalisation. This is said to severely restrict the capacity of states, weakening them in the face of financial markets and multinational corporate behemoths (Crouch 2011, 2018, 2020). In particular, the power of global unregulated financial markets permits them to frustrate the taxation and public expenditure plans of social democratic governments, by withdrawing capital or speculating against the currency.

These are, of course, not new problems. Discussions of globalisation often fuse together a number of strands. It is essential to distinguish between the development of communication and transport technologies, that break down physical barriers to trade and travel between places, and the neoliberal aegis under which this progress has developed since the 1970s. The latter entailed the erosion or destruction of regulatory barriers to the flow of capital – whether financial or material means of production, and the exchange of goods and services. It also facilitated the development of 'offshore' finance. This covered up 'the great tax robbery' (Brooks 2013), whereby the very few individuals and institutions of 'high net worth' are able to shield massive amounts of income and wealth from exposure to governments, thus avoiding or evading taxation. Such filching of public assets massively reduced the revenue base for governments, which is necessary for welfare and collective services such as health, education, and infrastructure (Shaxson 2012, 2018; Bullough 2018; Bernstein 2017).

The power of financial capital to flow among jurisdictions was already a problem during the social democratic era, from at least as early as 1955 (Blakeley 2019 pp. 40–45), and indeed was a major factor undermining it. Harold Wilson famously railed against the role of financial speculation against the pound by 'the gnomes of Zurich', which shipwrecked the 1964 Labour government's plans for boosting economic growth and public spending.

However, the formal abandonment in the early 1970s of the Bretton Woods regulation of currency flows marked a key turning point in the destruction of postwar social democracy. Thereafter, would-be social democratic governments faced massive obstacles to expanding social welfare spending, let alone more explicit forms of redistribution or empowerment in favour of labour. This was illustrated most vividly in the early days of neoliberal hegemony by the capital flight that defeated President Mitterand's attempt to introduce 'a French road to socialism', essentially a revival of the post-war social democratic Keynesian-welfarist settlement (Blakeley 2019 pp. 138–140).

It is vital to distinguish the technological and geophysical aspects of globalisation from the neoliberal auspices under which these developed, although they are, of course, interlaced to an extent. The massive expansion of means of communication and transport in themselves have brought about huge advances in opportunities, conveying universal benefits. These are embodied, for example, in the technology I am using to process these words, and the ability, once they are completed, to make them available to anyone who wishes to read them, anytime and anywhere. Instead of presidential fireside chats on radio, we are treated continuously to Donald Trump's twittering – a change albeit not obviously a beneficial one.

Along with these opportunities comes new exposure to risks, illustrated dramatically in early 2020 by the sudden global spread of the coronavirus.

In principle, the greater possibilities of international co-ordination brought by globalisation could make for easier and more effective co-operative action against such new scourges. However, the difficulties of actually achieving this are a vivid demonstration of the downsides of *neoliberal* globalisation. A key paradox is that deregulation at both the international and national level has permitted, indeed stimulated, the growth of transnational giant industrial and financial corporations. These have the capacity to dictate to the countries in which they operate, because of their power to cripple them by withdrawing their assets and resources to more friendly – that is, less regulated – regimes, forcing a race to the bottom. In turn, the consequent high levels of unemployment or insecure, low-paid work, and growing poverty and precarity are major factors underlying the rise of populist, right-wing, protectionist, and nationalist movements. This was exemplified in the heart of capitalism by the 2016 US election of Trump and the Brexit referendum in the UK. Support for these right-wing shifts flourishes as the mass anger and resentment caused by deteriorating material circumstances and lack of cultural recognition are projected onto external scapegoats, such as migrants, multinational governance institutions (like the UN or EU), and globalisation itself. This makes international co-operation to combat mutually threatening risks – such as pandemics and climate change – much harder, precisely when it is needed most. Nonetheless, it can be achieved *in extremis*, as illustrated by the successful international co-ordination to prevent the precipitate and potentially existentially calamitous collapse of the global banking system, which was spearheaded by Gordon Brown in 2008 (Tooze 2018 Part II; Blakeley 2019 pp. 168–179).

As Tooze has argued, this suggested that the thesis of globalisation making governments impotent was exaggerated. But in the end, only the surface of the problems was scratched, and the structures of the US-dominated financial system largely escaped unscathed after the emergency first-aid of bailing out the banks:

> At the height of the crisis, encouraged by Barack Obama's victory, Brown tried to offer a sweeping vision of global solutions for a global age. But the

134 Conclusion

new team in Washington was not interested in a rerun of the Anglo-American condominium at Bretton Woods.

(www.theguardian.com/commentisfree/2018/jul/29/
city-of-london-desperate-gamble-china-vulnerable-economy)

Soon after Gordon Brown's success as saviour of the world, the British electorate booted him out of office in 2010. They had largely bought into the Conservative narrative that the crash had been due to Labour's profligate spending, 'maxing out the nation's credit card'. The Tory-dominated Coalition government initiated the austerity policies that 'broke Britain' and produced a 'Lost Decade' (Toynbee and Walker 2020) – and maybe longer. As many have concluded, the bailout was 'socialism for the banks', but immiseration for the masses. Whilst the 2008 international rescue illustrates the possibilities of government action, despite the structural pressures of globalisation, it also showed that the balance of forces in favour of the wealthy and powerful remains formidably stacked against the prospects of social justice.

Nonetheless, it is technically feasible to clip or even eliminate the power of global financial markets to undermine the prospects of social democratic government policies. In the wake of the collapse of Bretton Woods in 1971, the Nobel Prize–winning American economist, James Tobin, proposed a financial transactions tax (he suggested about 0.1%) on all exchanges among currencies (www. ft.com/content/6210e49c-9307-11de-b146-00144feabdc0), drawing on an idea originally suggested by Keynes in the 1930s. His explicit purpose was 'to throw sand into the wheels of global finance', not to raise revenue. He suggested pitching it at a low level, so that it would inhibit short-term speculative exchanges which often involved huge amounts of 'hot' money, but not harm everyday trade or travel. Unsurprisingly, whilst neoliberalism was in its pomp the proposal was rejected by governments. However, in the wake of the 2007/8 financial crisis, several European and other governments have viewed it favourably, not only as a way of stabilising the system but also as a revenue-raising measure. This developed into the campaign for a 'Robin Hood' tax, led by several NGOs in the international aid field, together with social democratic leaders such as Jeremy Corbyn in the UK and Bernie Sanders in the USA (www.robinhoodtax.org.uk/).

Following the 2007/8 crisis, an array of voices called for some functional equivalent of Bretton Woods that could stabilise the financial markets' threat to national governments' economic and social programmes. Several of these advocate going beyond the Bretton Woods dollar-based arrangements, reviving Keynes' rejected proposal for an international currency (which he had called Bancor), to be governed by global governance institutions centred on a substantive World Bank. The IMF discussed this favourably in 2011, although it has not developed further so far:

Called, for example, bancor in honour of Keynes, such a currency could be used as a medium of exchange. . . . A global currency, bancor, issued by a global central bank . . . would be designed as a stable store of value. . . . As trade and finance continue to grow rapidly and global integration increases, the importance of this broader perspective is expected to continue growing.

(IMF 2010 pp. 26–27)

The private markets have gone one step ahead in appropriating the idea of Bancor, adopting the name for a blockchain protocol that allows users to convert among different tokens, introducing greater liquidity into the anonymous market for Bitcoin and other forms of cryptocurrency. This is, of course, the very opposite of Keynes' original conception which was intended to preserve the power of governments to pursue social democratic objectives, not to create a further shadow realm in which political democracy held no sway.

There has also been much lip service, and a modest amount of action, addressing the issue of tax havens and other aspects of tax avoidance and evasion. Few, if any, election manifestos of political parties running for election (including conservative ones) fail to include commitments to 'crack down' on such egregious misappropriation of public funds. Social democratic candidates differ only in the extent to which they are pledged not only to tougher and more effective enforcement of existing law, but also to legal change to close loopholes enabling avoidance, which are exploited by an army of accountants and lawyers advising the wealthy (Brooks 2013, 2019; Murphy 2016, 2017; Sikka 2018). Succeeding in these pledges is critical to the implementation of social democratic political economy in a globalised world, and the tackling of the newish wicked problems of climate change and pandemics.

These issues certainly require some international co-operation in achieving measures such as the Tobin/Robin Hood taxes, and a Bretton Woods–style regulation of financial flows. Brexit has made this more difficult, but the key challenge is to attain the election of social democratic governments. This means tackling the barriers stemming from moral economy and from the problem of agency. In effect, this must reverse the trajectory not only of the past decade of neoliberal retrenchment since the financial crash, nor its doubling down since 2016, but also the halfcentury since the 1970s – a tall order by any reckoning!

But such 'impossible' shifts have happened before. Indeed, a key example is the 1970s revival of neoliberalism itself. This overwhelmed the seemingly entrenched, and functional post-war mixed economy, welfarist settlement. The impossible dream of Hayek and his associates, fantasised about in the heady air of Mont Pellerin in 1947, but marginalised in academic culture and economic policy until the 1960s, eventually came to be fulfilled. Is it possible that the apparently immovable cultural and institutional blocks in the way of social democracy, and its criminological sensibility, might be shifted?

Moral economy barriers

As discussed in Chapter 2, 'economics' as a discipline must be distinguished from the broader political economy out of which it developed. Since the early 1960s,

136 Conclusion

when British professor Richard Lipsey wrote a (still standard) textbook on what he called 'positive economics', and mathematical approaches drove out all others from the citadels of the discipline, economics has suffered from 'physics envy'. This accompanied a renaissance of belief in the magic of the market, associated above all with the Chicago School (Friedman 1962). The notion of an inevitable imbrication of politics and economics became anathema to the profession, despite its distinguished history from Adam Smith and the nineteenth-century classical political economists to the Keynesians. *A fortiori* the idea of 'moral economy' raises the hackles of mainstream economists. It also antagonises those Marxists who espouse the materialist determinism expressed most sharply in the preface to the 1859 *Critique of Political Economy*.

In recent years, however, the idea of moral economy has become increasingly influential (with echoes in criminology, e.g. Karstedt and Farrall 2006). It has three distinct aspects. First, the recognition that economies are always embedded in moral notions of what ought to be. The supposedly objective positive science is itself heavily shaped by tacit, hidden values, and utopian notions such as free markets and perfect competition. Second, the workings and impact, both of economies and of economics, can and must be evaluated in relation to normative conceptions of welfare and human flourishing. This has become especially urgent in the face of the looming crimes and disasters of the twenty-first century: ever greater injustice, instability, and the undercutting of the material conditions of human survival by existential risks, above all climate change and pandemics. Third, the study of the inter-relationship of ethics and economies is a valid and already flourishing intellectual enterprise.

The argument of this book has been that a social democratic political and moral economy, which was eclipsed by the post-1970s neoliberal hegemony, is necessary for all these reasons. However, the changes in political economy went hand in hand with alterations of moral economy and dominant social imaginaries. A 'new spirit of capitalism' emerged, co-opting but perverting the cultural liberalism of the 1960s counter-culture. As Margaret Thatcher expressed her basic intention in a 1981 interview: 'Economics are the method; the object is to change the heart and soul' (www.margaretthatcher.org/document/104475). And she succeeded in this, consolidating a new neoliberal consensus. This was best expressed by its continuation under New Labour, as Thatcher herself recognised when she declared her greatest achievement was Tony Blair (https://conservativehome.blogs.com/centreright/2008/04/making-history. html). Much the same was true of her US counterpart, President Ronald Reagan, as the two most recent Democrat presidents, Bill Clinton and Barack Obama, observed themselves (www.theguardian.com/politics/2013/apr/08/margaret-thatcher-dies-tributes-obama).

The changes in moral economy wrought by neoliberalism are complex and deep. The most crucial are: a) the replacement of reciprocal by egoistic individualism; b) an upending of what is understood by compassion; c) the compartmentalisation of

Conclusion **137**

injustice and oppression, and of struggles against them; and d) the financialisation and commercialisation of everyday culture and aspirations.

Egoistic vs. reciprocal individualism

Individualism has many meanings: ontological, methodological, political, ethical, and more. Dictionary definitions tend to contrast it with socialism, simply taken as a collectivist perspective both in terms of its analysis and morality. Some versions of socialism clearly are collectivist, as are some versions of conservatism with their veneration of 'imagined communities' like the 'nation' (Anderson 1983). But it is certainly possible for forms of individualism to be combined with socialism (Wood 1972). Debates about the meaning of individualism cannot be engaged with at length here. But it will be presumed that many varieties of socialism share with liberalism, and some conservatism, a valorisation of individual welfare as the ultimate reference point of evaluation.

Maximising individual satisfaction and minimising its frustration, whether by material deprivations or unnecessary restrictions of liberty, is the touchstone of justice and social policy for these approaches. This is always subject, however, to consideration of individuals' impact on the equally valid claims of other individuals to happiness, concern, and respect. I am calling this 'reciprocal' individualism, which is grounded in an overarching sense of the fundamental equality of worth of all people. It is the ground zero of social democracy, found in such varying versions as the biblical 'Love your neighbour as yourself' (Leviticus 18:18), Marx's 'from each according to their ability, to each according to their needs', and Rawls' sophisticated elaboration of a theory of justice (Rawls 1971). By labelling this 'reciprocal' I do not wish to import the calculative selfishness of 'you scratch my back, and I'll scratch yours'. Rather, it is the vision that empathises with others because people see through the face-to-face encounter (Levinas 2005) a spark of the same image in which they themselves were formed. 'Bread for all . . . before cake for anyone' is the succinct expression of this philosophy by William Beveridge, key architect of the post-war welfare state (Renwick 2017).

However, this ethic has been overturned since the 1970s by the neoliberal revolution. Reciprocal individualism has been supplanted by egoistic or 'possessive' individualism. The latter was identified by Macpherson's classic critique of formative liberal political philosophy as an ideological construction, which mirrors the reality of social relations in capitalist market societies (Macpherson 1962; Cunningham 2018). In essence, this conception contends that an individual is the sole proprietor of their skills, with no obligations to others or to society. The capacities possessed by individuals are like any commodity, traded on the formally free labour market. The primary goals sought by possessive individuals are egoistic, the maximum satisfaction of consumerist desires. This mirrors the actual plight of individuals – whether workers or capitalists – in capitalist markets, but it is projected in liberal ideology as basic and eternal human nature.

138 Conclusion

Throughout history, including during the earlier periods of capitalist development, the possessive ethic has been challenged by reciprocal individualism, articulated, for example, by Christian socialism: 'Do as you would be done by' (Kingsley 1863/2016). Since the 1970s, however, egoistic individualism has become dominant, championed explicitly by Margaret Thatcher, for example, despite her avowed Christianity (Filby 2015). In one of her best-known interviews she explicitly inverted the biblical Golden Rule: 'Love your neighbour herself'. She castigated people with problems for

> casting their problems on society and who is society? There is no such thing! There are individual men and women and there are families and no government can do anything except through people and people look to themselves first. It is our duty to look after ourselves and then also to help look after our neighbour and life is a reciprocal business. . . . There is no such thing as society. There is living tapestry of men and women and people and the beauty of that tapestry and the quality of our lives will depend upon how much each of us is prepared to take responsibility for ourselves and each of us prepared to turn round and help by our own efforts those who are unfortunate.
>
> *(www.margaretthatcher.org/document/106689)*

This seems to be arguing that, contrary to the general reading of the biblical Golden Rule, one should love oneself first and then perhaps our neighbour as an act of charity. She calls life a reciprocal business but means by that not that our concern and respect for others derives from our common humanity, but from calculative exchanges driven by the participants' egoistic goals. Responsibility is to oneself primarily, not any notions of duty to others in need.

In another controversial *bouleversement* of the standard reading of a Christian text, she interpreted the lesson of the Good Samaritan narrative as celebrating not the virtue of helping a stranger in distress but of his accumulation of wealth. This enabled the eponymous Samaritan to come to the rescue. 'No-one would remember the Good Samaritan if he'd only had good intentions; he had money as well' (www.margaretthatcher.org/document/104210; Spencer 2017). A little hard to reconcile with St. Paul's famous words: 'For the love of money is the root of all evil' (I Timothy 6:10).

Margaret Thatcher's pronouncements were highly controversial, not least with Church leaders. However, the idea that putting oneself first is nothing but common sense, indeed virtuous in promoting liberty and affluence, has become taken-for-granted common sense. When the (fictional) corporate raider Gordon Gekko said in the 1987 film *Wall Street* that 'greed, for lack of a better word, is good. Greed is right, greed works. . . . Greed, in all of its forms; greed for life, for money, for love, knowledge has marked the upward surge of mankind', it caused a frisson amongst opponents of neoliberalism. But it was recognised as giving a clear voice to the emerging hegemony of egoistic individualism. And it now rules the world's most powerful nation, as declared by Trump:

> My whole life I've been greedy, greedy, greedy. I've grabbed all the money I could get. I'm so greedy. But now I want to be greedy for the United States. I want to grab all that money. I'm going to be greedy for the United States.
> *(www.vox.com/2016/1/29/10866388/donald-trump-greedy)*

MAGA: Make America Greedy Again?

Whatever happened to compassion?

It might be supposed that the dominance of egoistic individualism would some-how lower overall compassion. Compassion is not a synonym for pity but implies feelings of empathetic concern for the suffering of others, stimulating impulses to alleviate their pain as much as possible. It presupposes the same sense of funda-mental equality, reciprocal individualism, as the social democratic ethic in general. People in trouble stimulate the thought 'there but for the grace of god go I', not sentiments of blame for either failure or wrongdoing. Unlike pity, compassion is not *de haute en bas*; it is based on identification, not superiority. 'I know, or at least can imagine, what you are going through'.

Because neoliberalism emphasises solely individual responsibility for one's actions, precluding notions of social causation, it has an elective affinity with blam-ing victims of misfortune rather than encouraging compassion. Certainly there is considerable evidence of changes under neoliberalism in how people in trouble of different kinds are viewed by others, manifested, for example, in the many reports of the British Social Attitudes Survey, published since 1983 (www.natcen.ac.uk/our-research/research/british-social-attitudes/).

However, what can be discerned in the data is a shift in conceptions of who should be the object of compassion, rather than some overall hardening of the habits of the heart (Bellah et al. 1985/1996). There has been a marked revival of Victorian conservative moralistic notions of the 'deserving' and 'undeserving', with significant shifts in the criteria of merit.

The British Social Attitudes Survey suggests a complex array of views on inequality, with clear distinctions according to political identification and educa-tion. Thus, whilst the majority of the population believes that sharp differences in income are necessary and justifiable to reward greater talent and effort (BSA 36, 2019: Table 4), the proportion questioning this in the wake of the 2008 financial crisis has increased. There are also growing differences between Conservative and Labour voters, with a substantial fall in the proportion of the latter seeing eco-nomic inequalities as justified (ibid. Table 7). These patterns and trends are paral-leled in views on poverty and welfare. The proportion of people who think the unemployed are primarily responsible for relieving their own plight has markedly

140 Conclusion

increased. In 2001, 88% agreed that government should be mainly responsible for ensuring unemployed people have enough to live on, but by 2011 this had fallen to 59% (BSA 29, 2012 p. 1). Whereas in 1991 27% believed unemployment benefits were too high and discouraged work, by 2011 this had more than doubled, to 62% (ibid.). Whilst this view was held by a majority in all groups in 2011, it was less frequent amongst Labour or Liberal Democrat than Tory voters, and amongst those actually receiving benefits (ibid. Table 1.6). Overall, what the BSA

> data clearly show is that . . . the public is becoming less supportive of the government taking a leading role in providing welfare to the unemployed, and even to the elderly in retirement. There is less enthusiasm about public spending on all types of benefits and an increasing belief that the welfare system encourages dependence.
>
> *(BSA 29, 2012 p. 17)*

The changes in public attitudes away from seeing welfare recipients as unfortunate people deserving compassion but as responsible for their own plight is congruent with the broader change from reciprocal to egoistic individualism. It has also been inflamed relentlessly by negative mass media depiction of welfare recipients in highly pejorative terms. 'Beveridge envisaged a social-security system based on reciprocity, which provided a platform for all citizens; now, the poor were to blame for their condition, including the sick and disabled' (Toynbee and Walker 2020 p. 133). This was exacerbated by TV 'benefits porn' in the guise of documentaries 'such as *Benefits Street*, caricaturing claimants as exemplars of folly, fraud, addiction, criminality and idleness' (ibid.).

The trends in the nature and ambit of compassion are also illustrated by the shifting conception of victims of crime. An idealised and unrepresentative image of 'the victim' has become the iconic rationale for the concept of crime in neo-liberal criminal justice. Media narratives, and public and political discourse about crime, pivot around a notion of innocent and attractive victims (ideal typically angelic young children). They are brutalised by monstrous violence, perpetrated by bestial offenders who are beyond the pale of human concern (Reiner 2007 pp. 141–151). Criminal justice should solely be aimed at rectifying the violations of the victim, by inflicting pain on the perpetrator. Understanding offenders, let alone exhibiting any concern for them, is seen as a betrayal of the victim, in a zero-sum game conception of compassion. As the ideal type victim is constructed on dimensions of age, race, gender, and respectability (a stand-in for class), the boundaries of compassion are rationed on the basis of who is like 'one of us'. This is a far cry from the inspirational words of that notorious bleeding heart liberal, Winston Churchill: 'The mood and temper of the public in regard to the treatment of crime and criminals is one of the most unfailing tests of the civilisation of any country' (https://api.parliament.uk/historic-hansard/commons/1910/jul/20/class-iii#S5CV0019P0_19100720_HOC_288). The growth of compassion for

Conclusion **141**

victims of crime, expressed in a variety of policy reforms to ameliorate their previous insensitive treatment, is welcome. But the withdrawal of compassion for those accused or convicted of offences should not be regarded as a corollary of concern for actual or potential victims. Their interests are better served by understanding how to prevent recidivism and offending.

A final illustration of the shrinking, or at least shifting, boundaries of concern under the aegis of neoliberalism is the treatment of migrants and asylum seekers. As several criminologists have charted in recent years, there has developed a system of 'crimmigration', in which formerly administrative forms of regulating migration have become criminalised in terms of formal law and enforcement practice:

> What is emerging . . . is a global trend towards a transnational "crimmigration control system" that immobilizes the purportedly "undesirable" sector of our global society. The institutionalised use of crime control techniques within a regulatory system of population management demands critical analysis.
> *(http://britsoccrim.org/documents/Bowling2015.pdf)*

The pioneering paper on the concept of crimmigration (Stumpf 2006) located its source in the expanding ambit of those deemed by states and laws (in mutual interaction with media and public opinion) to be 'outsiders', not meriting the membership rights and privileges of citizens. David Goodhart, head of the Demography, Immigration and Integration Unit at the right-wing think tank Policy Exchange, has distinguished two contrasting and conflicting tribes in contemporary politics: people of Anywhere vs people of Somewhere (Goodhart 2017). The former are characterised as highly educated, urban, cosmopolitan professionals, the latter those left behind by globalisation, which destroyed the economic base of local communities dependent on manufacturing and extractive industries (in the US Rust Belt, much of the UK, and elsewhere in the global North). The Somewhere tribes bemoan the erosion of the stable locales they were rooted in and the traditional values of nation, community, and family. Their sense of neglect and frustration at cultural and political exclusion by liberal, cosmopolitan elites helps explain support for Brexit, Trump, populism, nostalgic nationalism, hostility to immigration, and embrace of authoritarian law and order politics.

Descriptively, this analysis has some plausibility, but it points to symptomatic rather than root causes of the *ressentiment* of those groups and areas that suffered from globalisation. The neoliberal financialised framework within which globalisation developed since the 1970s forced the destruction of secure, relatively well-paid job markets, protecting the dominance of a small, wealthy elite. The latter, immeasurably aided by the media they controlled, succeeded in scapegoating and demonising a powerless array of minorities, asylum seekers, and other migrants, welfare recipients, and street criminals. This diversion of anger shielded the far more harmful predations and violence of suite criminals, including the social murder wave caused by austerity.

142 Conclusion

Compartmentalisation of injustice and oppression

Social democracy in all its versions has a clear central focus on the pursuit of equality, balanced by liberty and democracy. Rooted in ancient and pre-modern conceptions of justice, social democratic political movements arose during the nineteenth century as a critique of capitalist political and moral economy. For most of its history the core explicit target has been inequality and oppression arising out of economic and social class. That itself gave rise to various jostling conceptualisations and priorities.

The key contrast in interpretations of class remains the tension between Marxist and Weberian analyses. The former posits class as based on ownership and control of capital, in the sense of the key means of production. It is thus seen as an objective relation of differential power and privilege, which may or may not correspond to class consciousness, or to corresponding cultures, identities, and styles of life. Whilst Weber also rooted class in economic position, he did so in terms of place in the markets for labour and goods, not in relations of production. He famously distinguished class from other dimensions of stratification: status (i.e. varying levels of cultural prestige) and power in ruling hierarchies. Empirical sociology has been dominated by Weberian conceptualisations in terms of market position, identity, and lifestyle (notably Goldthorpe et al. 1980), which are more susceptible to measurement. An influential recent sophisticated example is Savage 2015, which adds in an admixture of Bourdieu's analysis of class and human capital (Riley 2017 is a cogent critique of Bourdieu's analysis).

The empirical Weberian accounts provide useful pictures of shifting lifestyles, prestige rankings, and consumption patterns over time and space, yielding valuable insights into the dynamics of capitalist societies. However, the Marxist conceptualisation of dominance conferred by ownership and control of industrial and financial capital provides the root cause explanation of inequality. In these terms, the key split is between (some of) the top and the bottom levels of the class schema described by empirical studies:

> We demonstrate the existence of an 'elite', whose wealth separates them from an established middle class, as well as a class of technical experts and a class of 'new affluent' workers. We also show that at the lower levels of the class structure, alongside an ageing traditional working class, there is a 'precariat' characterised by very low levels of capital, and a group of emergent service workers.
>
> *(Savage et al. 2013)*

These finely observed gradations in the middle help explain many important phenomena such as voting and consumption behaviour. However, the competition for material and cultural resources amongst the middle and lower layers disguises the basic power difference among all of them, and the top sections of the elite who control the commanding heights of economy and society.

The distracting effect of small differences in class position and culture is one way that compartmentalisation of inequality enables the economically powerful and privileged 1% to divide and rule. But this is magnified hugely by the many other dimensions of injustice and oppression which – although present throughout history – have become more apparent sites of conflict since the 1960s. These include gender, ethnicity, generation, sexuality, religion, and physical disability. All of these have been the focus of movements to achieve equality, especially since the 1960s, largely spearheaded by the groups themselves in campaigns for justice and autonomy. Critical criminologists have championed these advances in human emancipation and social justice, ever since the emergence of a self-conscious critical criminology during the 1960s (van Swaaningen 1997; DeKeseredy 2010; DeKeseredy and Dragiewicz 2017), and have played a crucial role through research and activism.

Considerable advances have been achieved on all these issues, in law, policy, and public support. In the UK, these culminated in the 2010 Equality Act, which amalgamated 40 years of legislation seeking to promote 'a more fair and equal society', establishing an Equality and Human Rights Commission to monitor and enforce the law (www.equalityhumanrights.com/en/equality-act-2010/what-equality-act). A variety of specified 'protected characteristics' are listed, which the Act and Commission are mandated to safeguard against discrimination. These are: age, disability, gender reassignment, marriage and civil partnership, pregnancy and maternity, race, religion or belief, sex, and sexual orientation. Most of these had been the subject of specific legislation since 1970. The 2010 Act was the last significant achievement of the outgoing Labour government, but the Coalition and Conservative governments since then have added significant steps. Notable amongst them has been the establishment of gay marriage (in England and Wales by the 2013 Marriage Act, and subsequently throughout the UK).

Progress on all these dimensions of injustice has been paralleled throughout the Western world. In 2019 the US House of Representatives passed the Equality Act to add the protection of a similar range of characteristics to existing civil rights legislation. However, its fate in the Republican-dominated Senate is unlikely to be favourable. Indeed, with the US Supreme Court having a clear conservative majority following the appointment of two judges nominated by Donald Trump, the state of play in the long-running culture wars seems to have shifted towards the fundamentalist religious Right. Such achievements as legal abortion and the civil rights advances of the 1960s are under threat. This is, of course, subject to vigorous contestation from liberals and the Left.

Social democrats are and have been crucial champions of the emancipatory movements and achievements since the 1960s. Although major changes occurred during the neoliberal era, for the most part they were opposed by conservative politicians until the twenty-first century. It is important to stress, however, that despite the massive strides towards emancipation and justice achieved, there is a highly significant absence. Inequalities of class (in the Weberian and *a fortiori* the Marxist senses) dropped out of the mainstream political picture, whether under

144 Conclusion

conservative or 'third way' social democratic governments. Whilst the latter did continue to emphasise a fight against poverty, especially amongst children, this was attenuated by their enthusiastic espousal of conditionality in welfare, as they accepted the neoliberal resuscitation of notions of undeserving claimants (Levitas 2005; Lansley and Mack 2015; Armstrong 2017).

The marginalisation of class, in mainstream political discourse but also in left and liberal scholarship too, has only advantaged the very powerful. Class inequality is a bleeding wound cutting across many of the other types of injustice and oppression. This has become ever more apparent as austerity policies were adopted after 2010 by conservative governments, under the guise of dealing with the fallout from the 2007/8 financial crisis. This is brought out dramatically by the experience of disabled people (Ryan 2019), and how women and ethnic minorities have suffered most from cuts in public expenditure (Sanders and Shorrocks 2019). These inequalities are mutually reinforcing, BAME women suffering the most under austerity (ibid.). The complex interactions among different forms of deprivation and disadvantage are captured by the concept of intersectionality (Crenshaw 1991; Collins and Bilge 2016; Collins 2019). All the various dimensions of disadvantage cut across each other. A rich white, straight woman is in a very different position from a poor one. But so too is a rich white woman from a rich white man . . . and so on. Each aspect has the capacity to affect power and life chances for good or ill. Nonetheless, stressing this also obscures the way that the political economy of neoliberalism has adversely affected the majority of people of all kinds: male/female, black/white, young/old, gay/straight, and so on.

Until very recently, class largely dropped out of the picture of mainstream political argument. Focussing on a miscellany of movements perpetuated this forgetting, which benefitted the top layers of the various intersectional hierarchies. The virtue of the social democratic tradition is that, by its emphasis on the essential entitlement of people to equal concern and respect, it potentially encompasses all forms of oppression as departures from justice, liberty, and democracy, which can only be fully pursued together.

Financialisation and commercialisation of everyday culture

The term 'financialisation' signifies an 'increasing role of financial motives, financial markets, financial actors and financial institutions in the operation of the domestic and international markets' (Epstein 2005; Blakeley 2019 p. 11). This captures the macroeconomic transformation that has occurred worldwide since the 1970s. What this section is concerned with is the ramifications for the moral economy of everyday life. Financialisation oiled the wheels of the cultural change from reciprocal to egoistic individualisation, a restricted view of compassion, and the eclipse of concern with class. It signifies a commercialisation of aspiration and culture, a transformation of aspirations, dreams, and everyday reality. The pursuit of the good has been materialised into the consumerist pursuit of goods, a seductive, dazzling

Conclusion **145**

invitation to acquire possessions and pleasurable experiences way beyond ancient notions of bread and circuses (Hall et al. 2020). But with the same effect: distracting from the power and privileges of the elite who sedate the mass of the population with baubles.

Financialisation is the essential means of this transformation. Since the 1970s the real wages of workers have remained largely static, as discussed in Chapter 1. The legitimacy of neoliberalism was maintained by a series of financial strategies borrowing against the future: inflation, public debt, and expanding private debt. The latter was facilitated by financial instruments allowing greater mass borrowing to maintain, indeed enhance, standards of consumption. These included hire purchase, credit cards, privatisation of public utilities in which people were invited into stock ownership, easier mortgages to permit mass home ownership, and a shift of the risk of pensions from state and corporations to the public. Such devices propped up the consumerist boom, premised on a 'live now, pay later' ethic.

Even more significantly, they changed the perspective of the public at large into a consciousness of themselves as mini-entrepreneurs and rentiers. Instead of seeing the very rich as stealing public goods for self-enrichment, people were invited to see themselves as wealthy – but not yet. In the words of Del Boy in the quintessential 1980s comedy series *Only Fools and Horses*, 'this time next year we'll be millionaires'.

A token of this intended shift to a property-owning democracy, albeit an increasingly unequal one, is the way that news bulletins since the 1980s have come to incorporate business and financial reports. The stock market reports come alongside the sports results. In the UK this transition to a financialised society had its roots in the mid-1950s, as the social democratic consensus morphed into the 'never had it so good' era of consumer affluence. It was in 1955 that the Eurodollar market began, when a major high-street bank, the Midland, fobbed off the Bank of England's attempt to restrict its taking deposits denominated in US dollars (Blakeley 2019 pp. 40–41). Ultimately, this crack in the Bretton Woods structure led to the collapse of the whole edifice in the 1970s, ushering in neoliberal hegemony. Not coincidentally, 1955 was also the year that commercial television launched in the UK, with the ratings for many years dominated by consumerist ITV quiz shows such as 'Double Your Money'. And 1955 also marked the onset of the unremitting rise in recorded crime of the next four decades. As Margaret Thatcher intended, the result has been a transformation of dreams into the bottom line of material wealth. The vice of acquisitiveness transmuted into the virtue of aspiration, of the basest kind.

The problem of agency

This book has argued that what once was an ideal which worked, social democracy, was wrecked during the 1970s and displaced by neoliberal hegemony. This hugely benefitted the commercial elite who instigated many of the problems undermining

146 Conclusion

social democracy, such as unregulated, destabilising financial flows. Whilst inequality and insecurity rose for most people, this was disguised by debt-based economic and cultural diversions.

The 2007/8 financial crash exposed the frail foundations of neoliberal political economy, but the perpetrators were shielded by 'socialism for the banks', with a punitive austerity for everyone else. The anger this created was projected on to a variety of scapegoats: over-spending social democratic governments, the undeserving poor, migrants, ethnic minorities, cosmopolitan liberal elites. Eventually this produced the political upheavals of 2016: the EU referendum leave vote, the election of Donald Trump, and the emergence of populist (bordering on fascist) leaders, in a growing number of countries.

It has been increasingly evident for many years that the world confronted the Rosa Luxemburg choice: socialism or barbarism. In addition to (and largely arising from) the economic trends towards gross inequality and insecurity, there lurked the ever more visible and terrifying spectres of climate change, pandemics, and fears about the threats of artificial intelligence (AI). It became 'easier to imagine the end of the world than the end of capitalism' (Fisher 2009 Chap.1). As I am writing these words, in imposed isolation because of the coronavirus pandemic, these considerable concerns have been wrapped up in a pervasive and ubiquitous sense of apocalypse now, that humanity is on the precipice of existential risks to its future (Ord 2020).

This chapter has outlined the various blocks to any resuscitation of the pursuit of social democratic values, constituted by the political and moral economy of neoliberalism: financialised globalisation, egoistic individualism, compassion limited to those who are 'one of us', the diffusion of concerns about class injustice and oppression into a variety of specific struggles, the commercialisation not only of everyday life but of dreams, aspirations – the very soul of being human.

Ways to combat each of these have been suggested, and there are a growing number of plausible agendas for what is to be done. Corbyn lost the 2019 British general election badly, yielding the Tories a substantial majority, with fateful consequences for all who have lost out over the decade of Conservative austerity (Toynbee and Walker 2020). Nonetheless, the platform on which Labour stood embodied a social democratic ethos, offering prescriptions for tackling the massive problems people face.

Much the same can be said of the policy agenda on which the self-labelled democratic socialist Bernie Sanders ran for the 2020 US presidential election. This aimed to establish 'a 21st Century Economic Bill of Rights that guarantees all of our people the right to the basic necessities of life – and guarantees those rights regardless of Americans' income, race, religion, gender, country of origin or sexual orientation (https://berniesanders.com/issues/). Sanders has been beaten in the primaries by former Vice President Joe Biden, with a track record to the right of the past two Democrat presidents, Bill Clinton and Barack Obama (Marcetic 2020). His chances of winning against Trump are at best evens, but in any event the 2020 presidential election certainly seems unlikely to be a victory

Conclusion **147**

for social democracy, despite hopes created by the rise of a considerable movement supporting it, paralleling similar developments in the UK (Murray 2019; Aronoff et al. 2020).

The failure of the resurgent social democratic left to achieve electoral success, despite programmes aimed at addressing the interests of the many, not the few (in Corbyn's slogan), is deeply disappointing for those who share the analysis of this book that social democracy is the only alternative to barbarism. I would argue that what needs to be tackled is not so much assembling a new set of specific solutions – the programmes of both Corbyn and Sanders, and indeed Elizabeth Warren who was knocked out of the Democratic leadership race in early 2020 – offer that in spades. Empirical evidence suggests that a majority of people on both sides of the Atlantic view the key elements of social democracy favourably (Kenworthy 2014; Hindmoor 2018). But when these are assembled under a package labelled socialist, decades of media and politicians rubbishing the "S' word come to the fore, at least to date (Nichols 2015; Manwaring and Kennedy 2017).

As Marx wrote nearly two centuries ago in his *Theses on Feuerbach*, 'The philosophers have only interpreted the world, in various ways. The point, however, is to change it'. The crucial issue to confront is the perennial puzzle for the Left, the problem of agency. In Marx's own analysis, the problem would be solved by changes in political economy and social relations as capitalism developed, producing its own 'gravediggers'. The key elements of these processes were: a) the insecurity and impoverishment inherent in the trade and financial cycles of capitalism, producing regular immiseration, and b) the nature of productive relations under the mass production, 'Fordist' phase of capitalism, assembling masses of workers into identical conditions of alienation and exploitation, facilitating a sense of solidarity. The essence of revisionist social democracy, from Bernstein to Crosland, was that Marx's anticipations were refuted by the development of capitalism since the late nineteenth century (in the global North at any rate). The basic issues of inequality, poverty, and instability had not and could not be solved by undiluted capitalism, but the system was being transformed into a mixed economy that considerably improved the lot of most people. This meant that there are no inevitable processes producing the 'gravediggers' of capitalism. Making the majority of the population agents of their own liberation is an uphill struggle for hearts and minds, conducted by social democrats on hostile terrain, without guarantees (Hall 1996; Gilroy et al. 2000; Burczak et al. 2018). It has been and remains an uphill – often Sisyphean – struggle for two major reasons. First, there are psychodynamic processes that facilitate the receptiveness of the disadvantaged to ideologies reproducing their subjugation. Second, the mass media and other influences on mass consciousness remain largely dominated by capitalist interests.

The psychodynamics of ressentiment

In some ways the message of right-wing nostrums is easier to sell at a cognitive level. The balanced budget and 'no magic money tree' ideas, which conservatives

148 Conclusion

use to justify austerity as a way out of recession, appeal to the common experience of household budgeting. Thatcher, Reagan, Cameron, and leaders used these homely analogies adroitly. The arguments of Keynesian and Modern Monetary Theory assert the radical difference facing governments that can create their own money supply and are harder to grasp (Wray 2017; Mazzucato 2018; Kelton 2020). In the field of crime policy, punitive responses appeal immediately to the ancient sense of *lex talionis* as raw retribution for pain inflicted by another. The search for understanding causes and thus preventing future harms requires some standing back and the challenge of empathising with those who have done wrong.

Nonetheless, the historically widespread support for economic and social policies that safeguard economic and political elites above all cannot be explained only by cognitive simplicity. The Frankfurt School grappled in the 1930s to understand the sources of the fascism that ultimately exiled them and engulfed the world. Prominent amongst these was Erich Fromm, who specifically tackled the issue of crime and popular punitiveness, deploying a combination of political economy and psychoanalysis (Fromm 1930/2000a, 1931/2000b; Anderson 1998; Anderson and Quinney 2000; Cheliotis 2013).

Fromm's essays recognised the reality that conventionally defined crime does indeed harm vulnerable victims. He also accepted that socio-economic pressures lead some deprived people to commit crimes, especially when times are hard. But to explain why only some resort to harming others, he postulates psychodynamic processes separating them from their fellows in the same plight. Whilst conventional everyday crimes are indeed a problem, the hatred levelled at the offender (but not the elites who direct the economic system leading to the crimes) is excessive and partly misdirected. The roots of this, Fromm argues, lie in sado-masochistic psychic processes. The aggressive energy stoked by the suffering of the masses is directed inwards, rather than at the powerful father figures of the dominant elites. It is then projected outwards with even greater ferocity against scapegoats lower in the pecking order: convicted criminals, but also ethnic and other minorities, and foreigners, especially immigrants. The deep psychodynamic sources of populist punitiveness and authoritarianism certainly make tackling it challenging, especially when it is further fuelled by misinformation from a corporate-dominated mass media.

The media

The mass media–shaping of public debate constitutes perhaps the most formidable barrier to the election of social democratic governments, especially in the UK and USA. The relationship between mass media representations and public opinion is a complex, interactive process. Research on media effects has always questioned the 'hypodermic syringe' model implied in simple denunciations of the media as propaganda (or 'fake news'). Since Lazarsfeld's development in the 1940s of the two-step model of communications, it has been accepted that mass media content is filtered by opinion leaders and other aspects of the social contexts in which they are received. More recently, with the increasing dominance of social

Conclusion **149**

media, the idea of direct 'one step' impact has returned. This is reinforced by the hugely sophisticated targeting of messages to specific population sectors, facilitated by algorithmic mining of data gathered by social media usage, a key aspect of 'surveillance capitalism' (Zuboff 2019). The covert political influence of firms like Cambridge Analytica has been uncovered by *The Observer*'s Carole Cadwalladr and other investigative journalists, revealing huge threats of the subversion of democracy (www.theguardian.com/uk-news/2019/jul/20/the-great-hack-cambridge-ana lytica-scandal-facebook-netflix; www.theguardian.com/uk-news/2020/jan/04/cam bridge-analytica-data-leak-global-election-manipulation). Nonetheless, the mediating role of global opinion leaders such as celebrities, in some forms of social media, notably Twitter, suggests the two- (or more) step model remains pertinent. And this all reminds us of the continuing relevance of McLuhan's maxim that 'the medium is the message' (McLuhan 1967). The various forms of media not only convey 'messages', but also diverse sensory effects that may reinforce or under-cut the content of texts.

These health warnings about the complex dialectics among media content, forms, and effects should not detract from what is so obvious as to verge on the banal. From the standpoint of any form of socialism, the mass media in all capitalist societies operate as the propaganda arm of the corporate elite. They are a large part of the explanation of the greater electoral success of conservative parties over the past two centuries (apart from in Scandinavia). The evidence for this is meticulously presented in Herman and Chomsky's powerful analysis of the media 'manufacturing consent' (Herman and Chomsky 2002). The thesis is amply confirmed by numerous studies, many focussing on the presentation of 'law and order' (Cohen 1972; Cohen and Young 1973; Glasgow Media Group 1976, 1980, 1982; Chibnall 1977; Hall et al. 1978; Chomsky 2008; Philo 2017; Basu 2018; Basu et al. 2018; Edwards and Cromwell 2018; Bowling et al. 2019 Chap. 10).

This is largely a consequence of the political economy of media organisations, which varies somewhat among different societies over space and time. In the countries most marked by neoliberalism (primarily the USA, UK, and Australia), almost all mass media are owned and controlled by large globalised corporations, with a direct interest in protecting and reproducing the political and moral economy within which they flourish. They also depend for their profitability on the advertising they carry for other multinational commercial behemoths. In the UK, for example, just over 90% of national newspaper circulation is accounted for by four media conglomerates (Media Reform Coalition 2019 Table 3), with Rupert Murdoch's News UK itself accounting for 36.35%. The BBC remains dominant in terrestrial TV, with 31% viewing share compared with 23% for ITV, 10% for Channel 4, and 9% for Sky (ibid. Figure 2). The BBC also leads on radio listening with 51.7% audience share compared with 45.7% for all commercial stations (ibid. Figure 3). The BBC has been under pressure to compete with its commercial rivals ever since the dawn of neoliberalism, and this has become a serious threat to its financing by license fee under recent Conservative governments.

150 Conclusion

The overwhelming majority of newspapers in terms of ownership and readership are openly Conservative supporting and indeed clearly inclined towards the Tory right wing. The exceptions are *The Mirror, I,* and *The Guardian,* primarily leaning towards the right or centre of the Labour Party (since the Liberal Democrats joined the Conservative-led Coalition in 2010). The commercial TV channels do not exhibit explicit party political support, but the very nature of their dependence on regular advertising means they present a consumerist lifestyle. Commercial talk radio is largely dominated by right-wing chat and phone-in hosts.

Content analysis of BBC news and documentaries suggests a generally middle of the road perspective, memorably summed up by Stuart Hall (referring to its lunchtime radio news programme) as 'a world at one with itself' (Hall 1973). The plain result of all this is that (despite persistent right-wing claims of liberal or Left bias), even mild social democratic viewpoints get short shrift. This is shown by studies of the negative coverage given Jeremy Corbyn as Labour leader from the time of his election in 2015 (Cammaerts et al. 2016; Bassett 2019).

Media power in the criminal justice field has been illustrated many times. Most people derive their 'knowledge' of crime and criminal justice from the media rather than direct or even vicarious experience, so media (mis)representations are significant in framing policy discourse (Greer and Reiner 2012). Media crime stories overwhelmingly reflect a 'law and order' perspective (ibid.).

More broadly, the media are a significant factor in explaining a major mystery. The economic and financial collapse since 2007/8 might have been taken as discrediting the neoliberal model. Instead, its savagely deflationary prescriptions for dealing with the sovereign debt and deficit crises (resulting *inter alia* from governmental support for banking) remain the orthodoxy guiding government policy. This zombie neoliberalism survives largely because most of the media supported it (Basu 2018). But media power has limits.

The hold of zombie neoliberalism is vulnerable in view of the widespread harms perpetrated by the austerity policies of Conservative-led governments since 2010. So far, however, aided and abetted by gung ho media cheerleading, the anger generated by cuts has been displaced onto a series of scapegoats, such as welfare recipients, migrants, and the EU.

Social democratic governments have been elected, despite this dominance of global media corporations supporting conservatism. Partly this has been in countries, notably Scandinavia, where the political economy of the media is less neoliberal. In the UK, before the advent of neoliberalism the media world was more diverse. Until 1964 there was an explicitly socialist mass circulation newspaper, *The Daily Herald,* in which the Trades Union Congress (TUC) had an ownership share. In 1964 it was renamed as *The Sun* and sold to Rupert Murdoch in 1969. He transformed it into the best-selling tabloid in Britain, with an aggressively right-wing populist stance. *The Mirror* has been the only consistently Labour-supporting national newspaper, since the 1945 general election. Until the late 1960s, it was the best-selling newspaper but has since been overtaken by *The Sun,* coinciding with the advent of neoliberalism. The only Labour government to be elected since then, led by Tony Blair, assiduously sought (and got) the support of Murdoch, to whom the transmogrification into New Labour made it an acceptable choice.

The right-wing character of the media in neoliberal countries presents a fortified line against the election of a socialist government. It is unlikely to be successfully attacked head on, but perhaps it could be circumvented, like the supposedly impregnable Maginot Line in 1940. This would require stressing the potential widespread gains to most people from a fairer and more democratic political economy. It is also vital to counter some of the crucial myths deployed against Labour, notably its fiscal irresponsibility. So far, Labour leaders have failed to attempt this.

Public opinion

Opinion polls regularly portray populist punitiveness (Pratt 2006), suggesting that policing and punishment have become too liberal, and advocating tougher sentencing. This coexists with more nuanced views, however. When details of cases are given to people, their ideas about appropriate sentences are not out of line with judicial practice (Hough and Roberts 2017). Surveys also record considerable public support for social causation explanations, alongside the headline punitiveness, which are often based on lack of accurate information about the pattern of crime, especially nationally, and of sentencing practice.

More broadly, however, there is evidence that public attitudes are becoming more deeply shaped by the neoliberal hegemony of recent decades, as indicated by the British Social Attitudes Surveys cited earlier. Fifty years ago, at the dawn of neoliberal hegemony, Rawls's theory of justice assumed plausibly as a premise that popular decision-making was strongly risk averse, governed by the 'mini-max' principle of minimising the possibility of the worst possible outcome (Rawls 1971 Chap. III, Section 26). But this has come to be replaced by cultural adulation of risk-takers and 'edgework'. The meaning of 'security' has shifted from a primary focus on social welfare to crime control and terrorism. Surveys still suggest some ambivalence, however. In Britain there remains considerable support for the National Health Service, for example, and a belief that inequality is too great – although there is resistance to higher taxation for these purposes. The post-crash furore about bankers' bonuses indicated some potential for arousing popular sentiment in favour of greater social justice, although this was soon diverted onto the EU, welfare recipients, and migrants.

The 2007/8 crisis triggered some temporary self-questioning even by the erstwhile bastions of belief in unfettered economic and financial globalisation.

> 'Banks are global in life but national in death', opined Mervyn King, then Governor of the Bank of England.
> *(www.ft.com/content/3ae6432c-2307-11e9-b20d-5376ca5216eb)*

> 'I discovered a flaw in the model', declared Alan Greenspan, then Chair of the Federal Reserve, and a devotee of the libertarian Ayn Rand.
> *(www.ft.com/content/aee9e3a2-a11f-11dd-82fd-000077b07658)*

152 Conclusion

The banks were the first to rediscover the merits of Keynesian public spending in 2008 – for themselves as beneficiaries!

There developed hot pursuit of ways of regulating financial flows and excessive risk-taking. Fundamental assumptions of corporate and financial law were placed under the microscope: who is the lender of last resort? What are the perils of limited liability? Should a Tobin tax be introduced? Can the threat of capital flight be challenged? Global corporations depend upon special legal rules and national support structures which could and should be changed, as radical critics had long argued (Bakan 2005; Tombs and Whyte 2015). The growth of UK Uncut, the international Occupy, and other fair tax and anti-globalisation movements suggested increasing space for arguments about fairness. The stock of Keynes, and even of Marx, rose (Skidelsky 2010; Eagleton 2011; Backhouse and Bateman 2011). There has been a powerful and continuing growth of critiques of neoliberal arguments in other disciplines, notably economics and political science.

There has been little echo in criminology of these broader critiques of neo-liberalism (apart from Hall et al. 2008; Hall 2012; Hall and Winlow 2015; Currie 2016; DeKeseredy and Currie 2019). The main exceptions have been primarily in the political economy of punishment (Cavadino and Dignan 2006; Lacey 2008; Wacquant 2009; Bell 2011; Melossi et al. 2018).

This book argues for the need to bring political economy *and* ethical critique back in! Critical work in recent years has largely focussed on cultural analysis, or particularistic interventions into specific issues (of huge value), but within an assumption of the impossibility of attacking fundamental causes.

Nearly 30 years ago, Stan Cohen concluded his seminal book on social control with a parable pointing to a perpetual dilemma:

> A fisherman sees a body floating down stream, and jumps in to rescue it. The same happens a few minutes later, and then again, and again. Finally, the fisherman ignores the tenth body and starts running upstream. "Why aren't you rescuing that poor man?" shouts an observer. The fisherman replies that he's going to find out how to stop these poor people getting pushed into the water in the first place.
>
> *(Cohen 1985 p. 236)*

Critical criminology must work on both levels: piecemeal intervention *and* political economy addressing root causes. The fundamental lesson of historical experience and empirical evidence is: 'No justice, no peace'.

The chink of ambivalence in popular attitudes to criminal justice issues, and economic/social matters more generally, suggests that anxieties might be tapped to support an analysis of these problems in terms of fundamental causes, as in the heyday of social democracy. But as in the 1940s, this probably requires a massive jolt towards realising the human interdependence that underlies reciprocal, not egoistic, individualism – a functional equivalent of the drawing together stimulated by war.

From disaster capitalism to disaster socialism: twenty-first century existential problems

Historical experience suggests that right-wing and free market forces are much more adept than the Left at swiftly seizing advantage of economic, social, and natural shocks and crises. This has aptly been named 'disaster capitalism' (Klein 2007). A plethora of examples exist of how Western corporations are faster than vultures to feed off the profit opportunities in collapsing societies (ibid., Klein 2018; Lowenstein 2015). 'Never let a serious crisis go to waste', as Obama's then Chief of Staff Rahm Emanuel put it in 2008, though it was the neoliberals who implemented his advice (Mirowski 2014). As Jonathan Swift wrote in 1710, 'False-hood flies, and the Truth comes limping after it'. There are many fundamental reasons why this is the usual pattern. It is easier for small but very powerful elites to exert their interests rapidly, and they enjoy the inestimable advantage of controlling the communications media.

In the past decade, Gramsci's epigrammatic definition of 'crisis' has frequently been quoted: 'The crisis consists precisely in the fact that the old is dying and the new cannot be born' (Gramsci 1930/1971 pp. 275–276). A crisis opens up possibilities, making the future especially unpredictable and rife for change – for better or worse. 'A crisis can conclude well or badly, but the point is that its outcome is fundamentally uncertain. To experience a crisis is to inhabit a world that is temporarily up for grabs', as William Davies puts it (www.theguardian.com/commentisfree/2020/mar/24/coronavirus-crisis-change-world-financial-global-capitalism).

The intensity and global scale of the now-raging coronavirus pandemic could well shake up the fundamentals of the dominant political and moral economy:

> The immediacy of this visceral, mortal threat makes this moment feel less like 2008 or the 1970s and more like the other iconic crisis in our collective imagination – 1945. Matters of life and death occasion more drastic shifts in policy than economic indicators ever can. . . . Rather than view this as a crisis of capitalism, it might better be understood as the sort of world-making event that allows for new economic and intellectual beginnings.
>
> *(ibid.)*

Compounding the tragic loss of life and suffering stemming from the disease itself, the economic consequences of the global shutdowns seem to already be dwarfing not only the 2008 financial crisis, but the 1929 Wall Street Crash and ensuing Great Depression. The world faces a new Greater Depression, beyond the scale even of the one that led to the massive killing fields of World War II (www.project-syndi cate.org/commentary/coronavirus-greater-great-depression-by-nouriel-roubini-2020-03).

The existential threats which have been concretised by the coronavirus pandemic are the outcome of a series of interlocking spectres that have haunted the world for decades (Ord 2020). They may yet turn out differently from the repeated

154 Conclusion

triumphs of disaster capitalism. This is because the scale of the health and economic crisis is forcing neoliberal governments into massive intervention into economy and society, analogous to the total mobilisation of wartime. Chancellor of the Exchequer Rishi Sunak announced a series of support steps 'on a scale unimaginable only a few weeks ago. . . . This is not a time for ideology and orthodoxy, this is a time to be bold – a time for courage'. The avid Churchill fan, Prime Minister Boris Johnson, explicitly likened it to the war effort: 'We must act like any wartime government and do whatever it takes to support our economy. . . . This enemy can be deadly, but it is also beatable' (www.theguardian.com/uk-news/2020/mar/17/rishi-sunak-pledges-350bn-to-tackle-coronavirus-impact).

There has been a rapid succession of breathtaking steps, leading the current right-wing UK government ever further away from the neoliberal holy grail they have pursued for nearly half a century. 'The last vestiges of Thatcherite individualism are being torched. Social partnership is back with a vengeance', argues Will Hutton (www.theguardian.com/commentisfree/2020/mar/22/rishi-sunak-wartime-finance-for-wartime-economic-conditions-coronavirus). Much more will follow the rescue finance announced recently under the rubric 'whatever it takes':

> It is wartime finance for wartime economic conditions. Over and above the multiple bailout packages currently being negotiated will come state direction and manufacture of vaccines, key medical products, respirators, and the takeover of private hospitals. Key workers – in the NHS, police, transport and food supply chain – will have to be marshalled in their millions. . . . Rationing of key foodstuffs will need to be imposed. The only way to head off a full-scale collapse of sterling and protracted economic depression will be to defer Brexit.
>
> *(ibid.)*

Hutton and several others have raised the possibility of a wartime coalition analogous to the one formed in 1940.

The changes away from neoliberalism that are being forced by the pandemic emergency go way beyond political economy. They transform everyday interactions, and arguably the moral economy of egoistic individualism itself, towards greater reciprocity and solidarity. On the other hand, there have been disturbing (almost unbelievable) reports from police of vandalism and other attacks on emergency vehicles and staff (www.theguardian.com/uk-news/2020/mar/24/uk-police-chiefs-coronavirus-could-bring-out-worst-in-humanity).

It is hard to quantify what's actually happening, but stories of anti-social behavior seem to be outstripped by accounts of local initiatives creating community support and neighbourhood co-operative mutual aid groups:

> Tens of thousands of people have joined community efforts to look after the most vulnerable in society by volunteering to pick up shopping, deliver medicine and even offer music lessons to defeat boredom. Despite some

concerns raised over the safeguarding of the elderly, by (March 16), more than 720 local mutual aid groups had been set up by citizens from Wythenshawe to Woking, aimed at helping neighbours in self-isolation and boosting morale.

(www.theguardian.com/society/2020/mar/16/community-aid-groups-set-up-across-uk-amid-coronavirus-crisis)

These are often co-ordinated virtually, via social media such as Facebook or What's App (www.theguardian.com/commentisfree/2020/mar/22/facebook-powerful-crisis-coronavirus-communities-online).

Similar changes are happening in countries around the world, including the other bastions of neoliberalism, the USA (though dragged back by Trump) and Australia. The change in mood is illustrated by almost unbelievable *volte face* comments in the citadels of right-wing thought:

There is a growing consensus – in rhetoric, at least – that free-market capitalism is incapable of addressing this national emergency. ITV's political editor, Robert Peston, writes in the Spectator [a right-wing weekly] demanding Boris Johnson "borrow from Corbyn's playbook to prevent a coronavirus crash"; ConservativeHome demands the government "tear up the rulebook – we need Big State Government on a scale unknown in modern times"; whilst a former Tory minister calls for the temporary nationalisation of any troubled business.

(www.theguardian.com/commentisfree/2020/mar/18/coronavirus-exposed-extent-uk-social-crisis?)

Despite current UK government policy coming to resemble Labour's electorally rejected Manifesto more than its own, this is far from any permanent or solid conversion to social democratic political or moral economy, except 'for the duration' (in the wartime phrase). Nonetheless, it does signify a build-up of plausibility for Labour's nostrums, and those of Democratic Socialists in the USA.

This faith in a possible better future, arising out of the ashes of death and destruction (as in 1945), is enhanced when we consider that the coronavirus pandemic does not stand alone as an existential threat to human existence. The deadly impact of climate change is impending, unless current economic and social trends are rapidly reversed. Hopefully, most of the population now understands this, thanks to the valiant efforts of activists such as Greta Thunberg, Extinction Rebellion, and others (Klein 2014, 2019; Monbiot 2016, 2017; Raworth 2018), but little has been done as yet.

During the twenty-first century, there has developed a flourishing branch of critical criminology devoted to 'green criminology' (Brisman and South 2014; South and Brisman 2014; Sretesky et al. 2014; White and Heckenberg 2014; Nurse 2016; Lynch et al. 2017). Like critical criminology in general, green criminology is not bound by legal or state definitions of crime. It is concerned with expanding

156 Conclusion

the intellectual and policy horizon to the much broader harms threatening the global environment, including non-human beings (South and Beirne 2006; Beirne and South 2007; Beirne 2018). Probably the main stream in this rapidly expanding sub-discipline is the political economy of environmental harms, their sources, perpetrators, and the implications for global security and justice (Lynch 2019). This is well aligned to the thesis advanced here.

It is becoming clear that the profound existential threats of climate change and pandemics (complicated hugely by the growth of antibiotic resistance) are inter-related in aetiology and spread. All are largely rooted in the insecurities, inequalities, and injustices generated by neoliberal globalisation. Neoliberalism also makes their alleviation, let alone resolution, vastly more problematic. The unceasing drive for profits pushes relentless expansion of markets for natural resources into previously unexplored areas. It generates ever greater urbanisation, deforestation, and exploitation of new territories and species, releasing more toxic gases and novel viruses. As historian of pandemics Laura Spinney writes, controlling the

> animal-human interface is obviously important, but it shouldn't blind us to the bigger problem, which is those globalised industries. Economists use the term "tragedy of the commons" to describe a shared resource – common grazing land, say – that is spoiled by individuals acting in their own self-interest. . . . In the case of those industries, it would be more accurate to say that they have excluded the nearly 8 billion of us who depend on the commons from participating in their governance. Yet we are bearing the costs of their industrial exploitation, in the form of pandemic disease.
> *(www.theguardian.com/commentisfree/2020/mar/25/new-virus-china-covid-19-food-markets; Wallace 2016 Morens et al. 2020)*

The 'silent tsunami' of antibiotic resistance makes these threats vastly greater. England's former Chief Medical Officer, Dame Sally Davies, called for an Extinction Rebellion wave of protest to alert the public to the dangers (www. theguardian.com/society/2019/apr/29/antibiotic-resistance-as-big-threat-climate-change-chief-medic-sally-davies). Much of the problem is rooted in the perverse incentives created by leaving research to private pharmaceutical corporations. The development of the drugs needed by public health often provides smaller profits than those for less serious conditions that affect wealthier people using private medicine. Socialising the pharmaceutical industry is the only effective solution. 'Nationalised or state-run "utility" drug companies may be the only answer to the lack of investment in new antibiotics, former banker and superbug tsar Lord Jim O'Neill has suggested. The drastic measure would be intended to ensure that the development and production of new antibiotics were not at the mercy of capitalist market forces – which may seem at odds with O'Neill's background as a chief economist at global banking giant Goldman Sachs. 'It's what happened in finance in the end. If you're not going to do it yourself, we're going to turn certain parts of

Conclusion **157**

your business into being a utility' (www.theguardian.com/business/2019/mar/27/nationalised-drug-companies-may-be-needed-to-fix-antibiotics-market).

Ironically, one of the few positive developments against these health risks has come from an area often portrayed as another existential threat, the development of artificial intelligence (AI) (Bridel 2018; Wark 2019; Ord 2020 Chap. 5). AI has been used successfully to develop new antibiotics (www.theguardian.com/society/2020/feb/20/antibiotic-that-kills-drug-resistant-bacteria-discovered-through-ai). Nonetheless, the debate has been captured largely by more dystopian scenarios. These depict AI as developing an interest in its own autonomy and perhaps domination (fictionalised in *Westworld, Blade Runner*); or eroding democracy through sophisticated surveillance and targeted propaganda (Zuboff 2019; Wylie 2019; Kaiser 2019; Foroohar 2019); or displacing not only unskilled labour but also the professions, and even the knowledge industries themselves (Susskind and Susskind 2017; Susskind 2020).

Against the dystopian forebodings about the development of technology and AI, some have argued that they offer possibilities of finally realising a benign social democratic future (Mason 2015, 2019; Bregman 2018; Bastani 2019; Phillips and Rozworski 2019). In these visions, the abundance created by machines is a necessary condition for distributive justice – to each according to their need. It could also reduce the pressure to labour, allowing people to realise themselves in unalienated work and leisure, a hope shared by Marx, Engels, and Keynes (Marx and Engels 1844/2000; Keynes 1930/2010 Chap. 25; Skidelsky and Skidelsky 2012).

Moreover, the development of computing power and AI arguably has reached a stage in which an economy with central planning and public democratic control of its commanding heights becomes feasible. It would no longer be plagued by the Hayek problem of lack of information about granular local information, which markets are fine tuned to. Is this the same old unrealisable dream that failed in the USSR and many other places, as neoliberals argue? Not so. The massive global reach of multinational corporations demonstrates that it is now possible to govern complex enterprises co-ordinating resources and people on a vast scale:

> Planning exists all around us, and it clearly works, otherwise capitalists wouldn't make such comprehensive use of it. That's the simple message . . . that strikes at the heart of the dogma that "there is no alternative." Today, this Thatcherite slogan is already wilting under the pressure of its own success. It has created an anti-social compact: a world of rising inequality and widespread stagnation. But it is under attack from within. . . . From Amazon's warehouses to all major branches of industry, the capitalist system operates without price signals and markets.
>
> *(Phillips and Rozworski 2019 p. 242)*

As the subtitle of their book puts it: 'the world's biggest corporations are laying the foundations *for* socialism' (ibid.). A new 'fully automated luxury communism' beckons (Bastani 2019; Sunkara 2019; Gilbert 2020). There are, of course,

158 Conclusion

many significant matters that need to be addressed as part of these programmes, but they show that a better future is already feasible. Two crucial specific steps to facilitate it are: a) the now much touted idea of universal basic income, to smooth disruptions, as people are displaced from jobs, or have significantly reduced working hours (Mason 2015 Chap. 10; Standing 2017, 2020). The current state promises of substantial handouts to workers, threatened with impoverishment by the coronavirus-compelled business shutdowns, suggest this can no longer be the unthinkable it has been labelled as; and b) the second prerequisite is the socialisation of finance, converting it to an essential utility, not hoarded in privatised, offshored piggy banks for the 1% (Pettifor 2017; Blakeley 2019 Chap. 7). Again, the coronavirus pandemic has already forced the USA, UK, and other governments to measures of intervention that amount to virtual takeover as in wartime (www. theguardian.com/commentisfree/2020/mar/14/this-tory-budget-is-keynes-reborn-will-hutton; www.theguardian.com/commentisfree/2020/mar/22/rishi-sunak-wartime-finance-for-wartime-economic-conditions-coronavirus).

Perhaps the most significant development for putting this all together is the concept of the Green New Deal. The Green New Deal is a well-developed plan, built by far-sighted economists and climate change thinkers over many years (Raworth 2018; Klein 2019; Pettifor 2019). The New Economics Foundation and the Green New Deal Group first suggested it as a response to the financial crisis, publishing an influential 2008 pamphlet (https://greennewdealgroup.org/; https://neweco nomics.org/uploads/files/GND_2019_WEB.pdf). Since then, many groups have campaigned assiduously for the idea, which has become the cornerstone of social democratic parties' programmes around the world.

The essence of the concept echoes Keynes' solution to the Great Depression of the 1930s, anticipated in practice by Roosevelt's original New Deal. On the one hand, there are unemployed resources, especially labour; on the other hand, many human needs cannot be satisfied by the market because those who would benefit cannot pay. So for government to finance the use of idle resources to provide goods satisfying social needs has a multiplier effect – in the words of 1980s neoliberalism, it's a win-win. The workers employed on socially beneficial projects in turn spend their earnings on goods the manufacture of which gives work to others, and so on in a virtuous circle. The Green New Deal does the same. It brings together underused resources, notably workers who are far from idle but are under utilised in part-time, insecure, 'gig' jobs, or under threat of losing better jobs to machines; and puts them to work providing vital projects. The Green element comes in because these projects aim to convert the economy to one that uses fewer or no fossil fuels, and other environment-degrading processes. Many specific examples are given in the New Economics Foundation document cited earlier. But especially important are its proposals for radical change in the system for financing such works:

• Developing a wide-ranging package of other financial innovations and incentives to assemble the tens of billions of pounds that need to be spent.

Conclusion **159**

- Re-regulating the domestic financial system to ensure that the creation of money at low rates of interest is consistent with democratic aims, financial stability, social justice and environmental sustainability.
- Breaking up the discredited financial institutions that have needed so much public money to prop them up. . . . We are calling for the forced demerger of large banking and finance groups. Retail banking should be split from both corporate finance (merchant banking) and from securities dealing. . . .
- Finance will have to be returned to its role as servant, not master, of the global economy, to dealing prudently with people's savings and providing regular capital for productive and sustainable investment. Regulation of finance, and the restoration of policy autonomy to democratic government, implies the re-introduction of capital controls.
- Subjecting all derivative products and other exotic instruments to official inspection. . . . Anyone trying to circumvent the rules by going offshore or on to the internet should face the simple and effective sanction of 'negative enforcement' – their contracts would be made unenforceable in law. Ultimately our aim is an orderly downsizing of the financial sector in relation to the rest of the economy.
- Minimising corporate tax evasion by clamping down on tax havens and corporate financial reporting. Tax should be deducted at source (i.e. from the country from which payment is made) for all income paid to financial institutions in tax havens. International accounting rules should be changed to eliminate transfer mispricing by requiring corporations to report on a country by-country basis.

(https://neweconomics.org/2008/07/green-new-deal/)

The replacement of neoliberalism is not only possible, but happening on a daily basis in response to the disaster of the coronavirus pandemic (www.theguardian.com/world/2020/mar/31/how-will-the-world-emerge-from-the-coronavirus-crisis). The question for the future is whether the outcome will be more like what happened after World War I or after World War II. In 1918 governments promised 'a land fit for heroes'. Socialist revolutions occurred in several countries. Only the USSR revolution was lasting, and sadly it failed to produce anything that could be seen as congruent with social democratic values. There was a wave of labour militancy elsewhere, including the USA and UK. Nonetheless, in the Western world capitalism was restored, and indeed 'roared' during the twenties. The bubble burst with the 1929 Wall Street Crash, and the ensuing Great Depression. As anticipated by many thinkers (notably Keynes 1919), the failures of the post-World War I peace settlements culminated in the even more bloody and devastating conflict of World War II. The determination, shared by most people, not to repeat the interwar mistakes resulted in the social democratic consensus analysed in Chapter 1.

Once again today, the world order is being shaken to its roots. Will the result be a return to 'normality' as after the 2007/8 financial crisis? Or given the widespread

160 Conclusion

realisation of the problems of neoliberal capitalism, and the strengthening of state intervention to tackle the plague, will it be something more 'socialist'? The wheel is spinning, and there are potentially two contradictory outcomes. In the 1930s the discontent of the mass of the population resulted in many countries in fascism or *National* 'Socialism'. The trend towards this pole has been under way for several years, manifested in spiralling racism, xenophobia, nationalism, and protectionism, generally analysed as a rise of 'populism' and the radical right (Hall and Winlow 2017; Eatwell and Goodwin 2018; Mounk 2018; Snyder 2018; Norris and Inglehart 2019; Mudde 2019).

However, as argued earlier, there has also been resurgence on the Left. This has been much enhanced by the exercises in co-operation street by street during the coronavirus crisis. As I am writing these words in London on 26 March 2020, I have interrupted to go to my window for a nationally co-ordinated 'clap for the carers' in honour of the NHS and other vital emergency workers, who are risking life and limb pretty much 24/7 to save others. This spirit must prevail, or the result will be the barbarism Rosa Luxemburg warned against a century ago.

Over the rainbow: make love, not war

In September 1939, on the eve of six years of bloody conflict and the greatest crimes of all time, the poet W.H. Auden sat in a Manhattan bar. The poem he wrote – *September 1st. 1939* – remains resonant, and has been revived at many subsequent moments of existential despair, such as 9/11. It captures the anguish, fear, and uncertainty of our time of renewed existential threats to humanity:

> 'Uncertain and afraid
> As the clever hopes expire
> Of a low dishonest decade. . .
> The unmentionable odour of death
> Offends the September night'.

He concluded with words that still inspire, desperate hope against apparent hopelessness, the fragile flashes of scattered beacons of justice against an otherwise all-encompassing despair:

> 'Hunger allows no choice
> To the citizen or the police;
> We must love one another or die. . .
>
> Yet, dotted everywhere,
> Ironic points of light
> Flash out wherever the Just
> Exchange their messages: . . .

Beleaguered by the same
Negation and despair,
Show an affirming flame'.

Utopian perhaps. But as Oscar Wilde declared in his 'Soul of Man Under Socialism': 'A map of the world that does not include Utopia is not worth even glancing at, for it leaves out the one country at which Humanity is always landing. . . . Progress is the realisation of Utopias' (www.wilde-online.info/the-soul-of-man-under-socialism-page11.html).

References

Aronoff, K., Dreier, P. and Kazin, M. (Eds.) (2020) *We Own the Future: Democratic Socialism – American Style* New York: New Press.

Anderson, B. (1983) *Imagined Communities* London: Verso.

Anderson, K. (1998) 'The Young Erich Fromm's Contribution to Criminology' *Justice Quarterly* 16/4: 667–696.

Anderson, K. and Quinney, R. (Eds.) (2000) *Erich Fromm and Critical Criminology: Beyond the Punitive Society* Urbana: University of Illinois Press.

Armstrong, S. (2017) *The New Poverty* London: Verso.

Attlee, C. (1955) 'Foreword' to Sillitoe, P. *Cloak without Dagger* London: Cassell.

Backhouse, R. and Bateman, B. (2011) *Capitalist Revolutionary: John Maynard Keynes* Cambridge, MA: Harvard University Press.

Bakan, J. (2005) *The Corporation* London: Constable.

Bassett, L. (2019) 'Actually Existing Corbynism' *Renewal* 27/3: 37–45.

Bastani, A. (2019) *Fully Automated Luxury Communism* London: Verso.

Basu, L. (2018) *Media Amnesia* London: Pluto.

Basu, L., Schifferes, S. and Knowles, S. (Eds.) (2018) *The Media and Austerity* Abingdon: Routledge.

Beirne, P. (2018) *Murdering Animals* London: Macmillan.

Beirne, P. and South, N. (Eds.) (2007) *Issues in Green Criminology* Abingdon: Routledge.

Bell, E. (2011) *Criminal Justice and Neoliberalism* London: Macmillan.

Bellah, R., Madsen, R., Sullivan, W., Swidler, A. and Tipton, S. (1985/1996) *Habits of the Heart* Berkeley: University of California Press.

Bernstein, J. (2017) *Secrecy World* New York: Macmillan.

Bittle, S., Snider, L., Tombs, S. and Whyte, D. (Eds.) (2018) *Revisiting Crimes of the Powerful* Abingdon: Routledge.

Blakeley, G. (2019) *Stolen* London: Repeater Books.

Bowling, B., Reiner, R. and Sheptycki, J. (2019) *The Politics of the Police* 5th ed. Oxford: Oxford University Press.

Bregman, R. (2018) *Utopia for Realists* New York: Little Brown.

Bridel, J. (2018) *New Dark Age* London: Verso.

Brisman, A. and South, N. (2014) *Green Cultural Criminology* Abingdon: Routledge.

Brooks, R. (2013) *The Great Tax Robbery* London: Oneworld.

Brooks, R. (2019) *Bean Counters* London: Atlantic.

BSA (2012) *British Social Attitudes 29* London: NatCen.

BSA (2019) *British Social Attitudes 36* London: NatCen.

162 Conclusion

Bullough, O. (2018) *Moneyland* London: Profile.

Burczak, T., Garnett, R. and McIntyre, R. (Eds.) (2018) *Knowledge, Class and Economics: Marxism without Guarantees* Abingdon: Routledge.

Cammaerts, B., DeCillia, B., Magalhães, J. and Jimenez-Martínez, C. (2016) *Journalistic Representations of Jeremy Corbyn in the British Press* London: Media@LSE.

Cavadino, M. and Dignan, J. (2006) *Penal Systems: A Comparative Approach* London: Sage.

Cheliotis, L. (2013) 'Neoliberal Capitalism and Middle-Class Punitiveness: Bringing Erich Fromm's "Materialistic Psychoanalysis" to Penology' *Punishment and Society* 15/3: 247–273.

Chibnall, S. (1977) *Law and Order News*. London: Tavistock.

Chomsky, N. (2008) *Media Control* New York: Seven Stories Press.

Cohen, S. (1972) *Folk Devils and Moral Panics* London: MacGibbon and Kee.

Cohen, S. (1985) *Visions of Social Control* Cambridge: Polity.

Cohen, S. and Young, J. (Eds.) (1973) *The Manufacture of News* London: Constable.

Collins, P. (2019) *Intersectionality as Critical Social Theory* Durham, NC: Duke University Press.

Collins, P. and Bilge, S. (2016) *Intersectionality* Cambridge: Polity.

Cooper, V. and Whyte, D. (Eds.) (2017) *The Violence of Austerity* London: Pluto.

Crenshaw, K. (1991) 'Mapping the Margins: Intersectionality, Identity Politics, and Violence Against Women of Color' *Stanford Law Review* 43/6: 1241–1299.

Crouch, C. (2011) *The Strange Non-Death of Neoliberalism* Cambridge: Polity.

Crouch, C. (2018) *The Globalisation Backlash* Cambridge: Polity.

Crouch, C. (2020) *Post-Democracy After the Crises* Cambridge: Polity.

Cunningham, F. (2018) *The Political Thought of C.B. Macpherson* London: Macmillan.

Currie, E. (2016) *The Roots of Danger* New York: Oxford University Press.

De Giorgi, A. (2006) *Rethinking the Political Economy of Punishment* Aldershot: Ashgate.

DeKeseredy, W. (2010) *Contemporary Critical Criminology* Abingdon: Routledge.

DeKeseredy, W. and Dragiewicz, M. (Eds.) (2017) *Routledge Handbook of Critical Criminology* 2nd ed. Abingdon: Routledge.

DeKeseredy, W. and Currie, E. (Eds.) (2019) *Progressive Justice in an Age of Repression* Abingdon: Routledge.

Eagleton, T. (2011) *Why Marx Was Right* New Haven: Yale University Press.

Eatwell, R. and Goodwin, M. (2018) *National Populism: The Revolt Against Liberal Democracy* London: Penguin.

Edwards, D. and Cromwell, D. (2018) *Propaganda Blitz* London: Pluto.

Epstein, G. (Ed.) (2005) *Financialisation and the World Economy* Cheltenham: Edward Elgar.

Farrell, G., Tilley, N. and Tseloni, A. (2014) 'Why the Crime Drop?' in M. Tonry (Ed.) *Why Crime Rates Fall and Why They Don't* Chicago: University of Chicago Press.

Filby, E. (2015) *God and Mrs. Thatcher* London: Biteback.

Fisher M. (2009) *Capitalist Realism* Ropley: Zero Books.

Foroohar, R. (2019) *Don't Be Evil* London: Penguin.

Friedman, M. (1962) *Capitalism and Freedom* Chicago: University of Chicago Press.

Fromm, E. (1930/2000a) 'The State as Educator: On the Psychology of Criminal Justice', in K. Anderson and R. Quinney (Eds.) *Erich Fromm and Critical Criminology: Beyond the Punitive Society* Urbana: University of Illinois Press.

Fromm, E. (1931/2000b) 'On the Psychology of the Criminal and the Punitive Society', in K. Anderson and R. Quinney (Eds.) *Erich Fromm and Critical Criminology: Beyond the Punitive Society* Urbana: University of Illinois Press.

Gilbert, J. (2020) *Twenty-First Century Socialism* Cambridge: Polity.

Gilroy, P., Grossberg, L. and McRobbie, A. (2000) *Without Guarantees: In Honour of Stuart Hall* London: Verso.

Glasgow Media Group (1976) *Bad News* Abingdon: Routledge.

Glasgow Media Group (1980) *More Bad News* Abingdon: Routledge.

Glasgow Media Group (1982) *Really Bad News* London: Writers and Readers Publishing.

Goldthorpe, J., Llewellyn, C. and Payne, C. (1980) *Social Mobility and Class Structure in Modern Britain* Oxford: Oxford University Press.

Goodhart, D. (2017) *The Road to Somewhere* London: Penguin.

Gramsci, A. (1930/1971) *Selections from the Prison Notebooks* London: Lawrence and Wishart.

Green, P. and Ward, T. (2017) 'Understanding State Crime', in A. Liebling, S. Maruna, and L. McAra (Eds.) *The Oxford Handbook of Criminology* 6th ed. Oxford: Oxford University Press.

Greer, C. and Reiner, R. (2012) 'Mediated Mayhem: Media, Crime, Criminal Justice', in M. Maguire, R. Morgan, and R. Reiner (Eds.) *The Oxford Handbook of Criminology* 5th ed. Oxford: Oxford University Press.

Hall, S. (1973) 'A World at One With Itself' in S. Cohen and J. Young (Eds.) *The Manufacture of News* London: Constable.

Hall, S. (1996) 'The Problem of Ideology – Marxism without Guarantees' *Journal of Communication Inquiry* 10/2: 28–44.

Hall, S. (2012) *Theorizing Crime and Deviance* London: Sage.

Hall, S., Critcher, C., Jefferson, T., Clarke, J. and Roberts, B. (1978) *Policing the Crisis* London: Macmillan.

Hall, S., Kuldova, T. and Horsley, M. (Eds.) (2020) *Crime, Harm and Consumerism* Abingdon: Routledge.

Hall, S. and Winlow, S. (2015) *Revitalizing Criminological Theory* Abingdon: Routledge.

Hall, S. and Winlow, S. (2017) 'Ultra-realism', in W. DeKeseredy and M. Dragiewicz (Eds.) *Routledge Handbook of Critical Criminology* 2nd ed. Abingdon: Routledge.

Hall, S., Winlow, S. and Ancrum, C. (2008) *Criminal Identities and Consumer Culture* Cullompton: Willan.

Hayek, F. (1944/2001) *The Road to Serfdom* Abingdon: Routledge.

Herman, E. and Chomsky, N. (2002) *Manufacturing Consent* New York: Pantheon.

Hillyard, P., Pantazis, C., Tombs, S. and Gordon, D. (Eds.) (2004) *Beyond Criminology* London: Pluto.

Hillyard, P. and Tombs, S. (2017) 'Social Harm and Zemiology', in A. Liebling, S. Maruna, and L. McAra (Eds.) *Oxford Handbook of Criminology* 6th ed. Oxford: Oxford University Press.

Hindmoor, A. (2018) *What's Left Now?* Oxford: Oxford University Press.

Hough, M. and Roberts, J. (2017) 'Public Opinion, Crime, and Criminal Justice', in A. Liebling, S. Maruna, and L. McAra (Eds.) *Oxford Handbook of Criminology* 6th ed. Oxford: Oxford University Press.

IMF (2010) *Reserve Accumulation and International Monetary Stability* Washington, DC: International Monetary Fund Policy Paper https://www.imf.org/external/np/pp/eng/2010/041310.pdf

Kaiser, B. (2019) *Targeted* London: HarperCollins.

Karstedt, S. and Farrall, S. (2006) 'The Moral Economy of Everyday Crime' *British Journal of Criminology* 46/6: 1011–1036.

Kelton, S. (2020) *The Deficit Myth: Modern Monetary Theory and How to Build a Better Economy* London: John Murray.

Kenworthy, L. (2014) *Social Democratic America* New York: Oxford University Press.

Keynes, J.M. (1919) *The Economic Consequences of the Peace* London: Macmillan.

Keynes, J.M. (1930/2010) *Essays in Persuasion* London: Macmillan.

Kingsley, C. (1863/2016) *The Water Babies* London: Macmillan.

Klein, N. (2007) *The Shock Doctrine* London: Allen Lane.

Klein, N. (2014) *This Changes Everything* London: Allen Lane.

Klein, N. (2018) *No Is Not Enough* London: Penguin.

Klein, N. (2019) *On Fire* London: Allen Lane.

Lacey, N. (2008) *The Prisoners' Dilemma: Political Economy and Punishment in Contemporary Democracies* Cambridge: Cambridge University Press.

Lansley, S. and Mack, J. (2015) *Breadline Britain* London: Oneworld.

Levinas, E. (2005) *Humanism of the Other* Champaign: University of Illinois Press.

Levitas, R. (2005) *The Inclusive Society?* London: Macmillan.

Lowenstein, A. (2015) *Disaster Capitalism* London: Verso.

Luxemburg, R. (1899/2006) *Reform or Revolution?* New York: Dover.

Luxemburg, R. (1915/2010) The Crisis of German Social Democracy (The Junius Pamphlet)', in P. Le Blanc and H. Scott (Eds.) *Socialism or Barbarism* London: Pluto.

Luxemburg, R. (1918/2006) *The Russian Revolution in Reform and Revolution and Other Writings* New York: Dover.

Lynch, M. (2019) 'Green Criminology and Environmental Crime: Criminology That Matters in the Age of Global Ecological Collapse' *Journal of White Collar and Corporate Crime* 1/1:50–61.

Lynch, M., Long, M., Stertesky, P. and Barnett, K. (2017) *Green Criminology* Oakland: University of California Press.

Macpherson, C. B. (1962) *The Political Theory of Possessive Individualism* Oxford: Oxford University Press.

Manwaring, R. and Kennedy, P. (2017) *Why the Left Loses* Bristol: Policy Press.

Marcetic, B. (2020) *Yesterday's Man: The Case Against Joe Biden* London: Verso.

Marx, K. and Engels, F. (1844/2000) *Economic and Philosophical Manuscripts of 1844 in Early Writings* London: Penguin.

Mason, P. (2015) *Postcapitalism* London: Allen Lane.

Mason, P. (2019) *Clear Bright Future* London: Allen Lane.

Mazzucato, M. (2018) *The Value of Everything* London: Allen Lane.

McLuhan, M. (1967) *The Medium is the Massage* London: Penguin.

Media Reform Coalition (2019) *Who Owns the UK Media?* https://www.mediareform.org.uk/wp-content/uploads/2019/03/FINALonline2.pdf

Melossi, D., Sozzo, M. and Brandariz, J. (Eds.) (2018) *The Political Economy of Punishment Today* Abingdon: Routledge.

Mirowski, P. (2014) *Never Let a Serious Crisis Go to Waste* London: Verso.

Monbiot, G. (2016) *How Did We Get into This Mess?* London: Verso.

Monbiot, G. (2017) *Out of the Wreckage* London: Verso.

Morens, D., Daszak, P. and Taubenberger, J. (2020) 'Escaping Pandora's Box – Another Novel Coronavirus' *New England Journal of Medicine* https://www.nejm.org/doi/full/10.1056/NEJMp2002106

Mounk, Y. (2018) *The People vs. Democracy* Cambridge, MA: Harvard University Press.

Mudde, C. (2019) *The Far Right Today* Cambridge: Polity.

Murphy, R. (2016) *The Joy of Tax* London: Corgi.

Murphy, R. (2017) *Dirty Secrets: How Tax Havens Destroy the Economy* London: Verso.

Murray, A. (2019) *The Fall and Rise of the British Left* London: Verso.

Nichols, J. (2015) *The 'S' Word* London: Verso.

Norris, P. and Inglehart, R. (2019) *Cultural Backlash* Cambridge: Cambridge University Press.

Nurse, A. (2016) *An Introduction to Green Criminology and Environmental Justice* London: Sage.

Ord, T. (2020) *The Precipice* London: Bloomsbury.

Pettifor, A. (2017) *The Production of Money* London: Verso.

Pettifor, A. (2019) *The Case for the Green New Deal* London: Verso.

Phillips, L. and Rozworski, M. (2019) *People's Republic of Walmart* London: Verso.

Philo, G. (Ed.) (2017) *Message Received* Abingdon: Routledge.

Piketty, T. (2020) *Capital and Ideology* Cambridge, MA: Harvard University Press.

Pratt, J. (2006) *Penal Populism* Abingdon: Routledge.

Rawls, J. (1971) *A Theory of Justice* Cambridge: Harvard University Press.

Raworth, K. (2018) *Doughnut Economics* London: Random House.

Reiner, R. (2007) *Law and Order: An Honest Citizen's Guide to Crime and Control* Cambridge: Polity.

Reiner, R. (2016) *Crime: The Mystery of the Common-Sense Concept* Cambridge: Polity.

Reiner, J.T. (2018) *New Directions in Just War Theory* Carlisle, PA: Strategic Studies Institute.

Reiner, J.T. (2019) *Michael Walzer* Cambridge: Polity.

Renwick, C. (2017) *Bread for All* London: Allen Lane.

Riley, D. (2017) 'Bourdieu's Class Theory' *Catalyst* https://catalyst-journal.com/vol1/no2/bourdieu-class-theory-riley

Roeder, O., Eisen, L-B. and Bowling, J. (2015) *What Caused the Crime Decline?* New York: Brennan Center for Justice, New York University Law School.

Rogers, P. (2010) *Losing Control: Global Security in the 21st Century* 3rd ed. London: Pluto.

Ryan, K. (2019) *Crippled: Austerity and the Demonisation of Disabled People* London: Verso.

Sanders, A. and Shorrocks, R. (2019) 'All in this together? Austerity and the gender-age gap in the 2015 and 2017 British general elections' *British Journal of Politics and International Relations* 21/4: 667–688.

Savage, M. (2015) *Social Class in the 21st Century* London: Penguin.

Savage, M., Devine, F., Cunningham, N., Taylor, M., Yaojjun, L., Hjellbrekke, J., Le Roux, B., Friedman, S. and Miles, A. (2013) 'A New Model of Social Class? Findings from the BBC's Great British Class Survey Experiment' *Sociology* 47/2: 219–250.

Shaxson, N. (2012) *Treasure Islands* London: Macmillan.

Shaxson, N. (2018) *The Finance Curse* London: Bodley Head.

Sikka, P. (2018) 'Rising to the Challenge of Tax Avoidance' in J. McDonnell (Ed.) *Economics for the Many* London: Verso.

Skidelsky, R. (2010) *Keynes: The Return of the Master* London: Penguin.

Skidelsky, R. and Skidelsky, E. (2012) *How Much Is Enough?* London: Allen Lane.

Snyder, T. (2018) *The Road to Unfreedom* London: Vintage.

South, N. and Beirne, P. (Eds.) (2006) *Green Criminology* Aldershot: Ashgate.

South, N. and Brisman, A. (Eds.) (2014) *Routledge International Handbook of Green Criminology* Abingdon: Routledge.

Spencer, N. (2017) *The Political Samaritan* London: Bloomsbury.

Sretesky, P., Long, M. and Lynch, M. (2014) *The Treadmill of Crime: Political Economy and Green Criminology* Abingdon: Routledge.

Standing, G. (2017) *Basic Income: And How We Can Make It Happen* London: Pelican.

Standing, G. (2020) *Battling Eight Giants: Basic Income Now* London: I.B. Taurus.

Stumpf, J. (2006) 'The Crimmigration Crisis: Immigrants, Crime, and Sovereign Power' *American University Law Review* 56/2: 367–419.

Sunkara, B. (2019) *The Socialist Manifesto* London: Verso.

166 Conclusion

Susskind, D. (2020) *A World Without Work* London: Allen Lane.

Susskind, R. and Susskind, D. (2017) *The Future of the Professions* Oxford: Oxford University Press.

Tombs, S. and Whyte, D. (2015) *The Corporate Criminal* Abingdon: Routledge.

Tooze, A. (2018) *Crashed* London: Allen Lane.

Toynbee, P. and Walker, D. (2020) *The Lost Decade 2010–2020* London: Guardian Faber.

Tudor, H. and Tudor, J.M. (Eds.) (1988) *Marxism and Social Democracy* Cambridge: Cambridge University Press.

van Swaaningen, R. (1997) *Critical Criminology* London: Sage.

Wacquant, L. (2009) *Punishing the Poor: The Neoliberal Government of Social Insecurity* Durham, NC: Duke University Press.

Wallace, R. (2016) *Big Markets Make Big Flu* New York: Monthly Review Press.

Walzer, M. (2015) *Just and Unjust Wars* 5th ed. New York: Basic Books.

Wark, M. (2019) *Capitalism Is Dead: Is This Something Worse?* London: Verso.

White, R. and Heckenberg, D. (2014) *Green Criminology* Abingdon: Routledge.

Wood, E.M. (1972) *Mind and Politics: An Approach to the Meaning of Liberal and Social Individualism* Berkeley: University of California Press.

Wray, L.R. (2017) *Why Minsky Matters* Princeton: Princeton University Press.

Wylie, C. (2019) *Mindf*ck: Inside Cambridge Analytica's Plot to Break the World* London: Profile.

Zuboff, S. (2019) *The Age of Surveillance* London: Profile.

INDEX

accentuating the negative 115
Adam Smith Institute 20
agency problem 145–152; mass media and 148–151; psychodynamics of ressentiment and 147–148; public opinion and 151–152
American Dream 25, 106
Anglocentrism 89
Animal Farm 38
anomie theory 64
Aron, R. 20
Arpaio, J. 118
artistic critique of capitalism 24
Attlee, C. 12
Auden, W. H. 160
austerity policies 53, 111–112, 148

Ball, J. 40
barriers to social democracy 131–152; agency 145–152; moral economy 135–145; political economy 132–135
Bauman, Z. 31
BBC 149–150
Bebel, A. 9
Beccaria, C. 62
Bernstein, E. 9–10, 34, 36
Beveridge, W. 12
Beveridge Report, 1942 1, 12
Biden, J. 146–147
Black-Merton-Scholes formula 22
Blair, T. 11, 22, 26–27, 73, 74–75, 113, 127, 151
Blum, L. 10
Bolsheviks 10, 11

Boltanski, L. 24, 25
Bonger, W. 32, 37, 39, 64, 99–102, 108
Bourdieu, P. 49
Boutellier, H. 31
Braithwaite, J. 95
Bratton, W. 58
Bretton Woods 14, 16, 21, 132, 134–135, 145
Brexit 18, 23, 117, 133, 141
British Crime Survey (BCS) 69–72
British Labour Party 10, 26–27, 32, 98, 127; moral concerns in 30
British Report of the Committee on Homosexual Offences and Prostitution 110
British Social Attitudes Survey 139–140, 151
British Social Democratic Federation (SDF) 9
British Social Democratic Party (SDP) 11, 26
Brown, G. 134
Butler, R. A. 12, 104

Cadwalladr, C. 149
Cambridge Analytica 149
Cameron, D. 116, 127, 148
Capital 29–30
capitalism 147; critique of 24, 32–34; disaster 153–160; liberal 60–61; long waves of capitalist political economy and 85–88; as prone to extreme individualism 100–101
capital punishment 112
Case, A. 96
Cato Institute 20
causes of crime 63, 67, 74, 98, 104–105, 108, 111, 114, 130–131
Centre for Policy Studies 20

168 Index

Chiapello, E. 24, 25
Chicago School 136
Christian socialism 30, 138
Churchill, W. 12, 154
citizenship, inclusive 88–93, 113
Clarke, K. 116–117
Clarkson, J. 54
class 130, 140–141; financialisation and commercialisation of everyday culture and 144–145; injustice, oppression, and 142–144
class incorporation 87
Clinton, B. 22, 73, 136, 146
Clinton Democrats 4, 22, 23, 113
Cloward, R. 64, 106
Cohen, S. 99, 152
Colquhoun, P. 63–64
Commentaries on the Laws of England 109
communism 8, 19, 27, 30, 157; vs. social democracy 10–11
Communist Manifesto, The 33
communitarianism 38
compartmentalisation of injustice and oppression 142–144
compassion 139–141
conceptions of crime 52–56
Conservative-Liberal Democrat Coalition 116
conspicuous consumption 25
consumerism 25, 57, 67, 74, 112, 131
contested neoliberalism 27, 38, 87–88
controls, crime 58–59
Cook, T. 127
co-operative movement 38
Corbyn, J. 11, 147
counterculture 24–25
COVID-19 pandemic 125, 153–155, 158, 159
crime: causes of 63, 67, 74, 98, 104–105, 108, 111, 114, 130–131; charting recent trends in 69–72; complex preconditions in 56–59; criminalisation, growth of citizenship and 66–69; criminal justice conceptions of 54; defined 51–52; legal conceptions of 52; mass media and policy conceptions of 54–56; media on 150; multiple causes and trends in 59–60; new law and order consensus on 113–115; normative conceptions of 52–53; political and moral economies of criminalisation and 73; public discussions of 95–98, 104, 107; social and individual explanation of 98–108; social/cultural conceptions of 53–54; trends in 58–60, 66, 70, 72; victimless 109

Crime: A Challenge For Us All 32
Crime Commission 107
Crime Survey for England and Wales (CSEW) 70–72
crime trends 58–60, 66, 70, 72
criminalisation: crime, growth of citizenship and 66–69; long waves of 88; political and moral economies of 73
criminal justice: coalition 116–117; limits of 110–111
criminal opportunities 57–58
critical criminology 152, 155–156
critique of capitalism 24, 32–34
Critique of Political Economy 136
Critique of the Gotha Programme 35
cultural conceptions of 53–54
cultural criminologists 66
culture, neoliberal 23–26
culture of control 114
cybercrime 59
cyberterrorism 59

Daily Herald, The 150
Dangerfield, G. 84
Darwin, C. 16
Darwinism 40
Davies, S. 156
Davies, W. 153
deaths of despair 96
Deaton, A. 96
Dei Delitti e Delle Pene 62
de Jouvenel, B. 20
democracy 4, 5, 142, 144–145, 149, 157
democratic socialism 7, 27–29
deregulation 21–22
desubordination 115
Devlin, Lord Justice 53
Diggers 40
dimensions of justice 37–38
disaster capitalism 153–160
disaster socialism 153–160
Durkheim, E. 53–54, 64, 95
Dworkin, R. 31

effectiveness of criminal justice 110–111
egoism 2, 137–139
Ehrlichman, J. 5
Eisenhower Report on Violence 107–108
Emanuel, R. 153
Engels, F. 8–9, 33, 128, 130, 157; on morality 29; on 'social murder' 53
Enlightenment, the 62
equality 35–36, 143
ethics 31–32

Index

ethnicity 36, 37–38, 51, 89–90, 101, 143
European Court of Human Rights 116–117
Evolutionary Socialism 10
Extinction Rebellion 155

Fabian gradualism 11, 34–35
Fabian Society 10, 34
Farrall, S. 50
Ferguson, A. 62
filleted Marxism 106
financial crisis of 2007/8 7, 39, 93, 111, 125, 144, 151, 153, 159
financialisation and commercialisation of everyday culture 144–145
Five Giants 1
Floyd, G. 118
Fonseca, M. 52
Fordism 25, 147
formal social control 36
Foucault, M. 31, 64–65
Frankfurt School 148
free market perspective 19–20
French Socialist Party 10
Friedman, M. 19, 60
Friendly Societies 38
Fromm, E. 148
Fry, M. 103
fully social theory 65

Gallie, W. B. 27–28
Garland, D. 61, 69
gender 2, 24, 36, 85, 89–90, 98, 101, 130, 140; dimensions of justice and 37–38; relationship between crime and 51
General Household Survey (GHS) 70
German Social Democratic Workers' Party 9
Giddens, T. 26–27
Gilded Age 13
Glass-Steagall Act 22
Golden Rule 30, 31, 32, 138
Goldwater, B. 96, 106
Goodhart, D. 141
Good Samaritan 138
gradualism 34–35
Gramsci, A. 153
Grayling, C. 117
Great Depression 153, 158, 159; *see also* New Deal
Great Society programme 12, 64, 106–107
Green, T. H. 11
green criminology 155–156
Green New Deal 158–159
Greenspan, A. 151

Grunhut, M. 103
Guardian, The 150
Guesde, J. 10
guild socialism 38

habitus 49
Hall, S. 65, 150
Harcourt, W. 89
Hart, H. L. A. 53
Harvey, D. 86–87
Hayek, F. von 19, 157
Healey, D. 30
Hegel, G. W. F. 27, 60
hegemonic neoliberalism 87–88
Heritage Foundation 20
Hillesum, E. 101
Hinton, E. 107
Hirsch, F. 25
Hobhouse, L. T. 11, 27
Hobsbawm, E. 89
Howard, M. 58
Hume, D. 62
Hyndman, H. 9

ideology, neoliberal 19–20
Ignatieff, M. 39
inclusive citizenship 88–93, 113
individualism: decontextualisation and 115; egoistic vs. reciprocal 137–139, 154
inequality 1, 13, 14, 24, 40, 89, 91–93, 96; capitalism and 33; compartmentalisation of injustice and oppression and 142–144; contested neoliberalism and 87–88; cultural meaning of 64, 66; democracy and 35; dimensions of 37–38; gross forms of 28; leading to crime 32, 59, 74–75, 98; neoliberalism and 116; political economy and 15–16, 73; social democracy and 130, 146; social mediating processes in 101
inflation 21
informal social control 34, 59
Institute of Economic Affairs 20
institutionalisation 85
International Clearing Union 14
International Monetary Fund 14

Jaures, J. 10
Johnson, B. 93, 117–118, 154
Johnson, L. 12, 17, 64–65, 96, 106
Journal of Political Economy 60
justice: dimensions of 37–38; equality and 36; state as instrument of 38–39; *see also* social democratic criminology

170 Index

Kalecki, M. 16
Kantian ethics 31
Karstedt, S. 50
Kautsky, K. 9, 128
keeping calm slogan 111–112
Kennedy, J. F. 17, 106
Kennedy, R. 107
Kerner Commission on Violence and Civil
  Disorders 107
Keynesianism 1, 2, 4, 11–12, 14–15,
  134–135, 148, 157; ideology in 19–20;
  political economy and 15–19; privatised 22
Khan, S. 117
King, Mervyn 151
King, Martin Luther, Jr. 2, 93, 107
Kingsley, C. 32
Kolakowski, L. 34–35
Kondatrieff cycles 85

labelling of crime 56
law and order 93–94, 113–115; explaining
  the rise of 115–116; media and 150
*Lectures on Justice, Police, Revenue and
  Arms* 62
left realism 102
legal conceptions of crime 52–53
Lenin, V. 10
les trentes glorieuses 11–13, 125
Levellers 40
liberal capitalism 60–61
liberal elitism 67
liberty 26–27, 85, 127; modernism and
  40–41; quiet optimism and 36–37;
  restrictions on 24; social democrats and 31
Lippman, W. 19
Lipsey, R. 136
Loader, I. 67
long waves of capitalism 85–87
long waves of criminalisation 88
Luxemburg, R. 5, 128–130

Macpherson, C. B. 137
Mannheim, H. 32, 39, 103–105
Marshall, A. 33, 89–92
Marshall, T. H. 11, 27, 91–92
Marx, K. 8–9, 24, 33, 39, 92, 130, 137,
  157; on agency 147; on equality 35; on
  morality 29
Marxism 8–9, 16, 27, 66, 128, 142; filleted
  106; morality and 29–30, 136; Willem
  Bonger and 99
mass media and crime 54–56, 148–151
May, T. 116
McLuhan, M. 149

means of crime 57
Merton, R. 32, 40, 64, 98; 1960s
  presidential commissions and 106–108
Miliband, E. 11
Mill, J. S. 37, 53
Miners' Strike, 1984/5 4, 87, 98
Mirror, The 150
Mitterand, F. 133
modernism/modernity 40–41
Modern Monetary Theory 148
money illusion 21
Mont Pelerin Society 19–20
moral economy 109; compartmentalisation
  of injustice and oppression and 142–144;
  compassion and 139–141; egoistic vs.
  reciprocal individualism and 137–139;
  financialisation and commercialisation
  of everyday culture and 144–145; social
  democracy barriers in 135–145
morality 29–30
More, T. 40, 111
motivation of crime 56–57
Murdoch, R. 149, 150–151

National Violence Commission 107
neo-liberal counter-revolution 87
neoliberal hegemony 126, 129, 132, 136,
  145, 151; social democracy and 15, 23,
  38; social democratic criminology and
  50, 61, 87–88, 93, 113
neoliberalism 1, 2, 4, 7, 66, 68, 126;
  'buying time' for 20–23; contested
  27, 38, 87–88; counter-revolution,
  1979–2008 87–88; culture of 23–26;
  globalisation and 133; ideology of
  19–20; law and order consensus and 116;
  media and 149–150; moral economy and
  136–145; political economy and 16–19;
  problem of agency and 145–152
New Criminology, The 65
New Deal 12, 22, 27, 106, 107, 126, 158
New Economics Foundation 33, 158–159
New Labour 4, 11, 22, 34, 75, 98, 113,
  115, 129, 136, 151
new right populist vigilantism 117–118
newspapers 150
new spirit of capitalism 24–26
New Spirit of Capitalism, The 23
Nietzsche, F. 31
Nixon, R. 4–5, 16–17, 93, 97, 107
normative conceptions of crime 52–53

Obama, B. 52, 118, 136, 146, 153
Observer, The 149

offenders, concern for 108–110
Ohlin, L. 64, 106
oil shock 14–15
O'Neill, Lord J. 156
Only Fools and Horses 145
opportunity for crime 57–58
overcriminalisation 110
Owen, R. 8

Parker, T. 93
Patel, P. 117–118
Peasants' Revolt 40
penal modernism 41
penal welfarism 68–69
Phillips, L. 157
Pigou, A. C. 33
Polanyi, M. 20
police, science of 62–65
policing by consent 113
Policing the Crisis 65
Policy Exchange 20
political economy 15–19; criminology's
    roots in 62–65; eclipsed in criminology
    65–66; history of criminology and
    60–62; social democracy barriers in
    132–135
politicisation of law and order 97–98,
    113–116, 126–127
Popper, K. 19–20
populism 23, 117–118, 160
positional goods 25
postmodernism/postmodernity 31, 64–65
postwar consensus 23, 132
post-World War II era 1
primacy of the ethical in social democracy
    29–32
privatised Keynesianism 22
*Protestant Ethic and the Spirit of Capitalism,
    The* 23
psychodynamics of ressentiment 147–148
public opinion and crime 151–152

race 24, 37, 38, 89, 97, 130, 140, 143
Radzinowicz, L. 103
Rand, A. 151
Rawls, J. 27, 36, 137
Raworth, K. 125
Reagan, R. 4, 20–21, 34, 66, 87, 92, 136;
    austerity polities and 148
reciprocal individualism 137–139
reductive determinism 50
Rehn-Meidner model 18–19
'Ridley Plan' 4
risk society 75

Road to Serfdom, The 19, 126
Robbins, L. 20
Roosevelt, F. D. 12, 27, 158
Ropke, W. 19
Rorty, R. 31
Rougier, L. 19
Rozworski, M. 157
Russian Social Democratic Workers 10

Sanders, B. 146, 147
Savage, M. 142
science 39–40; of police 62–65
September 1st. 1939 160
sexuality 2, 24, 38, 51, 53, 89, 101, 130, 143
Smith, A. 60, 62–63, 136
social and individual explanation of crime
    98–108
social control: formal 36; informal 34, 59
social critique of capitalism 24
social/cultural conceptions of crime 53–54
social democracy 1–3, 7–8, 125–126; vs.
    communism 10–11; core meaning and
    values 26–41; criminal justice system
    and 2–3; decline of, 1970–2008 14–15;
    from disaster capitalism to disaster
    socialism and 153–160; equality and
    35–36; gradualism and 11, 34–35;
    historical overview of 8–26; hopefulness
    and 160–161; key barriers to reviving
    131–152; les trentes glorieuses and
    11–13; meaning of 27–29; modernism
    and 40–41; plea for 73–76; primacy of
    the ethical in 29–32; quiet optimism of
    36–37; science and 39–40; socialism or
    barbarism and 128–131; before World
    War I 8–10
social democratic criminologists: British
    102–106; European 99–102; US
    106–108
social democratic criminology (SDC)
    32, 49–50; aetiological crisis for 37;
    charting recent crime trends and 69–72;
    coalition criminal justice and 116–117;
    concern for offenders and victims in
    108–110; crime, criminalisation, and
    growth of citizenship and 66–69; crime
    in its place and 95–98; crime's complex
    preconditions and 56–59; criminology's
    roots in political economy and 'science
    of police' and 62–65; essentials of
    50–51; explaining crime 51–56;
    history and achievements of 84–88;
    ideal type in 94–112; keeping calm
    and 111–112; law and order consensus

and 93–94, 113–116; limits of criminal justice and 110–111; Mannheim and Wootton on British 102–106; Merton and United States' 106–108; multiple causes and crime trends and 59–60; new right populist vigilantism and 117–118; political and moral economies of criminalisation and 73; political economy and history of criminology and 60–62; politics of law and order and 88–94; problems and prospects for reviving 128; repression of 112–113; science and 39–40; social and individual explanation of crime and 98–108; *see also* justice
socialism 8–10; Christian 30, 138; disaster 153–160; or barbarism 128–131; utopian 8, 29, 130
social media 149, 155
social murder 53, 96
Social Reform or Revolution? 10
"Soul of Man Under Socialism, The" 3
Soviet Union, the 10, 11, 24, 129
Spinney, L. 156
stagflation 15, 17
state, the (as instrument of justice) 38–39
Stephen, F. 53
Straw, J. 40
Streeck, W. 23
St Simon, Henri de 8, 60
Suicide 64
Sun, The 150
Swift, J. 153
syndicalism 38

Tawney, R. H. 11, 27, 30, 75
Tax Payers' Alliance 20
Taylor, I. 103
Thatcher, M. 4, 20–22, 34, 66, 87, 92, 136, 145; austerity politics and 148; egoistic individualism and 138, 154; politicisation of law and order under 97–98, 114
Theses on Feuerbach 147

Third Way 27, 34, 73, 129, 144
Thunberg, G. 155
Tobin, J. 134, 152
Tooze, A. 22, 133–134
totalitarianism 19, 38
Truman, H. 107
Trump, D. 18, 93, 126, 139, 141; 2020 election and 146–147; law and order consensus and 118; rise of populism and 23, 117, 133, 146
Twitter 149
Tyler, W. 40
tyranny of the majority 28

utilitarianism 31
utopian socialism 8, 29, 130

values issues in politics 29
victim culture 115
victims of crime 108–110, 114
Vietnam War 17, 107
von Mises, L. 19

Wallace, A. R. 16
Wallas, G. 11, 27
Walzer, M. 29
War on Crime 4–5, 107
War on Poverty 4–5, 106–107
Warren, E. 147
Wealth of Nations, The 60
Weber, M. 23, 24, 40, 142
welfare states 11–12, 67, 89
What is to Be Done? 10
Wilde, O. 3, 161
Wilson, H. 30, 32
Wilson, J. Q. 95–96, 100
Wood, E. M. 86
Wootton, B. 39, 103, 105–106, 111
World Bank 14

Young, J. 37

zemiology 53, 95, 131
Zombie neoliberalism 88

Printed in the United States
By Bookmasters